WORK SIMPLIFICATION

Work Simplification

GERALD NADLER, Ph.D.

Professor and Head of Department of Industrial Engineering
Washington University, St. Louis, Missouri

McGRAW-HILL BOOK COMPANY, INC.

New York   Toronto   London

1957

WORK SIMPLIFICATION

PREFACE

Everyone should use work simplification. Although logical, this has not been considered true or important, or put into practice, until recently. Now this concept guides most new applications of work simplification programs. In fact, letting everyone know about work simplification through training sessions is usually the way work simplification is started in many organizations today.

The realization of this fact has come to many people in industrial engineering, the field of endeavor which has sponsored and nurtured the growth of, and new technique developments in, work simplification. The author, like others, has come to this conclusion through many activities in work simplification: installing work simplification programs in industrial plants; conducting work simplification training programs for supervisors; indoctrinating personnel in work simplification in hospitals, chemical plants, homes, and offices; teaching work simplification at adult education levels; presenting a one-hour credit course on work simplification for 17 weeks over education television station KETC in St. Louis; offering work simplification in intensive course format; and many other ways, like consultation work, or advice to others for establishing work simplification programs.

Much of the material in this book has been adapted from the author's book, *Motion and Time Study*. Because the book has been used in many of the above situations, many ideas for presenting the topics to different groups have developed. In addition, the type of presentation in the present book was developed when the work simplification subject matter was presented on television. With the experience of many work simplification training programs in many work areas, it has been possible to develop the material for ease of presentation to any group.

This book is written to explain what the techniques are and how they are used. Very little information is given about why the techniques work, or about the background and development of the concepts. This is a "how-to-do-it" book. Yet, the very presentation of all the material in a problem-solving-approach context encourages people to think about simplifying their work. Throughout the entire presentation, much emphasis has been placed on the human being: operators, unions, management, and the individuals included in each group.

Many techniques are presented, but some are omitted. The techniques included are those which seem to be applicable to more than two or three types of activity. Some specialized work situations might require special techniques not discussed here, but the general presentation of the concepts in this book should aid any such situation.

The amount of detail and the accuracy required for using any given technique vary, depending on the requirements of the situation. The analyst must recognize that the techniques as presented are not used in exactly the same way each time. In some cases more detail is used; in others, less detail.

Once the technique is learned, it is easy to make the adjustments for the requirements of the situation.

There are two ways this book can be used for a training program for any organization:

1. When the people in the group are from the same area or work situation or when the individuals are from different organizations the material should be presented in virtually the same order as the chapters of the book. Each topic would be discussed briefly in one or more sessions (the number depends on the industry, instructor, etc.), all members assigned a specific problem or problems in that topic area to work for the next session. At the next session, the

problem is discussed, and a new topic is then taken up as indicated by the chapter order. Some chapters or techniques may be omitted if it appears that they are not suited to the organization or group. A typical outline, using *all* the techniques, would be as follows for two-hour sessions (the amount covered in any session will vary with the length of the session):

Session 1. Introduction and human relations. Problem-solving approach.

Session 2. How to get started. Present details of product process chart. Assign PPC problem.

Session 3. Discuss PPC made by students. Present concepts of form process chart. Assign FPC problem.

Session 4. Discuss FPC. Present concepts of man process chart. Assign MPC problem.

Continue through all the techniques. At the end of the discussion about the last technique, present concepts of *getting ideas*. Assign problems of making suggestion lists for PPC and FPC problems. Then continue the sessions until suggestion lists for all problems have been made. Repeat the procedure of this paragraph, but for making evaluation worksheets. Then repeat it again for making proposed charts. The remaining information in Chapters 15 through 17 would be presented as desired.

2. When the group is composed of people from different activities within the same organization, a different procedure should be used. Each technique for charting work is presented in four stages. These stages represent the second, third, fourth, and fifth steps of the logical approach to solving problems. A general outline follows for two-hour sessions:

Session 1. Introduction and human relations. Problem-solving approach.

Session 2. How to get started. Present details of product process chart. Require each student to obtain a product process chart from his own area of work.

Session 3. Discuss product process charts of students. Present basic information about getting ideas.

Session 4. Discuss suggestion lists of students. Present basic ideas about selecting best idea.

Session 5. Discuss evaluation worksheets for PPC from each student. Present basic concepts about designing proposed method.

Session 6. Discuss the proposals of students for PPC. Present concepts of FPC.

Session 7. Discuss FPC and suggestion lists made by students. Assign evaluation and formulation for FPC problem for next time.

Session 8. Discuss evaluation worksheet and proposed charts for FPC. Present MPC, and have students make MPC and suggestion list for next time.

Each session would continue in this general pattern until all the techniques have been covered. Then the remaining information starting with Chapter 15 would be presented as desired.

The author has had his ideas and concepts for this book shaped and developed by many persons to whom a deep debt of gratitude is due. In addition there are many companies whose practices are reported here. Some of them have been of special help to the author: Artcraft Venetian Blind Manufacturing Company, Frank Adam Electric Company, Ashby Metal Forming Company, Aeronautical Chart and Information Center, American Car and Foundry Company, Central Wisconsin Canneries, Halmar Dress Company, Hussmann Refrigerator Corporation, McQuay Norris Manufacturing Company, Jewish Hospital of St. Louis, McDonnell Aircraft Corporation, and Stix-Baer-Fuller Department Store. The opportunities presented by these organizations are gratefully acknowledged.

The help given by secretarial assistants was an important factor in putting this book together. Mrs. Lorraine Franzel did an excellent job in transcribing the dictated notes; Miss

Carol Ann Freeman produced the final manuscript from the corrected rough draft; and Miss Agnes Gillespie helped complete the various details required for such an undertaking. For this help, many thanks.

GERALD NADLER

CONTENTS

CHAPTER 1

INTRODUCTION

Work simplification is new, yet it is old.

The new part concerns the increased emphasis placed on work simplification for reducing costs, increasing productivity, etc. Our standard of living has been rising, and making increases in productivity and reducing costs help this rise.

It is old because in general terms it has always been applied. The ingenuity of people like Cyrus McCormick, Eli Whitney, Robert Fulton, and Thomas Edison was really an expression of the fundamental philosophy of work simplification. These people lived many years ago. Their work concerned seemingly complex situations, yet today it is recognized that the work that was simplified involved individual operations, not complex activities.

Today, simplifying complex work activities cannot depend completely upon individual ingenuity. There has to be an approach. There has to be a concept with which the work problem is attacked. There has to be work simplification.

Without question, one of the best advances in work simplification has been the concern for the human being. And here we find one of the beautiful aspects of work simplification: Not only does it provide us with the techniques used to design and improve work, but also it provides the framework around which it is possible to obtain more and better cooperation of people. Any person can apply these techniques, and those performing the work can benefit also when they understand work simplification.

1

WHAT IS WORK SIMPLIFICATION?

Many people think there are different names for work simplification. Motion study or methods study are sometimes used as synonyms for work simplification. The new term *work study* is very similar to work simplification. Some people even use the words "motion and time study" as a replacement for work simplification. In this book, work simplification includes elements of all these phrases.

Definition

Work simplification is the systematic analysis of any type of work to
1. Eliminate unnecessary work.
2. Arrange remaining work in the best order possible.
3. Make certain that the right method is used.

There is one important attribute of work simplification: The better ways for performing work which will be found will be the "best" for the conditions under which the work is performed. There is nothing which says that work performed under different conditions should be performed in exactly the same way. Washing dishes in the home is an example. The same method for washing dishes is not applicable in every situation. Kitchens vary. Arrangements vary. Types of dishes vary. These factors indicate that different methods would be used in different situations.

Systematic analysis

A "genius" can look at work and without special techniques see what it involves. However, there are very few geniuses. All of us generally need some aids to enable us to look at work. This is one of the most important aspects of work simplification. Work simplification provides a set of techniques which enables us to look at work in a completely different way. Even our own work can be scrutinized differently. Each one of us can learn so much more about work

with work simplification that it sometimes appears that a
new world has opened.

WHERE HAS WORK SIMPLIFICATION BEEN APPLIED?

As you can expect, work involves any type of physical
effort. There is absolutely no distinction as to where the
work occurs. Wherever human beings exert some effort,
there work simplification is applicable.

To show how this concept has universal application, it
would be wise to review some of the different situations
under which work simplification has been applied.

Past, or recurring, work

This area of application for work simplification seems
rather unusual. But actually it is important that work simplification be applied to activities which have been done
in the past and which may be done in the future. So often,
learning a little more about work done previously provides
the key for doing the work the right way in the future.

There are many illustrations where analysis of past performances of recurring work has saved much. Analyzing
records of inspections, production, down time, etc., frequently can tell where improvements may be made. Even
analyzing the methods of work done in the past when that
work was unsatisfactory might help straighten out the methods for future production.

Or take the nurse in a hospital writing out the complete
list of patients twice in a given day. By analyzing the lists
of previous days and weeks, it was learned that there was
almost no change in the lists between the time of the first
and second writing. Here, the analysis of past work permitted the elimination of work, one of the major objectives
of work simplification. Even the second objective of arranging work in the best order possible was met in this case. The
forms were redesigned to make listing easier.

Present work

You probably think this is the area in which work simplification has been applied most successfully. This is to be expected. Many procedures and methods have grown so rapidly and without planning that poor methods have naturally accumulated. We can expect to apply work simplification to present work for many years.

Fig. 1-1. Original workplace layout for identifying tubing. The tube was placed on the table until the work on it had been completed.

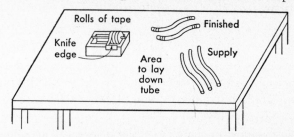

The job of identifying tubing was an expensive and lengthy one in an aircraft plant. Tubes of ⅛ to 2 inches in diameter had to be color-coded with colored self-adhesive tape at both ends. There were hundreds of different sizes and shapes of tubes. Two pieces of different-colored tape were required at each end. In the original method, performed at the workplace shown in Fig. 1-1, the operator would get a piece of tape and place it on one end of the tube. He would get another piece of the same-colored tape and place it on the other end of the tube. Then he would repeat the process for the second-color tape. While getting each piece of tape he would put the tube on the table.

In the improved method, a slightly different tape holder, as shown in Fig. 1-2, was used. The operator could insert the tube in the space between the tape roll holder and knife edge, lift up, pull the tape out of the tube, and then cut off the tape. The same method was used on the other end of the tube. Production increased 150 per cent.

FIG. 1-2. Improved workplace layout for identifying tubing. The tube was not placed on the table until the work on it had been completed.

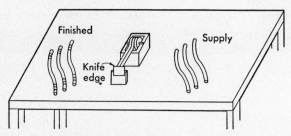

Future work (methods planning)

This is the most important way in which work simplification can be applied. Finding the better ways of doing work before work is ever done is without question the best way of using any technique. Better methods and larger savings can be obtained for production. Hard feelings and other human relations problems can be eliminated by installing proper methods before production. It seems quite clear that these are advantages that everyone should strive for.

One section of a large assembly involved placing a magnet and coil spring in a base. The coil springs were to be purchased outside the plant and shipped to the plant in boxes. A special operation would have had to be designed to separate these springs, which came tangled in the box. This would be a tedious and lengthy operation. Since the engineers had designed the spring in this way, the manufacturing department planned on setting up a special operation workplace and special tools and fixtures for an operator to separate the springs. At this point the foreman and the work simplification analyst got together.

It was found that the spring could be redesigned to eliminate the operation. The new spring, shown in Fig. 1-3, could be manufactured by the plant rather than be purchased outside, thereby making another reduction in costs. By the proper application of work simplification, the production problem was not encountered but was anticipated and solved before production.

FIG. 1-3. New and old spring design. The old springs frequently become jumbled, as shown.

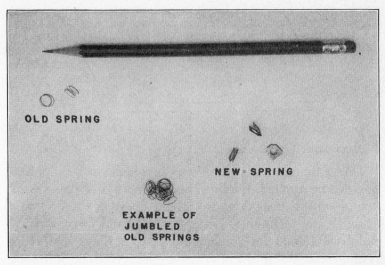

OLD SPRING

NEW SPRING

EXAMPLE OF
JUMBLED
OLD SPRINGS

Any industry or type of work

Work simplification has been applied in many areas and fields. Some areas where applications have been fruitful are department stores, chemical plants, farms, hospitals, restaurants, drugstores, forms systems, mail-order houses, food processing. Some of the illustrations given above show these different types of work, and the following example shows another case:

Shelled peas are sent to the processing plant in large hoppers measuring 30 by 30 inches across the top and 36 inches high. These hoppers are taken off the trucks, and the peas are inspected for grade. The hoppers are then rolled to a dump, and the peas are dumped. The hoppers are washed and returned to storage, from which they go to the empty trucks for return to the field. Figure 1-4 shows the original flow diagram of the hoppers on the unloading dock.

Using the same method of grading, dumping, and washing, the improved flow diagram is shown in Fig. 1-5. In this

FIG. 1-4. Original flow diagram of hoppers on unloading dock. (Reprinted with permission from G. Nadler, "Industrial Engineering Cuts Labor, Time, Handling," *Food Industries,* vol. 21, no. 5, May, 1949.)

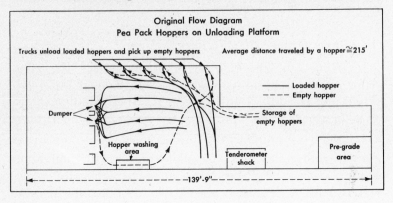

FIG. 1-5. Improved flow diagram of hoppers on unloading dock. (Reprinted with permission from G. Nadler, "Industrial Engineering Cuts Labor, Time, Handling," *Food Industries,* vol. 21, no. 5, May, 1949.)

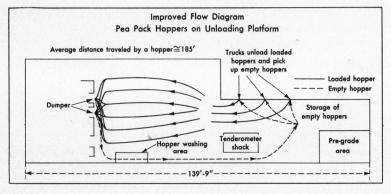

problem much confusion was eliminated, and steps were saved by the improved procedure. This was evident from the lines of flow of the original and improved method. Here again, the foreman of the unloading dock and the work simplification analyst had an excellent opportunity to work together to solve the problem.

Operations performed only once

Sometimes the question that bothers people is: "How many cycles or performances must be planned for a job before it is feasible to be analyzed by work simplification?" Without question, the only logical answer is: "One." Here is where the work simplification principles must become a part of the man, for this type of activity requires the individual doing the work frequently to plan before doing the work. This is another important reason why all operating personnel, whether in the office or plant, should learn about work simplification. Proper planning with work simplification should provide better ways of doing a job even though it is to be done only once. Included in this area are jobs done just a small number of times. Some illustrations of this activity are making special bus ducts, performing your own personal work, constructing a building, doing repair work on a machine, departmental moving, and putting down a new lawn.

WHERE IS WORK SIMPLIFICATION HEADED?

Work simplification is well established in businesses, offices, and production. But there is even a brighter future. Work simplification is producing many improvements in some of the areas usually considered outside its application. Some examples are hospitals, hotels, government activities (such as post offices and the ordnance and other branches of the armed services) and other nonrepetitive or nonprofit work activities. This whole area indicates an unusual opportunity for applying the techniques of work simplification.

Also, we know that automation is here. And work simplification has an important role in automation.

The easiest type of work to automate is that which has the least skills. One of work simplification's functions is to reduce the skills required for performing jobs. Then it is easier to mechanize and automate operations and processes. Work simplification has been reducing skills and simplifying work for many years, and this has been important for leading to automation.

Work simplification helps make job shop activities into better production line procedures. Some illustrations and the ways of arriving at such results are shown in later chapters of the book. But the important factor is to search out the components of the work performed in job shops to find that which occurs often. This work is simplified, making it more productive for the other activities. There are different ways to do this, but the work simplification approach is most important.

But this is not all. Work simplification will be needed even after automation. Some people have the idea that automation means there can be no more increases in production. This is not true. A big problem under automation will be how to increase the productivity of an automated plant. Here again work simplification will play an important role. It will be used to analyze where time was wasted, what happened on breakdowns, what is the correct method for the maintenance of the equipment, how many men are needed to do the work of maintaining and engineering an automated plant, how to set up methods for material control, how to maintain the methods for replacing and controlling tools, and even how to find new types of incentives for workers in automated plants. The work in an automated factory tends to remove the repetitive work. But it does not remove the nonrepetitive work, where work simplification will be needed for shaving costs.

EVERYONE IN WORK SIMPLIFICATION

If you are a worker, you should be interested in work simplification. You are a key person. If you are a foreman or supervisor, you should be interested in work simplification; in this case too you are a key person in work simplification. If you do any type of work or supervise any type of work, you should know about work simplification.

It is easy to see how everyone in a factory or office should cooperate in work simplification. But something else is meant here. Every person doing any type of work must participate in applying work simplification. Even the housewife should apply the techniques. It is important for everyone, including the housewife, to devote more time to civic and community affairs. Work simplification helps everyone, like the housewife, find better ways of doing their own work so that time will be available for such important duties.

Everyone must take part in work simplification. Everyone should know what work simplification is and what some of the techniques are. It is not always easy to do this. Certainly, you will not be a work simplification analyst just by reading this book. You must practice the techniques to become better able to simplify and improve work.

Learning about work simplification will make you learn about seeing your work in a way in which you have never been able to view your activity before. Actually, knowing more about your work makes it much more interesting. You may believe your work is different, that it is not susceptible to work simplification analysis, but regardless of what you do, at work or at play, it can be analyzed and, probably, can be improved. This book should assist you by giving you some of the techniques for the technical and human problems involved.

CHAPTER 2

PEOPLE AND PROBLEMS

Work simplification is good. Work simplification has been applied in many places. It will continue to be applied more and more. But this does not mean that there are no problems associated with the application.

WORK SIMPLIFICATION DEALS WITH PEOPLE

People apply it, and it is applied to people and their work. Although people are very interesting, they often present problems. These problems can become pronounced when the work of the individual is concerned. Before presenting the techniques for work simplification, it would be wise to point out some of the problems encountered with people, and how a work simplification analyst can overcome some of these problems and even use the techniques to help himself.

1. The people who are performing the jobs (operators, clerks, etc.)

Work simplification usually results in "changing" work. Because people are involved, the way they feel about these changes is very important. And experience has shown that the usual feelings of people on the job do represent difficulties or obstacles for the analyst when making the study and changes. (Here is a good reason why it is so important to apply work simplification before the work is done. Then there can be no problems with people wondering what changes mean to them.)

11

What *does* happen when you approach Joe, the man on the job? Although he may not say it in exactly the same words, there are several reactions:

Joe may wonder about the money connected with the job. "Who is going to get the extra savings? Will I get some of the financial benefits? What is going to happen to my take-home pay?" Of course, the reaction could take another form: "What is going to happen to my security on the job? With the increased production, it doesn't seem as if there will be enough work for me to do later. What will be done with me?"

These are questions concerning the economic fears Joe might have. They are important to him. Obviously, these fears are obstacles in applying work simplification.

Or Joe might say something else. This does not mean he is not worried about the economics, but the words he uses might be different. After all, we all resist change. We do not like to change the procedures and methods we are using. Or we do not like the fact that some people are "criticizing us," which is not really true. Sometimes Joe says, "This new method just won't work." Or he might say, "I've been turning out good parts. Why shouldn't I continue using my old method?" Of course, there are many other ways of expressing these psychological fears.

Or Joe might actually appear willing to go along with your change. However, after a while this cooperation might disappear. This change might be due to the group within which Joe works. Some of the other operators may have an influence on him, telling him he should not cooperate. This is "group action" and can represent a materially large obstacle to work simplification.

Generally, any one or combination of these reactions can present an obstacle to the successful application of work simplification. Knowing these, and that they will occur, is an important component of doing away with them.

2. Management

Including management among the groups of people representing an obstacle to work simplification is a serious matter. Management is not a conscious obstacle. But after all, management consists of people. And these people are similar to others in the way they react to various changes proposed.

The people involved sometimes think the analyst is criticizing them when he suggests changes. Or they might feel that they are quite successful now, so why change. Management people are sometimes resistant to change. It is even possible that a group of management personnel will have an obstacle-creating effect on certain individuals. One member of management might be willing to cooperate, but others might object and thus significantly reduce the degree of cooperation.

The most important thing to remember is that management is made up of people. They should be treated in overcoming obstacles like all other people.

3. You

When *you* apply work simplification, it is easy to realize the difficulties involved in the technical abilities required. You frequently know that it is hard to apply the principles of charts, rules, etc. The one thing you might forget is that you yourself are an obstacle to your own application of new techniques.

Your own personality will often cause obstacles. You are a human being. You must improve certain personal characteristics and traits to enable yourself to deal with people better when you are applying the techniques. The work simplification analyst is a human being too. You can easily have many of the above-mentioned difficulties and traits of the human being.

WHAT TO DO ABOUT THE OBSTACLES?

Many things. Let us look at each group.

1. The people performing the jobs

To eliminate the economic fears, management must make certain policies. In most cases, these policies are already in effect. Ordinarily, each employee is guaranteed a job should his be eliminated by work simplification. This should get more cooperation from the employees. Normal labor turnover can take care of people kept on the payroll after job elimination. If such a policy is not in effect, strong recommendations to this effect should be made.

Finding a way for employees to share in the results of the improvements represents a serious problem. Annual productivity wage increases can be included in labor contracts. A group bonus can be given to all people affected. A lumpsum payment can be given to the worker making a suggestion. Small wage increases might be given to the people affected. Management should be made to realize that some form of assistance can be provided.

Trying to take care of the other obstacles presented by the people doing the job is sometimes difficult. Telling them *what* is happening is, of course, the best policy. This is the same as saying you should educate them in terms of the what, why, and how of work simplification. A person usually fears what he does not know. It is also important that operators trust their supervision. They should know that their supervisors are interested in their work and welfare. They should expect to get all information concerning themselves as individuals or groups from their supervisors.

But the man applying work simplification must do other things to eliminate some of the obstacles. This is, of course, related to the proper personal approach to an individual doing the job:

1. The analyst should listen with humility rather than talk too much.

2. The analyst should tell the worker why he is doing something, what he is doing, how he is doing it, etc.

3. The analyst should get suggestions from each of the workers, since they know their job best. Getting ideas from workers, and trying to use some components of their ideas, frequently results in more production. Employees are better motivated to make a change "work out" when their own ideas are part of the change.

4. The analyst should put himself in the worker's shoes when approaching him. Each individual feels different on different days of the week and at various hours during the day. The analyst must attempt to anticipate reactions to his approach in order to meet them properly.

5. The analyst should eliminate the word "I" from his vocabulary. It is much better to say "we," whenever you talk with an operator, a supervisor, or anyone concerned with the work being studied. This properly emphasizes that no one person knows everything about the work.

6. Some difficulty may be encountered with an individual who has had a bad experience with work simplification in another plant. Or it might be that a relative of an individual has had the bad experience. This individual can cause trouble unless he learns why or how this application is or will be different from his previous experience. This can be done while he is a member of a group receiving training in work simplification, or by special attention from the analyst (or the supervisor).

2. Management

In most cases, a training program in work simplification is the best tool for overcoming management obstacles. When management know the why and how of work simplification, it becomes easier for them to understand and support the whole program, and the individual operation changes.

Training is important when work simplification is being applied by a group of supervisors. This group can be of great assistance in overcoming the management obstacles.

To do this, the supervisor, or anyone applying work simplification, should submit reports about the work simplification project. Facts are better than the usual opinion. The techniques, presented later, can be used as facts. Too often supervisors approach their own superiors with the statement "We ought to change to this because . . ." with substantiation amounting to only opinion. This should be changed with factual reports in terms of techniques and monetary values.

After the management is convinced of the merit of work simplification, then reports become summaries of accomplishments. The approach here is to use the old management adage "A program is good when it is successful."

3. The individual applying work simplification

Overcoming your own shortcomings is difficult. The analyst must recognize his own faults. Although this is difficult to do, there are some general rules which an analyst might follow to help overcome his faults:

The analyst should not act superior. This causes people to resent and resist the suggestions of the analyst.

The analyst should deal through proper channels. The analyst can talk to any person he wants to, but the supervisor should know what is going on beforehand.

The analyst must be able to handle the technical problems in work simplification. He must know when to hold down a display of his technical knowledge and pay more attention to the human relations. He must know when his technical knowledge must be used to maintain a certain amount of prestige and personal know-how. Good human relations by itself is not sufficient. Technical competence and the trust of the other people go hand in hand.

A good work simplification analyst and a good supervisor have many traits in common. Some guides to good human relations for analyst and supervisors are: [1]

[1] Arthur O. England, *Who, Me?* The National Foremen's Institute, New London, Conn., 1950.

"Tell your people how they are getting along.

Give credit when credit is due.

Tell your people in advance about changes that will affect them.

Ask for new suggestions.

Make all jobs seem important.

Be courteous in your treatment of others.

Be honest in all your dealings.

Make people feel they belong.

Treat people with dignity."

General approach

One of the best ways of overcoming all three sources of obstacles is to have a consistent and logical approach to solving the work simplification problem. Workers, management, and the analyst himself will be more completely convinced and capable, and the analyst will be able to work more readily and produce more consistently, when using such a logical approach.

The logical approach for solving problems is really very simple. Yet it is important for each individual to know exactly what this procedure is, so that each step is performed.

In general the logical procedure for solving work problems is:

1. *State the Problem.* Knowing the specific reason why you want to work on a job, the limits of the type of solution, and the tentative means by which the solution can be found helps make an important beginning for work simplification (see Chapter 3).

2. *Get Facts.* Getting all the information about the equipment, method, product, material, and sequence is necessary before a final solution can be found (see Chapters 3 through 11).

3. *Develop Possible Ideas.* With all the information, now we determine some of the ways the problem can be solved.

Imagination and ingenuity play an important role in this step (see Chapter 12).

4. *Pick the Best Idea.* From all the possibilities in step 3, the "best" idea or group of ideas must be selected for the solution of the problem (see Chapter 13).

5. *Detail How the Job Should Be Done.* Before trying to install any new procedures, the methods and approach should be well thought out and written to avoid trouble (see Chapter 14).

6. *Review the Job Design.* This is a stop-look-and-listen step. Is every possible improvement included, and are all details included (see Chapter 15)?

7. *Test the Job.* Sometimes an actual trial of the methods design can be performed. This is another stop-for-a-moment step (see Chapter 15).

8. *Install the Method.* If all difficulties have been eliminated in steps 6 and 7, then the method is ready for installation. This is sometimes an involved process, because training may be necessary for the operators. Certainly a method installed improperly is worth nothing, and this is not good after all the time and effort have been spent in developing the method (see Chapter 16).

9. *How Much Should Be Expected?* Is the goal of step 1 accomplished, and how much can we now expect from the performance of the operators (see Chapter 17)?

The rest of this book is organized on the basis of this logical approach. The various chapters will explain the techniques used in work simplification for the various steps. This logical procedure is also a good way of submitting reports. It shows that every possibility and difficulty have been considered.

Is logical approach needed?

You may object to the presentation of a logical procedure (or, as it is sometimes called, a scientific approach) by saying that you do not need it. Your experience tells you that you know how to do this anyway. There are several reasons why the logical approach is needed.

By saying that you do not need the logical approach, you say you will use intuition. Certainly, intuition has worked many times. But there are very few of us who can depend on this. Even if it has worked for us several times, it is stretching intuition or "luck" too far to expect it always to work.

In addition, many of us find the application of intuition difficult, because we do not have much of it. Therefore, those who rely on intuition must answer the question "How do you really know you have the best answer?" Because you have been successful? You might have been more successful. Because it does not take as long with intuition? This is correct. With intuition you may get an answer immediately but waste more time and effort in carrying out what the answer suggests than if you had used the logical, or scientific, approach.

The logical approach looks like the best way. Intuition is quite important, as pointed out in step 3. But following a step-by-step approach is more likely to result in more benefits for more jobs.

CHAPTER 3

GETTING STARTED

The first step in work simplification is to state the problem. Of course, this step involves more than just saying, "Operation 379 is a bottleneck; we have to find a way of increasing productivity." Let us review some of the components of this step to make certain all aspects of stating the problem are taken care of.

OVER-ALL PROBLEM

Most of the time, the word "problem" indicates there is trouble. However, in work simplification, the word "problem" refers to any work that is being performed. In other words, it is not necessary to have some work where difficulty is occurring, in order to apply work simplification. Any work at all is a problem, and it should be either eliminated or simplified. So it is not always necessary to have trouble to apply work simplification.

In every office, plant, or place where work is performed, there are some over-all, or long-range, objectives. These may be in terms of the whole function, a department, or an area within the department. In some cases, over-all objectives are least cost for a better product, better service for the least cost, materials savings programs, increased productivity programs.

Notice that some of these over-all objectives refer to problem situations, and others to normal situations where continuing progress is expected. Of course, these objectives are given to the analyst or supervisors by management. Such over-all objectives set the pace for the work to be done in designing and improving work.

WHICH WORK SITUATION SHOULD BE SELECTED?

Now, you must decide which of the many problems should be worked on first. Let us look at it this way:

If the company you are working for were losing money at the rate of 4 per cent of its sales, this would be a serious problem. The company's over-all objective would be to increase profits and reduce costs. Now there are many cost contributing centers in an organization. This part of step 1 tries to figure out which one of the many cost contributing centers should be attacked first. In one specific case of this type, it was decided that the assembly line, where 20 per cent of the payroll was located, would be a logical first problem. With 20 per cent of the payroll, there was a good potential for savings.

Or take a hospital. There is a shortage of nurses, yet each hospital would like to improve patient care. This represents a problem because it usually takes more nurses to provide better patient care. Yet the problems must be worked on. Therefore, eliminating or simplifying those activities which take nurses off the patient floors would be a good place to start. This is the first specific work situation to be selected.

Or take a housewife who does not get her housework finished. It seems that the over-all objective would be to reduce the amount of time and effort spent on housework. There are many household tasks, and the housewife must select one to start with, perhaps washing dishes. Of course, she, like other analysts, will go on to the next work situation after finding a better way for the first problem.

The major purpose of this part is to limit the actual work situation to which the analyst will apply work simplification.

This does not mean he will forget the rest of the work situations, but that they will be taken into consideration later. This might be shown graphically as in Fig. 3-1. Here is a department in a plant or an office with many jobs or work situations. Each work situation is represented by a dash line. Now, management wants to reduce costs. The problem is to decide which one of the many work situations would be good

FIG. 3-1. Graphical picture of jobs in a department. Because there are so many jobs, one should be selected for study.

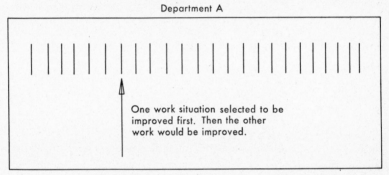

Each dash is a work situation or cost center

to start with. The analyst should look over the general objective and pick out the work situation with the most possibilities. The examples of the company losing 4 per cent of sales, the hospital, and the housewife showed how this was done.

Remember: Limit the problem. Get the problem down to the smallest activity that can be handled. This makes the problem realistic. Select the right problem to work on. Trying to solve the wrong problem to reach the goal can be disastrous to the work simplification program. Also, including too many work activities in a study can be bad, because it may be difficult to reach a good solution with so many work problems to keep track of and consider.

This part determines what is to be done. Other parts of this step determine where we should go with the problem.

SPECIFIC OBJECTIVES FOR SELECTED PROBLEM

We have an over-all objective for our area. Now we need a specific objective for the definite problem selected. This is necessary because we want to become more detailed in our objectives.

In the company losing money, the specific problem was the assembly line with 20 per cent of the payroll. The objective for this specific problem was to reduce the out-of-pocket expense and to increase productivity. Notice that those words are different from the words used for the over-all objective, "Eliminate the loss and increase profits." But the new words apply directly to the problem at hand.

In most cases such a specific objective can be stated. It should be stated to clear up in the analyst's mind what is to be done with the problem operation.

GENERAL APPROACH TO BE USED

This part makes plans about how to reach the objectives. One component of such plans is to make a preliminary investigation into whether or not the work itself is necessary at all. This question is important now and will be important throughout the entire process of work simplification. Certainly, if we can eliminate the work now, much time and effort can be saved.

If the operation is considered necessary, then the plans of the analyst should include questioning several areas. How should the workers be approached? How much time is available to solve this problem? What are the possible savings? What amount of money can be spent to meet the objectives set up for the problem? These and many similar questions, which pertain to individual organizations, must be reviewed to lay the plans for the analyst.

Answering these questions helps the analyst to decide what type of analysis should be made and into how much detail the analysis should go. If much time and money can be spent to analyze a situation, then the most detailed and accurate techniques should be used, and they should be used as fully as possible. You do not know at this point what the techniques will be, but after learning about them in the next few chapters, you should be able to make some of these decisions.

Mental approach

The procedures and information in this book provide the most detailed way of making a work simplification approach. There are many cases, as when there is not enough time or money, where not all the details are needed. The analyst should use the same logical approach, even though he might do it all mentally. This is entirely possible and would be determined by the general approach above. Using the logical approach for solving problems may be done mentally, or by writing out every step and using every technique in its most detailed fashion.

STARTING THE ANALYSIS OF WORK

We have limited the problem, know what it is to be, know where we want to go with it, and how we are going to go about it. This completes step 1. Now—to learn about the work situation itself in its entirety (step 2).

The work situation does not exist all by itself. It is affected by a number of different factors within itself and within the area where the work is done. Generally, all types of work are affected by five factors.[1] It is apparent that information should be gathered about these factors. The five factors are:

1. *Materials*
2. *Design* of product (which includes specifications, quality requirements, etc.)

---

[1] Although there can be many more factors, all the others can be grouped within the five enumerated. The five factors were first clearly separated and set forth by M. E. Mundel, *Motion and Time Study: Principles and Practice*, Englewood Cliffs, New Jersey: Prentice-Hall, Inc., 1950, pp. 23–24.

3. *Sequence* of work on the material to change it to the desired design

4. *Equipment,* tools, workplace, etc., used at the specific operation

5. *Method* utilizing the equipment, tools, and workplace to accomplish these specific operations being studied

This can be illustrated graphically, as in Fig. 3-2. Assume the hopper is a factory. The various materials needed for the product or service enter at the top. The material is processed by a series of operations to turn out the product or service, coming out of the bottom of the hopper. Circles in the hopper represent the operations used to modify the material to reach the product design. These are the modification operations (operation sheet) for the material. Notice the similarity between Figs. 3-1 and 3-2. Figure 3-2 organizes the operations to illustrate these five factors.

All types of work are affected by the same five factors. For example, if an analyst wanted to improve the work of washing dishes, he would find that the material is dirty dishes; the product design is clean dishes (the degree of cleanliness, or specifications, depends on the desires of the housewife and her family); the sequence of work on the material prior to and succeeding the operation to be studied is clear dishes from table, scrape dishes, stack dishes, wash dishes, dry, and replace in cabinet; the equipment being used for the operation of washing dishes might include water, soap water, washcloth, scouring pads; and the method being used for the job of washing dishes would be dependent upon the individual performing the operation. Notice that the individual operation being worked on (selected in the first step, stating the problem) is noted by the arrow in Fig. 3-2.

Other illustrations of how these five factors affect all types of work can be drawn easily from manufacturing. But to make it more interesting, let us look at the work of a clerk in a department store. This clerk works in the credit department, and her job is to answer the telephone when the sales-

Fig. 3-2. A portrayal of the relationship among the five factors affecting any work. If the work being studied is indicated by the arrow, notice how all the other factors are directly related. The hopper represents the whole plant or office.

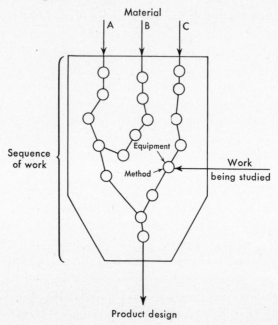

people in various selling departments inquire about the credit limits for certain customers. The material being worked on is the information from the clerk in the selling department. The design of the product is the answer which the credit-department clerk gives the salesgirl. The sequence of work includes the salesperson's dialing the telephone, transmitting her request, and the credit-department clerk's looking for the information in the files and giving information to the salesperson. The equipment being used for the operation includes telephone, file, paper and pencil. The method for accomplishing this operation is dependent on the credit-department clerk and how she utilizes the equipment.

To make a complete analysis, we should have information

about each of the five factors affecting the work situation under study. However, information about some of the items is relatively easy to gather. For example, there is usually no trouble in gathering information about the *materials* of the products or service. Usually a bill of material is available. In a like manner there seems to be no difficulty in gathering information, either by observation or from drawings or prints, about the *design* of the product. Likewise, in most cases little time is needed in gathering information about the *equipment*, tools, and workplace of the operation. Drawings and manufacturer's specifications are usually available. Equipment and workplace present some exceptions, and the techniques for gathering the slight information needed on certain operations will be described in later chapters.

The other two factors affecting work, *sequence* and *method*, usually represent items about which little is known in complete detail. This does not mean that the supervisors or foremen are not familiar with the procedure of their plant for producing a product. Rather, it means that the complexity of processing the material for a product or service does not allow familiarity with all the details concerning the work that are needed for the processing. Most foremen or supervisors know generally what method is being used for performing an operation, but it is unusual when complete details of hand and body motions being employed are known. Therefore, this book will deal mainly with the procedures and techniques for gathering information about the *sequence* and *method* of work. This does not mean the other three factors are not important. It merely means that this training will include only those techniques needed in finding information for these two factors.

GATHERING THE INFORMATION FOR THE ANALYSIS TECHNIQUES

In general, there are four ways information about the work can be gathered. These methods are observation, discussion

Table 3-1. When to Use Motion Pictures

General advantages:
1. Greater detail
2. Permits review of details in quiet surroundings
3. Greater convenience for study
4. Enlists cooperation of all concerned
5. More accuracy of times
6. Better training aids
7. Positive record
8. Evaluate methods changes before the change
9. Accurate portrayal of simultaneity

Speed	Situations	Special advantages (in addition to above)
1 FPS* 100 FPM	1. Three or more in a coordinate crew 2. Nonrepetitive work in one area 3. Long-cycle repetitive work 4. Gross body motion operations 5. Need for times in work load determination (for operations with characteristics of 1 through 4 above)	1. Lower film cost 2. Greater time coverage
8 FPS 500 FPM 10 FPS	1. Medium (0.75 to 2 min) cycles 2. Short-cycle nonrepetitive work 3. Need for times in work load determination	1. Slightly lower film cost 2. More cycles 3. Relatively continuous motions
16 FPS 1000 FPM	1. Short-cycle work 2. Need for measurement in work load determination 3. Skilled operation 4. Transfer operation to another plant 5. Comparison of methods 6. Finger or hand operations 7. Evaluation of equipment	1. Normal projection speed 2. Training film
24, 32, 64 FPS 1500, 2000, 4000 FPM	1. Motion and time study research 2. Especially skilled or complex operation 3. Evaluation of complex equipment usage	1. Fine detail 2. "Stop" skill frame at a time 3. Training in skills

* FPS = frames per second.   FPM = frames per minute.

with others, motion pictures, and past records. The most widely used procedures involve observing the work directly and, importantly, using discussion with others. This follows the human relations principles mentioned in Chapter 2. These two procedures do not involve anything more than their names imply. This is where the principles of good human relations are quite important.

Using past records, like quality, cost, and production, is not difficult. A foreman or supervisor can frequently find much information in his own files about past activities. For example, information about production from a previous production sequence may be required. Production records would provide these data. Actually, no difficulty should be encountered by using past records.

Motion pictures represent a very important way of gathering data in work simplification. There are many uses for motion pictures, and these are summarized in Table 3-1.

Table 3-1 should be used as a guide to indicate when motion-picture equipment for recording work situations might be requested. Motion pictures can be analyzed at the convenience of the analyst, and at a rate of speed for desired accuracy needed. In general, motion pictures are used for the analysis of work *methods*, rather than *sequence*.

A complete description of motion-picture equipment and the type needed in work simplification is included in another book.[2] The procedure for taking motion pictures is included in the same reference. The analyst should recognize when motion pictures would be most desirable for analyzing many of his work activities; then it is advisable to investigate the necessary motion-picture equipment.

ANALYSIS TECHNIQUES

Collecting the information does not complete the analysis. The information should be put into a graphical presentation.

[2] See G. Nadler, *Motion and Time Study,* New York: McGraw-Hill Book Company, Inc., 1955, chap. 4.

This enables the analyst to examine more logically the activities under study. This information can be presented to the worker, supervisors, and others involved. Data in graphical form, or in the form of the techniques to be presented, are better for general analysis and presentation. The manner of converting the collected data or information into these techniques will be presented in the following eight chapters.

These techniques involve written presentations. However, an analyst familiar with the symbols and concepts can make a mental analysis of work. This would involve noting mentally the particular symbol breakdown which normally would have been written.

Not all the following techniques are used for analyzing the work for every problem. Rather, these techniques are like the tools in a carpenter's kit. The carpenter knows how to use each of his tools, but it is his judgment which determines the tool to be used for a particular problem. The work simplification analyst selects the techniques to be used for a problem, according to his judgment of the situation. Supposedly he is familiar with each tool and knows where and how it can be used best.

Chapters 4 and 5 deal with techniques for analyzing *sequence*. The next five chapters concern techniques for analyzing *methods* of work. Chapter 11 concerns various techniques, some for analyzing sequence, some for method.

Important: Even though techniques will be presented for gathering information about only two (sequence and method) of the five factors affecting work, the analyst must gather information about the other three from usual sources (engineering, purchasing, accounting, etc.) in the organization.

CHAPTER 4

PRODUCT PROCESS CHART

When work simplification was defined, "systematic analysis of work" was the first phrase used. This is the key to gathering information about the work situation being studied.

What does systematic analysis mean? Basically, it means breaking work into basic components or units of accomplishment. A breakdown is essential for proper analysis. A person cannot get a complete understanding of any activity by merely "looking" or getting a superficial or over-all impression of it. Designing job methods is easier when each of the individual components is known. People are able to study only one thing at a time. Charting attempts to list, one thing at a time, all the components in the work. If the individual components are separated, they can be improved or eliminated.

A product process chart (PPC) is a technique used to get sequence information. The product process chart is the symbolic and systematic presentation of the procedure used to modify and/or work on a product. Generally, it is a good idea to chart as much of the work sequence as possible to get full information. Frequently, less than the whole sequence of work on the product will be all that should be analyzed. When deciding about the beginning and end points for charting less than a whole sequence, the analyst is guided by the first step, "state the problem." For example, it is unlikely that a PPC for a problem selected in a machine shop would include work in the foundry. Of course, the chart can be made for the entire process if desired.

The product process chart provides a presentation of everything (all the work) that happens to the product. The ability to chart everything is valuable; a mere listing of product modification operations is incomplete for analysis purposes.

When speaking of components of work, it is necessary to devise symbols or breakdowns which are similar from one situation to another. Obviously, this is what makes the breakdown so worthwhile. A well-trained analyst can always find similarities, or basic components, in all types of activity. This permits him really to tackle any job.

ANALYZING FUTURE WORK

Although the product process chart helps gather information about present work, one of its best uses is for planning future work. This is the best use of any chart. A product process chart for a sequence not yet in existence is a description of what the analyst and manufacturing supervisors think the sequence *would have been* if the product had been sent into manufacturing. Then, the product process chart permits various people and departments to work together and combine ideas to arrive at the most economical procedure before any of the work starts.

OTHER USES OF PPC

Some of the widely diversified activities where PPCs have been made include manufacturing chairs, tables, automobiles, electric motors, etc. But the PPC can be applied to a process which is used intermittently, like canning foods; or in the home, for charting light bulbs, firewood, groceries, etc.; or in the office, for charting supplies, books (see Chapter 5); or in libraries for checking out books; or for charting food in restaurants; or flowers in a florist shop.

SYMBOLS FOR PRODUCT PROCESS CHARTS

Table 4-1 gives the symbols for consistent work units used to break down any type of procedure of work on a product. Two sets of symbols are included: One is for a rough analysis, and the other is for a more detailed analysis. Most of the illustrations for a PPC use the most detailed set of symbols, because it is easy to see how the less detailed symbols could be used in place of them.

MAKING THE PRODUCT PROCESS CHART

A product process chart can be made on a form similar to that used in any of the illustrations in this chapter, or on any piece of blank paper. The chart is made by assigning to each step of the work sequence on the product an appropriate symbol from Table 4-1. A short explanation of exactly what each step accomplishes is written alongside the symbol.

There are usually five columns on the product process chart. These columns are:

1. A symbol column.
2. An explanation or description column, which adds pertinent information to describe the actual activity indicated by the symbol.
3. A distance column to indicate how far one unit of product travels for every move symbol.
4. A quantity column to indicate the number of material or product units worked on, handled, or started at the same time for each symbol on the chart.
5. An equipment column to note the equipment being worked on with each symbol (mainly the operation symbols). Obviously few storage symbols will have an equipment listing.

Sometimes a column is included for listing the amount of time the operation and movement symbols take. Because it is difficult to determine a time value for a storage symbol

Table 4-1. Product Process Chart Symbols

Geometric symbol	Name	Activity represented	Simplified symbols
(L)	Labor operation	Expenditure of labor or cost on product at one workplace which does not add value to the product.	Operation ◯
(M)	Modification operation	Modification (changing shape or size, machining, permanent assembly or disassembly, etc.) of product at one workplace. (Modification may be accomplished by machines and/or labor expenditure.)	
◯	Move	Change in location of product from one workplace to another workplace.	Same ◯
▽	Temporary storage *	Delay, waiting, or banking of product when *no* special order or requisition is required to perform next activity.	Storage ▽
▽̿	Controlled storage *	Delay, waiting, or banking of product when a special order or requisition is required to perform next activity.	
◇	Verification	Comparison of product with a standard of quantity or quality at one workplace (a specialized labor operation). (A control point established by management action.)	Same ◇

* In most literature, the temporary storage symbol is a double triangle, and the controlled, or permanent, storage symbol is a single triangle. Because the temporary storage symbol is used overwhelmingly more than the controlled storage symbol, the principles of methods design (Chap. 12) indicate that it is better to use the symbols as indicated here, i.e., single triangle for temporary storage, double triangle for controlled storage.

which is meaningful, a time column is not considered necessary.

To start the product process chart, the analyst records the
symbol for the first step of the phase of the sequence being
charted. Everything that happens to the product (lifted,
modified, packaged) is then classified by symbol. (When
the product is already being manufactured or worked on, it
is important to chart what *is happening* to the product, *not*
what *should be happening.* In many cases there is a difference between the two, usually with more inefficiencies
present than there should be. Because the improvement will
have to be evaluated in terms of the process now in use, it is
wise to use as the original method the actual, rather than
intended, procedure.) The symbols are placed vertically and
are connected to one another by a straight line in the order
of occurrence. This forms a column around which the other
columns are placed. All the other columns are filled in, in
relation to the symbol column. Only one symbol is placed
on one line of the chart. The information pertaining to that
symbol, required in each of the other columns, is located on
the same symbol line. Distances are measured from the
centers of workplaces.

Sometimes it is difficult to visualize exactly what is to be
charted on the product process chart. There are many things
occurring: a materials handler moving a pallet, a man modifying a product, material being stored in a storage rack, etc.
To avoid confusion, it is best for the analyst to assume that
he is one of the units being worked on. Then the question
of what to chart becomes one of "what happens to me as I
progress through the sequence." A symbol would be assigned
to each activity which occurred to the "analyst." For example, you may be following some dishes. If the family has just
eaten a meal, then the dishes are on the table. The analyst
would then assume that he is one of the dishes on the table.
Obviously, "he" is in storage—that is, not moving or being
worked on. Then "he" might be scraped; an operation symbol would be used. Or it might be a movement symbol to

the sink. If you assume you are one of the units being charted, it is easier to chart everything that happens to "you."

Explanation of symbols

The operation symbols are, in most cases, the most important activity on the chart. Certainly the work to be accomplished will be indicated by the operation symbols. The breakdown into labor and modification operation symbols is one of the most valuable aids in detailing a procedure.

In most cases, labor operation symbols do not add value to the final product. They add only expense to the product. Because the PPC tells what work is performed on the product, the expenditure of labor which does not modify the product is included. The labor operation symbol should be used when detail is required for such activity as stacking, unloading, shoveling, lifting of heavy or bulky parts. Technically, every time a product is picked up or put down, a labor operation symbol for detail should be used. Because this would make the chart rather lengthy, the labor operation symbol is used mainly for pickup and put-down of product or material only when it is large in size, unusual in shape, or heavy. This is done even though a detailed chart with a finer breakdown of symbols is used.

The verification symbol is a specialized type of operation. Sometimes both some operation and verification occur at the same time. When this happens, both symbols are recorded together on the same line, with the operation symbol placed inside the verification symbol.

Other information on chart

A product process chart, like all the other techniques presented in this book, is a flexible one. Although some specific suggestions have been given for making and using such a chart, an analyst can do pretty much anything he wants to do in relation to getting information onto the chart. The column of time values could be added. Special symbols for materials handling procedures could be used (see Table 11-1). The number of men used at each symbol could be indicated. The number of square feet used for storage space could be noted. Anything you feel will help should be put on the chart.

Amount of detail on chart

In almost all cases, only one symbol is used for each step of the process. However, it may be desirable to use more than one symbol for a particular activity. For example, a worker at one workplace may actually perform several important steps like assemble, test, and package. Instead of noting this all as one modification operation, or as a combination verification and operation, it might be better to note this with three symbols, as one modification operation, a verification, and another modification operation. *The amount of detail to be used on a chart depends on you.*

SUMMARY ON CHART

A summary should be placed at the bottom of each product process chart (as is done on most charts). The summary, illustrated in the following examples, shows the total number of symbols of each type in the chart and a summation of the distance moved for one part. For some of the more complex product process charts, a summary is not meaningful. If it is feasible, a summary should be made.

FLOW DIAGRAM

To help explain the product process chart activities, it is customary to make a flow diagram. A flow diagram includes the layout of the area in which the product is moving, with lines drawn to indicate the movement of the product. It is very valuable in pointing out the relationships between movements and workplaces. The flow diagram can be made on a form similar to that used in the flow-diagram illustration in this chapter or on a blank sheet of paper. It is almost always useful to make the diagram to the proper scale.

One of the most amazing results of making a chart, any chart or flow diagram, is the insight gained by the mere act of symbolizing the work. The information starts to generate ideas as to what can be done to improve or plan a situation. Although this chapter will not discuss the procedures for obtaining ideas about improvement or design, it is important for the analyst to record for future use (step 3, getting the ideas) any ideas he obtains while charting.

ILLUSTRATIONS

The illustrations given below were selected to show varying conditions under which a product process chart can be made. Each chart should be reviewed to learn how the five columns are used, the summary is made, special situations are handled, the flow diagrams assist in understanding the chart, etc.

A difficult problem in a textbook presentation of work simplification is how to describe adequately the actual process of what is occurring, and then demonstrate how the chart is a result of such a process. A complete description of one process will be given in the first illustration that follows; the reader should attempt to relate this description to the chart to make certain that he understands how a certain symbol was derived from a specific set of circumstances. Although the complete description for all the other problems in the book will not be given, the charts were made from actual situations, in the same way as indicated by this first illustration.

1. Handling hoppers on unloading dock

Figure 1-4 shows the original flow diagram for handling hoppers filled with shelled peas brought on trucks from the

fields. Analysis included the product process chart shown
in Fig. 4-1.

Peas are harvested and brought to viners located in several
convenient points in the countryside surrounding the cannery. The viners are machines which separate all the leaves,
vines, stems, pods, etc., from the peas, and move the peas

FIG. 4-1. Original product process chart of hoppers on unloading
platform.

ORIGINAL _____ PRODUCT PROCESS _____ **_OF_ CHART**

OF_ HOPPERS ON UNLOADING PLATFORM

Date 7/14/48 Part HOPPERS Operator _____ Mach_____

By E. D. No._____

QUANTITY	DIST.	SYMBOL	EXPLANATION	EQUIPMENT
1 6		▽	On Truck (Filled with Peas)	
2 I	6'	○	To Edge of Truck	
3 I		Ⓛ	Lifted to Platform	
4 ∽ I	40'	○	To Position Near Tenderometer Shack	
5 ∽ 25	Sample of Peas	▽	At Shack	
6	Grade Paddle			Tenderometer
7 I		Ⓛ	Hopper Turned Around	
8 I	40'	○	To Front of Dumper	
9 ∽ 20		▽	For Dumping	
10 I	20' Paddle	○	To Dumper	
11 I		Ⓜ	Peas Dumped from Hopper	
12 I	5' Peas	○	Backed Out	
13 I		Ⓛ	Turned Around	
14 I	25'	○	To Washer	Shower Spray
15 I		Ⓜ	Washed	
16 I	20'	○	To Scales	
17 I		◇	Check Empty Weight	Scale
18 I	30'	○	To Storage Through Rows of Hoppers	
19 ∽ 35		▽	Until Needed	
20 I	30'	○	To Truck	
21 I		Ⓛ	Lowered to Truck	
22 I	6'	○	To Position on Truck	
23 6		▽	On Truck	
24				
25	SUMMARY			
26	Ⓜ 2			
27	Ⓛ 4			
28	○ 10			
29	▽ 5			
30	◇ I			
31	DIST. 222'			
32				
33				
F I				

over a conveyor to hoppers. The hoppers are four-wheeled devices which measure 30 by 30 inches at the top and are 36 inches high. Each hopper holds about 400 pounds of peas. The hoppers are funnel-shaped at the bottom and have a slide door which permits unloading from the bottom of the hopper.

Six hoppers are placed in a truck, which takes them to the cannery. The truck is backed up to the unloading platform, and in most cases the floor of the truck is beneath the level of the unloading platform. After the gate of the truck is removed, the unloader starts to pull off one of the hoppers. When the hopper gets to the edge of the unloading dock, the unloader must lift the end of the hopper up to the end of the dock. The unloader pushes the other end of the hopper up to the dock and then rolls it to the ungraded area near the tenderometer shack. Frequently, the process of rolling the hopper to the tenderometer shack becomes involved and complicated because other rows of hoppers are lined up in front of the dumper, awaiting dumping. Likewise, there are frequently many hoppers awaiting grading at the tenderometer shack. The unloader gets the other five hoppers in the same way, and places all the hoppers from one truckload together, so that they are more easily identified.

A grader gets a sample of peas with a scoop from each hopper, keeping each hopper's sample separate from the others. Each sample is taken to the tenderometer shack, where a tenderometer is used to determine the tenderness of the peas. The tenderometer works on the principle of squeezing the peas to determine with how much pressure they resist the squeeze; the less pressure, the tenderer the peas. When the grade has been determined, a paddle with a grade number on it is placed in the hopper of peas.

Each hopper is rolled to the appropriate row of hoppers, each row based on its grade. There are four different grades of peas. In almost all cases, these rows of hoppers are in front of the dumping point. As a certain grade of pea is required in the processing, each hopper with that grade is rolled onto the dump one at a time, the door opened at the bottom of the hopper, and the peas dumped. After each hopper is emptied, it is rolled to the washing area, where it is sprayed with water to clean out most of the peas and other plant material which has stuck to the sides of the hopper. Each hopper is rolled to the scales, where the weight of the hopper is checked against a slip of paper giving the number of the hopper and its previous empty weight. If trucks are waiting for hoppers, the hopper is rolled to an empty truck and lowered from the dock to the truck. Six hoppers are placed on the truck in this way. If there are no empty trucks waiting for hoppers, the hoppers are rolled to the storage area where they remain until empty trucks are available.

This chart was made when the problems of confusion, delays, and extra cost on the unloading platform were brought to the attention of the industrial engineer. The specific goal was to eliminate these problems. The engineer decided that the best procedure for gathering the data was mainly by observation. The work was of the varied-cycle type dealing with hoppers (a piece of equipment which is considered a product, since work is performed on it). Since the work was varied-cycle, the chart shows a general method encompassing most of the situations which arose.

The product process chart of Fig. 4-1 was made with the more detailed symbols. As pointed out previously, it is possible to make a product process chart without this detail, by using the simple symbols shown in Table 4-1. A simplified version of this chart is shown in Fig. 4-2. A comparison between Figs. 4-1 and 4-2 will easily point out the differences in detail.

2. Copper bar processing

Ten-foot copper bars in ducts are used for carrying electricity through plants. Before being assembled in the duct, they are prepared for the assembly. The specific goal for

FIG. 4-2. A product process chart of the same activity shown in Fig. 4-1, except for the use of simplified symbols and detail.

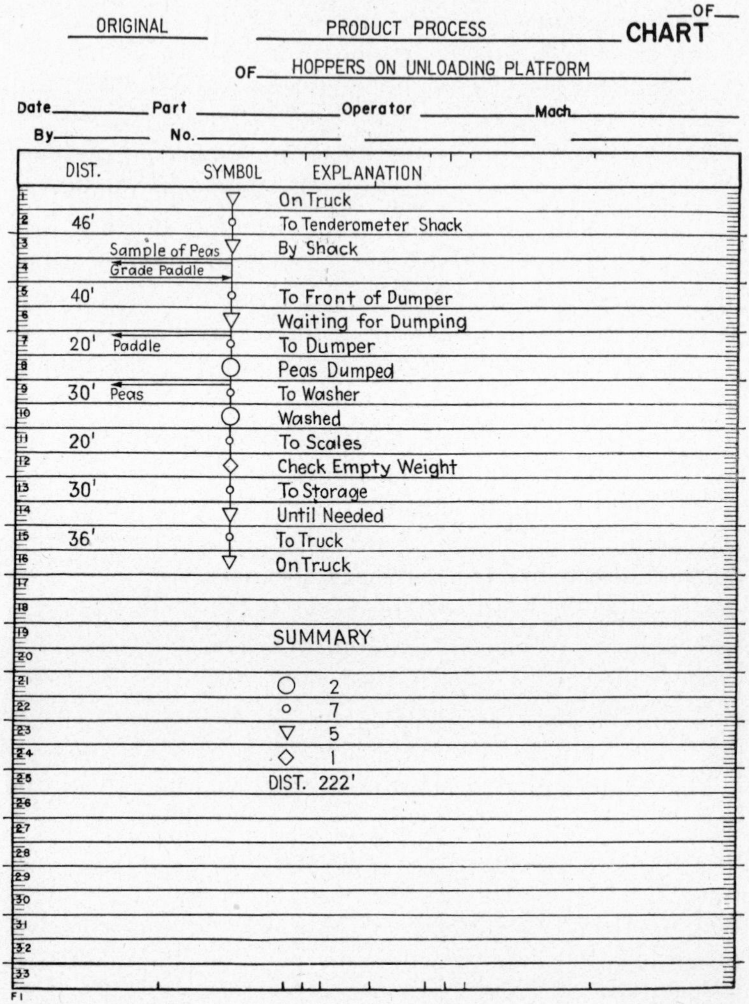

ORIGINAL   PRODUCT PROCESS   **CHART** ___OF___

OF___ HOPPERS ON UNLOADING PLATFORM _____

Date_____ Part _____ Operator _____ Mach_____

By_____ No. _____

	DIST.	SYMBOL	EXPLANATION
1		▽	On Truck
2	46'	○	To Tenderometer Shack
3	Sample of Peas	▽	By Shack
4	Grade Paddle		
5	40'	○	To Front of Dumper
6		▽	Waiting for Dumping
7	20' Paddle	○	To Dumper
8		○	Peas Dumped
9	30' Peas	○	To Washer
10		○	Washed
11	20'	○	To Scales
12		◇	Check Empty Weight
13	30'	○	To Storage
14		▽	Until Needed
15	36'	○	To Truck
16		▽	On Truck
17			
18			
19			SUMMARY
20			
21		○	2
22		o	7
23		▽	5
24		◇	1
25			DIST. 222'
26			
27			
28			
29			
30			
31			
32			
33			

F 1

each of the operations involved was to reduce the amount of handling. The chart was made by observing a few of the slightly varied cycles. The product process chart of Fig. 4-3 is a simple one. Because the bars were heavy, many labor operations appear on this chart. The flow diagram is given in Fig. 4-4.

FIG. 4-3. Original product process chart of copper bar processing.

ORIGINAL   PRODUCT PROCESS   1 OF 2 **CHART**

OF COPPER BAR PROCESSING

Date 12/27/51   Part COPPER BAR   Operator J. R. & M.S.   Mach PRESS, DRILL, SANDER

By G.E.M.   No. 1/8 x 1 1/2 to 1/4 x 3 –10' in Length (Approx. 30 #/BAR)

	QUANT.	DIST.		SYMBOL	EXPLANATION	EQUIPMENT
1	10-12 Boxes	15'		○	From Truck to Skid	Overhead Hoist
2	10-12 Boxes			▽	On Skid	
3	1 Skid			Ⓛ	Picked up by Hand Truck	Hand Truck
4	1 Skid	50'		○	To Storage Area	
5	1 Skid			Ⓛ	Skid Placed	
6	10 Skid			▽		
7	1 Skid			Ⓛ	Skid Picked Up	Hand Truck
8	1 Skid	60'		○	To Bar Storage	
9	1 Skid			Ⓛ	Skid Placed	
10	10-12 Boxes			▽		
11	1 Box	Strap		Ⓜ	Strap Broken	Steel Strap Break
12	1 Box	Nails Etc.		Ⓜ	Nails & Box Top Removed	
13	1 Box			▽		
14	2 Bars			Ⓛ	P U Copper Bars	
15	2 Bars	5'		○	To Storage Bin	
16	2 Bars			Ⓛ	Placed in Bin	
17	800 Bars	Boxes		▽	In Bin	
18	2-4 Bars			Ⓛ	Bars P U	
19	2-4 Bars	10'		○	To Press Table	
20	2-4 Bars			Ⓛ	Placed	
21	16-20 Bars			▽	On Press Table	
22	1 Bar			Ⓛ	Bars Placed Under Press	
23	1 Bar			Ⓜ	Holes Punched	Punch Press
24	1 Bar			Ⓛ	Other End of Bar Placed	
25	1 Bar			Ⓜ	Holes Punched	Punch Press
26	1 Bar			Ⓛ	Bar Lifted	
27	1 Bar	10'		○	To Skid	
28	1 Bar			Ⓛ	Bar Placed	
29	150 Bars			▽	On Skid	
30	150 Bars	20'		○	To Degreaser	
31	150 Bars			▽	By Degreaser	
32	1 Bar			Ⓛ	Bar Picked Up	
33	1 Bar	4'		○	To Degreaser	

F1

FIG. 4-3 (Cont.)

ORIGINAL　　　　PRODUCT PROCESS　　　CHART

OF　COPPER BAR PROCESSING

Date_____ Part _____ Operator _____ Mach_____
By_____ No._____

QUANT.	DIST.	SYMBOL	EXPLANATION	EQUIPMENT
1	1 Bar		(L) Placed in Degreaser	
2	1 Bar		(M) Degreased	Vapor Degreaser
3	1 Bar		(L) Bar Reversed	
4	1 Bar		(M) Degreased	Vapor Degreaser
5	15 Bars		▽ In Degreaser	
6	1 Bar		(L) Bar P U	
7	1 Bar	7'	○ To Sander	
8	1 Bar		(M) Sand One Edge 1ST End	Sander
9	1 Bar		(M) Sand Two Edge 1ST End	"
10	1 Bar	A	(M) Sand One Flatside 1ST End	"
11	1 Bar		(M) Sand Two Flatside 1ST End	"
12	1 Bar		(L) Reverse Ends	
13			Repeat A on 2nd End	
14	1 Bar	5'	○ To Silverplate Bucket	
15	1 Bar		(M) Silverplate 1st End	Silverplate Dips
16	1 Bar		(M) 1st Rinse	"　"
17	1 Bar		(M) 2nd Rinse	"　"
18	10 Bars		▽ In 2nd Rinse	"　"
19	1 Bar		(L) Reverse Ends	"　"
20	1 Bar		(M) Silverplate 2nd End	"　"
21	1 Bar		(M) 1st Rinse	"　"
22	1 Bar		(M) 2nd Rinse	"　"
23	10 Bars		▽ In 2nd Rinse	"　"
24	1 Bar		(L) Bar P U	
25	1 Bar	10'	○ To Skid	
26	1 Bar		(L) Bar Placed	
27	150 Bars		▽ On Skid	SUMMARY
28				(L) = 20
29				(M) = 20
30				○ = 11
31				▽ 12
32				Dist = 196'
33				

F I

Fig. 4-4. Flow diagram for original sequence of copper bar processing.

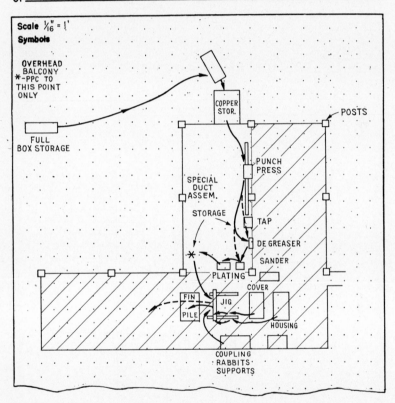

3. Planning for switch box assembly

Before starting production, the industrial engineer, fore-man of department, and production manager met to discuss the process to be used for assembly. They knew the floor space available for the assembly (Fig. 4-5) and decided to make a product process chart for the procedure according to the way present plans seemed to indicate the assembly would

FIG. 4-5. Flow diagram for original *planned* sequence of switch box assembly.

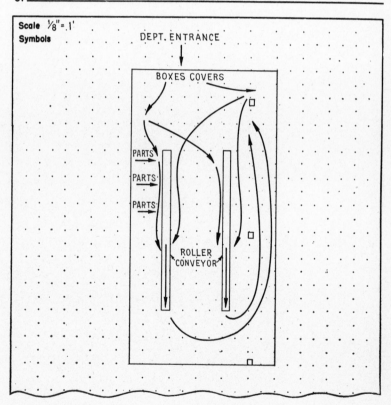

be done. This chart is shown in Fig. 4-6. Their goal was to assemble the box with the least cost. Two box sizes were required, for which two roller conveyors were to be set up. By discussion they charted, with minimum detail, what they thought would be the repetitive cycle. Because there was no

FIG. 4-6. Original *planned* product process chart for switch box assembly.

ORIGINAL PLANNED _____ PRODUCT PROCESS _____ **CHART** __OF__

OF ASSEMBLY SWITCH BOX (2 SIZES)

Date 3/12/53 Part SWITCH BOX PARTS Operator _____ Mach _____
By C.A. No. 7849 THROUGH 7862

QUANT.	DIST.	BOX EXPLAN.	QUANT.	DIST.	COVERS EXPLAN.
1 60-75 Boxes		▽ By Entrance to Dept. on Skid	120 Covers		▽ By Entrance
2 60-75 Boxes	12'	○ Pulled to Storage	120 Covers	12'	○ Pulled to Storage
3 300 Boxes		▽ On Skids	360 Covers		▽ On Skid
4 2 Boxes		Ⓛ P U	4 Covers		Ⓛ P U
5 2 Boxes	15'	○ To Assembly By Area	4 Covers	30'	○ To Assembly Parts
6 2 Boxes		Ⓛ Place	4 Covers		Ⓛ Place
7 20-25 Boxes		▽ Parts	50 Covers		▽ Parts
8 1 Box		Ⓜ Assem. 1st Set of Parts	1 Cover		Ⓜ Assemble Parts
9 1 Box	6'	○ To 2nd Assem.			← Hinges
10 10-15 Boxes		▽ On Conveyor Parts			
11 1 Box		Ⓜ Assem. 2nd Set of Parts			
12 1 Box	6'	○ To 3rd Assem.			
13 10-15 Boxes		▽ On Conveyor Parts			
14 1 Box		Ⓜ Assem. 3rd Set of Parts			
15 1 Box	6'	○ To Cover Assem.			
16 10-15 Boxes		▽ On Conveyor			
17 1 Box		Ⓜ Assem. Cover		CARTONS	
18 1 Box	7'	○ To Packing	150 Flat		▽ By Entrance
19 10-15 Boxes		▽ On Conveyor	150 Flat	40'	○ Pulled to Storage
20 1 Box		Ⓜ Assem. in Box; Label, Filler, Tape	450 Flat Ctns.		▽
21 1 Box		Ⓜ Assem. Other Matl.	1 Carton		Ⓜ Form and Fold Cartons
22 1 Box	10'	○ To Skid	1 Carton	8'	○ To Assembly
23 60 Boxes		▽ On Skid			
24 60 Boxes	30'	○ Pulled to Store			
25 300 Boxes		▽			
26 60 Boxes		○ Pulled to Dept. Ent.		SUMMARY	
27 60-120 Boxes		▽ At Entrance		Box Cover Carton	
28			Ⓛ	2 2 0	
29			Ⓜ	6 1 1	
30			○	9 2 2	
31			▽	10 3 2	
32			Dist.	92' 42' 48'	
33					

F I

FIG. 4-7. Original product process chart for processing laundry in a hospital. (Only the first of two pages is shown.)

ORIGINAL   PRODUCT PROCESS   1 OF 2 **CHART**

OF LAUNDRY IN HOSPITAL

Date 2/28/56   Part LINENS   Operator _____ Mach _____

By KC   No. _____

	QUANTITY	DIST	SYMBOL	EXPLANATION
1	∿ 200#/Truck	40'		To Sorting Room
2	∿ 2000#			
3	2#		Ⓛ	Sorted Into 8 Classifications
4	2#	8'		to Pile of Laundry
5	1000#			Wait for Sorting to Finish
6	15#		Ⓛ	Laundry Picked up and put into Truck
7	175#/Truck			In Truck
8	Truck	23'		To Scale
9	Truck			Weighed to Standard
10			Ⓛ	Linen Removed or Added as Needed
11	Truck	40'		To Storage
12	6–8 Trucks			In Storage
13	1 Truck	20'		To Washing Machine
14	2 Trucks			By Washing Machine
15	15#		Ⓛ	Loaded into Machine
16	350#			In Machine
17	350#		Ⓜ	Washed
18	850# +Water			Awaiting Removal
19	15#		Ⓛ	Unload into Extractor Basket
20	850#			In Basket
21	850#	15'		To Extractor
22	850#		Ⓛ	Hoist Attached
23	850#		Ⓛ	Hoisted and Placed in Extractor
24	850#		Ⓜ	Water Extracted
25	525#		Ⓛ	Hoisted up
26	525#	13'		To Portable Storage Table
27	525#			Await Dumping
28	263#		Ⓛ	Dump one Side
29	Rough Dry			OnTable Flatwork
30				Uniforms
31	15#	Ⓛ	Loaded Into Trucks	◇ Checked by Inspector Ⓛ Shaken
32	100#		In Truck	Ⓛ Loaded Into Truck ⒧Placed on Truck
33			To Tumblers	Await Move to Pressers, For Move

F I

production, the chart made is called an *original planned* product process chart.

4. Sorting laundry in hospital

Laundry in a hospital is brought to the sorting room in trucks and dumped into the middle of the room. From here the laundry is sorted into various classifications and placed in trucks. A load has to be weighed to limit the amount going into a washing machine. The trucks are rolled to a scale where they are weighed, and then rolled to the washer where the laundry begins its process through the washing machines. After washing, excess water is extracted, and the laundry goes in three different paths: one to the tumblers, the second to the flatwork ironer, and the third to the pressers. All this laundry eventually ends in the storeroom for distribution to the various floors. The product process chart is shown in Fig. 4-7. Notice how the labor operation symbols show the excess work. Also, notice how easy it is to make a chart if you assume that you are a "dirty pillow case." The major objective for studying this problem was to reduce the costs of processing laundry.

CHAPTER 5

FORM PROCESS CHART

Another technique for analyzing sequence of work is the form process chart (FPC). The FPC is the symbolic and systematic presentation of the procedure used to modify, work on, and handle a form or forms. In many ways the form process chart is similar to the product process chart in that it follows a "product." However, the product is paper work and/or information. This requires a new technique.

It has been estimated that 25 per cent of all work in this country involves paper work. This means that the wages paid for paper work run into billions of dollars. It has been estimated again that even if one-third of all paper work were eliminated, this would be a savings of somewhere around 25 billion dollars.

A form process chart is usually made for a procedure. In this it is similar to a product process chart, which is made for the manufacturing of a product. A product usually involves more than one component. A procedure or system usually involves more than one form. Although the form process chart can be made for one form or one copy, this is usually meaningless because of the usual interdependence among forms. Also changing one form cannot usually be done without reference to other forms. Interdependence of information and means of communication make the form process chart valuable.

The form process chart is not only for analysis of office work. The form process chart finds use in the factory too.

For example, production control procedures are based on forms. The same is true for maintenance work orders, petty cash vouchers, incentive reporting cards, etc. Form process charts have been applied to pharmacy prescriptions, laboratory research reports, medical and hospital activities, etc.

The FPC is used to assist in gathering information and presenting gathered data about the sequence of work on or with the form or forms, and for planning the design and the sequence for future systems, procedures, and forms. This latter use is one of the most important aspects of form process charts. More and more paper work is being handled through automatic data processing equipment, and the form process chart is highly useful for designing the required procedure.

As with every other chart, the form process chart gives facts about procedures or forms. At the present time, discussion about work methods center around people's opinions. Each and every chart presented in this book can be used as an excellent device for helping to sell ideas. In forms work, this is even more prevalent. In almost all cases a forms procedure is someone's opinion as to how the work should be done. These charts give facts, essential to establishing any design.

CHARTS HELP SELL

The selling feature of the graphic presentations or techniques (presented in Chapters 4 and 5 and the next few chapters) cannot be overemphasized. Too often a foreman will tell the superintendent, or an engineer will say, "I think we ought to make this change." If the superintendent disagrees, the idea is usually forgotten. However, if charts giving present and proposed methods, with improvements well annotated, were available, there would be a better chance of selling the idea. This is another way of saying that written facts are more acceptable to people than opinions. Of course, the charts are beneficial to proper planning because they force ideas to be written. This, then, makes good ideas easier to sell

SYMBOLS

The symbols for form process charts are given in Table 5-1. Many of these symbols are similar to those used on product process charts. However, because of the form, additional symbols are listed.

MAKING THE FORM PROCESS CHART

In making the form process chart, there are usually three, and possibly four, columns for following a copy of a form. The three basic columns are distance, symbol, and explanation. The fourth column could be the equipment column. For example, opposite an operation symbol the piece of equipment utilized, if any, might be listed, such as accounting machine, calculator, typewriter. Because different copies of the same form may follow different procedures in moving through a plant or office, the form process chart is not limited to a single column for the form, or "product," as on the product process chart. If two copies of the same form are followed, there would usually be two columns each of symbols, distance, and description; three copies would involve three columns each of symbols, distance, and description, etc. Since more than one form is usually on the chart, the form process chart can easily become complex and lengthy. However, the chart is graphic and, therefore, extremely valuable when compared to having no information. The columns on the chart are drawn vertically.

In addition to each set of columns for a copy of a form, it is desirable to superimpose somewhat broader categories. These categories are the department or area in which the work on the copy or form is performed. The column for the various departments or areas, in which the columns for the

Table 5-1. Form Process Chart Symbols

Geometric symbol	Name	Activity represented
(2)	Origination	Form being made out at one workplace. (Number in center represents number of copies made.)
◯	Operation	Modification of, or addition to, form at one workplace.
○	Move	Change in location of form from one workplace to another.
▽	Temporary storage	Delay or waiting of form where no special order is required to perform next activity (e.g., in desk basket).
▽	Controlled storage	Delay or waiting of form where a special order is required to perform next activity (e.g., in file cabinet).
◇	Verification	Comparison of form with other information to ascertain correctness of form.
⊢	Information transmission	Reading or removal of information on form for use by someone or some machine.
⊠	Disposal	Form destroyed.

various copies or forms are placed, is vertical and of variable width. In this way a form worked on in a given department is interrelated to other forms originated or worked on at the same time in the department. If necessary, additional sheets of the type shown in Fig. 5-2 can be pasted on either the side or the bottom of the original sheet to provide sufficient area for making the chart. If desirable, the definition of department or area can be reduced to include only one person. The responsibility for and the greater work load due to a form, forms, or copies are more easily pointed out by the department, area, or person differentiation. Relationships among departments and forms are clarified.

When departmental or area columns are used on a form process chart, the symbol columns are moved from department to department as required. In some cases, this can cause a complicated chart. Although complicated, the chart provides so much valuable information that it would be impossible to analyze the procedure any other way. The charts can become rather lengthy. In one case, an analysis of a production control system produced a chart which went around the room to a length of 32 feet and was 4 feet high. But the chart showed so many problems and difficulties that were not known before that the complication was well worthwhile.

INFORMATION TRANSMISSION SYMBOL

Every time the information transmission symbol is used, there should be an indication of the purpose for which the symbol is noted. Likewise, every operation symbol, and even origination symbol, should have an indication mark showing from where information came. In this way, it would be possible to chart all the details concerning use of, and transfer of, information.

On a form process chart the temporary storage symbol is not as important as on the product process chart. Actually, this symbol should be used mainly to indicate a long delay in the processing of forms, rather than all the actual waiting of forms as was done on the product process chart.

FLOW DIAGRAM AND SUMMARY

A flow diagram is made easily for some of the simpler form process charts. For the more involved ones a flow diagram would not be too clear or meaningful. The listing of departments on the chart itself helps eliminate the need for a flow diagram in many cases.

Similarly a summary can be made on a form process chart, but in most cases it is meaningless. As a chart becomes more complicated, the value of a summary decreases. The summary could be a total number of symbols required for each form, or a total number-of-symbols summary for all forms. However, a flow diagram and summary should be made whenever possible.

"RED TAPE"

Paper work has been one of the most insidious forms of increased work in industry and business. It is something that just seems to grow with the frequent comment "One more form won't hurt." Although there are indications that many savings can be made, people and paper work are obstacles. These are the paper work forms designed by people who wish to receive information at regular intervals. Frequently, they may oppose a suggestion that a form be eliminated even if the form serves no useful purpose. The very act of gathering information about the work on and with the forms leads to many ideas for improving the procedures. For this reason, it is necessary to record ideas as they occur. The very act of charting is beneficial. It tells what is occurring most and what is not occurring. This gives ideas, and although the third step, getting ideas, is supposed to show how we can obtain suggestions, it is wise always to record these anyway.

ILLUSTRATIONS

These illustrations should help clarify some of the uses and types of form process charts discussed above.

1. Order form

This company had initiated a large cost reduction program. One phase involved a review of forms and procedures. Specific goal for the analysis of this form was to reduce the time and money spent in working with it. The work on the form was repetitive, and the procedure used to gather the information was by discussion with the people involved. This form process chart (Fig. 5-1) does not involve a flow diagram, since it would not show any additional information. The detail of departments and areas already shown on the chart was sufficient.

2. Policy writing

A policy order (8309) is obtained by an agent and mailed to the office of the insurance company. The order is processed by the steps shown in Fig. 5-2. The specific goal for the typist operation was to decrease the time necessary for preparing the policy. The chart again was made mainly by discussion with the people involved, with some observation. The whole sequence was repetitive. A flow diagram was meaningful for this work, and it is shown in Fig. 5-3.

FIG. 5-1. Original form process chart for order form.

| ORIGINAL | FORM PROCESS | _OF_ CHART |

OF ORDER FORM (WITHIN COMPANY)

Date 12/13/51 Part ORDER FORM Operator _____ Mach _____

By A.E.S. No. 1880

ORDER DEPT.	FACTORY	SUPPLY ORDER FILLING	CENTRAL SUPPLY	PURCHASING DEPT.
1 Info Typed				
2 Copies Separated				
3 12345 Stapled		12345		
4 To File 6	6	In Basket		
5 With Orig. Order		600 To Stockroom		
6 Info From #2	To File	Order Filled		
7 To File		Lot #4 Quant. Added		
8	Out After #5 Recd.	300 To Packer		
9	Destroyed	Separated		
10	5	50 1234 Var. With Material	1234	
11	With Items Received		In Basket	
12	To Receiving File		Add Date, B/L No. and Route	
13			Staples Removed Carbon Out	
14			Separated	
15			1,2 100' To Records 3 To File 4 200'	4
16				In Basket
17			Separated	With Tables
18			Copies Pinned Together	To File
19			Quant. Deducted Stock Records	
20			2 Unit Price Added	
21			75' To Billing Clerk To Billing Clerk	
22			Extensions Added	
23			Extensions Copied	
24			Pin Removed Pin Removed	
25	2		Var. 300'	
26 Billing To #7			2	SUMMARY (FOR #1880)
27	With #5 (Receiving)		To File 15	(7 COPIES)
28 300 To Cent. Supply	Billing Added to Month Cost Stm		20	
29			10	
30			7	
31			4	
32			5	
33			1	

F 1

FIG. 5-2. Original form process chart for policy writing.

ORIGINAL _____ FORM PROCESS _____ CHART __OF__

OF_____ POLICY WRITING _____

Date 5/14/53 Part AGENT FORM 8309 Operator _____ Mach. _____

By F.M.D. No. POLICY 2805 _____ _____

	MR.H.	MR.R.	UNIT SUPVR.	CHECKER	ORDER CLERK	TYPIST
1	8309 In Basket					
2	If Complete					
3	In Basket					
4	50' To Mr. R.					
5		In Basket				
6		Read				
7		Sorted				
8		In Basket				
9		All Groups Follow Same Sequence				
10		50' To Unit Supvr.				
11			In Basket			
12			Read			
13			In Basket			
14			50' To Checker			
15				In Basket		
16				With Files		
17				Corrections		
18				In Basket		
19				50' To Unit Supvr.		
20			In Basket			
21			O.K. Placed			
22						
23			70' To Order Clerk			
24					In Basket	
25		SUMMARY			8309 Completed	
26		⊙ 1				
27		◯ 5			100'	
28		o 11				In Basket
29		▽ 15				2805
30		▽ 2				
31		+→ 4			70' To Checker	
32		◇ 3		25' Sep		
33				To Mail		

F 1

Fig. 5-3. Flow diagram for original sequence of policy writing.

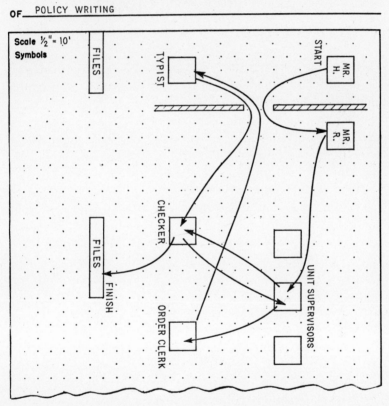

CHAPTER 6

MAN PROCESS CHART

Chapters 4 and 5 dealt with techniques used to analyze *sequence*. This is one of the items about which information should be gathered in the analysis-of-work step.

Now the next several chapters will present techniques used for analyzing *method*. This is the other item about which techniques have to be given for assistance in gathering complete information about work.

However, when it comes to analyzing method, or *how* an operation is performed, it becomes readily apparent that there are different physical characteristics of work being analyzed. In work simplification, there are different techniques to analyze work with different characteristics. Several chapters describe these characteristics of work, and the techniques.

The difference between sequence and method is shown by the operation symbols on the product process chart and form process chart. Here the labor or modification operation, or just plain operation, symbols indicated "what" happened to the product or paper. This is sequence. Method concerns *how* the work shown by the PPC or FPC operation symbol is performed.

The man process chart (MPC) is the first method technique we will discuss, because it is a general over-all one concerning a gross type of work.

The man process chart is the symbolic and systematic presentation of the method of work (series of steps) performed by a man when his work requires him to move from workplace to workplace. Notice that the type of work condition described concerns the movement of a man from workplace to workplace.

USES OF MAN PROCESS CHART

The man process chart is used to gather information and present facts gathered about the method of work being used on a job when the man goes from place to place. It is also used to help plan the method a man should use, when the work will require him to move from one workplace to another. Man process charts are used mainly when the work requires repetitive activity. However, noncyclic work can be analyzed more readily when the analyst thinks in terms of the symbols. Here the analyst looks at the noncyclic work and breaks it down mentally into the components indicated by symbols. This at least permits some degree of analysis where none might be possible otherwise.

Like all charts, the man process chart is valuable for selling ideas and presenting facts. In one case, a superintendent did not think an improvement for the operation of a stock handler would save sufficient time or money to pay for the changes. However, after the superintendent himself made a man process chart for the stock handler, he became an enthusiastic sponsor of the change. He learned how to make the man process chart through work simplification training programs in the company.

When everyone knows what the chart means, and what the symbols mean, then the charts become easier to use. Everyone should be able to apply work simplification and understand these simple symbols. It is easy for an analyst to use the chart he is making to explain the symbols. The very act of charting is a fascinating one to all people, and helps develop ideas by actually putting what is occurring on paper.

SYMBOLS

The symbols used to portray the activities of the man on a man process chart are given in Table 6-1. Two sets of symbols are given. The geometric symbols are used to make the usual man process charts. The time symbols permit a man process time chart to be made. The time symbols can

Table 6-1. Man Process Chart Symbols

Geometric symbol	Time symbol	Name	Activity represented
		Operation	Doing something at one workplace.
		Move without load	Change in location without load from one workplace to another or taking *more than* one step at one workplace.
		Move with load	Change in location with load from one workplace to another or taking *more than* one step at one workplace.
		Delay	Waiting, or idleness, or any activity which is not necessary for the method of work on the operation being charted.
		Hold	Maintaining an object in a fixed position (a special type of operation).
		Verification	Comparing product with a standard of quantity or quality (a special type of operation).
		Interval	Productive activity but not for job being charted.

be lengthened or shortened to correspond to the approximate time for a given activity. A man process time chart is not made often. The ability to lengthen and shorten time symbols helps explain certain types of activities.

MAKING THE MAN PROCESS CHART

Since a man process chart follows but one individual, it is made with a simple, or straight, vertical symbol line. There are three basic columns on the man process chart. The first column is for distance, the second is for symbols, and the third is for description. Other columns can be added to the man process chart, such as a cost-for-the-symbol column and a weight column. It may even be desirable to include an equipment column to note machines, trucks, etc., used by the man for each symbol.

The symbol column is made by placing vertically the symbols representing the activities of a man. A symbol is used for each step. Following strict definitions of each symbol, it is easy to define each step in the method. The move symbols are the main key. The movement symbols should be placed on the chart every time the man takes more than one step. A pivot on one foot is not considered a movement. Any activity which requires a man to move more than one of his feet is a movement, and should be charted as a move. This shows all activities of the man clearly. Although a man might be at only one machine, the MPC will show movements if he takes more than one step.

The "move with load" symbol should be used whenever the man is carrying, pushing, or pulling something, even though the object is not a product or a part of it, or is not the main function for the plant activity. For example, pushing an empty hand truck would be considered a move with load.

The interval symbol represents activity which the man being followed must do within his entire job. However, some of the man's activity, although productive, is not a part of the *operation, or work,* being charted. To avoid lengthy charting of activity which has no effect on the problem, this symbol is used to indicate the diversion of the man to some other activity. This symbol has been useful for clarifying operations which have been considered too complicated to analyze or too variable to chart with a man process chart.

FLOW DIAGRAM

A flow diagram should be made to accompany a man process chart. The flow diagram in this case is the layout of the area in which the man is working, with "flow" lines to indicate his movements from one place to another or when he takes more than one step.

SUMMARY

Because there is only one "item" being followed, a summary is very useful. It is the total number of each type of symbol, and the total distance traveled, placed at the bottom of the chart. The summary shows the general nature of the activities in the operation. This points out the type of activity which should be studied first for possible improvement or design.

ILLUSTRATIONS

The illustrations given below should help clarify how the man process chart can be made to present information. An illustration of a time chart will be shown to compare the type of information from the man process chart and the man process time chart.

1. *Filling containers with powdered material 39*

Materials handling in the packaging of powdered material is rather costly. This operation is concerned with the packaging of less-than-200-pound fiber containers. The present cost of packaging was approximately 10 cents per pound. Under the present volume requirements, a savings of only 10 per cent would amount to $9,200 per year. The specific goal was to reduce the cost for packaging and handling. The man process chart shown in Fig. 6-1 was made as a start for

FIG. 6-1. Original man process chart for filling containers with powdered material. (Only the first page of three is shown.)

ORIGINAL   MAN PROCESS   CHART   1 OF 3

OF FILLING CONTAINERS WITH POWDERED MATERIAL

Date 3/5/53   Part MATERIAL 39   Operator _____ Mach _____

By JWD   No. _____

	DIST.	SYMBOL	DESCRIPTION
1	15'	○	To Door
2		◯	PU Container
3	15'	○	To Container Storage
4		◯	Place on Stack
5		Repeat Above Activity Approx. 50 Times	
6	20'	○	To Containers
7		◯	Position 6 Containers
8	18'	○	To Stencil Storage
9		◯	PU Stencil and Brush
10	18'	○	To Containers
11		◯	Stencil 6 Containers
12	18'	○	To Stencil Storage
13		◯	Replace Stencil and Brush
14	18'	○	To Containers
15		◯	Remove Rims and Covers from 6 Containers
16	50'	○	To Scales with Rims and Covers
17		◯	Stack Rims and Covers
18	60'	○	To Bag Storage
19		◯	PU Six Bags
20	70'	○	To Containers
21		◯	Place Bags Down
22		◯	Place One Bag in each Container
23		◯	PU One Container
24	50'	○	To Scale Area
25		◯	Place Down
26	50'	○	To Containers
27		◯	PU One Container
28	50'	A ○	To Scale Area
29		◯	Place Down
30		Repeat A Four More Times	
31	15'	○	To Rims and Covers
32		B ◯	PU One Set
33		○	To Scales

analyzing the work. Then it was decided that a man process time chart would be desirable. The flow diagram of Fig. 6-2 indicates that there are many activities which take much

FIG. 6-2. Flow diagram for original method of filling containers with powdered material 39.

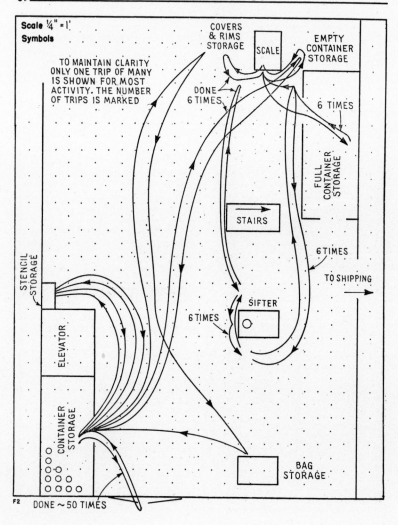

FLOW   **DIAGRAM** ACCOMPANYING ORIGINAL MAN PROCESS TIME _OF_ CHART

OF FILLING CONTAINERS WITH POWDERED MATERIAL 39

Scale ¼" = 1'
Symbols

TO MAINTAIN CLARITY
ONLY ONE TRIP OF MANY
IS SHOWN FOR MOST
ACTIVITY. THE NUMBER
OF TRIPS IS MARKED

COVERS & RIMS STORAGE

SCALE

EMPTY CONTAINER STORAGE

DONE 6 TIMES

6 TIMES

FULL CONTAINER STORAGE

STAIRS

6 TIMES

TO SHIPPING

STENCIL STORAGE

SIFTER

6 TIMES

ELEVATOR

CONTAINER STORAGE

BAG STORAGE

F2   DONE ~ 50 TIMES

longer than other activities. On the man process chart shown in Fig. 6-1 it becomes apparent that each line on the chart has but one symbol, and it appears that each symbol therefore takes about the same amount of time. The man process time chart was made to show that this was not true; each symbol takes a different amount of time. The man process time chart is shown in Fig. 6-3. (In this particular case mo-

FIG. 6-3. Original man process time chart for filling containers with powdered material 39. Time values were obtained from 1 FPS motion picture.

ORIGINAL   MAN PROCESS TIME   CHART $\frac{1}{}$ OF $\frac{2}{}$

OF FILLING CONTAINERS WITH POWDERED MATERIAL

Date 3/7/53 Part MATERIAL 39 Operator _____ Mach _____
By JWD No. _____ (TIMES FROM 1 FPS MOTION PICTURES)

ACCUM TIME	DIST	SYMBOL	(SECS)	DESCRIPTION	FRAME COUNTER
0	15'		3	To Door	420
			4	PU Container	
8	15'		5	To Container Storage	430
16			4	Place on Stack	435
				The Above Activity Repeated Approximately 50 Times	250
800 804	20'		5	To Container	255
814			23	Position 6 Containers	265
824	18'				275
834			4	To Stencil Storage	285
			5	PU Stencil and Brush	
844	18'		5	To Containers	295
854			31	Stencil 6 Containers	305
864					315
874					325
	18'		4	To Stencil Storage	
884	18'		4	Replace Stencil & Brush To Containers	335
894			28	Remove Rims & Covers from 6 Containers	345
904					355
914					365
	50'			To Scales with Rims & Covers	
924			13		375
			8	Stack Rims and Covers	385
934 939					390

FIG. 6-3 (Cont.)

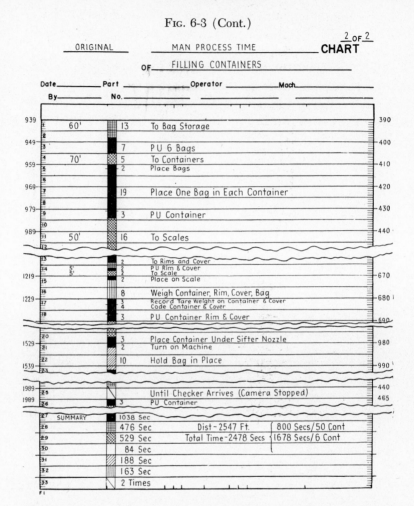

939	60'	13	To Bag Storage	390
949		7	P U 6 Bags	400
959	70'	5	To Containers	410
		2	Place Bags	
969		19	Place One Bag in Each Container	420
979		3	P U Container	430
989	50'	16	To Scales	440
1219	5' 5'	2 2 2	To Rims and Cover / P U Rim & Cover / To Scale / Place on Scale	670
1229		8	Weigh Container, Rim, Cover, Bag	680
		3 4	Record Tare Weight on Container & Cover / Code Container & Cover	
		3	P U Container Rim & Cover	690
1529		3	Place Container Under Sifter Nozzle	980
		2	Turn on Machine	
1539		10	Hold Bag in Place	990
1989			Until Checker Arrives (Camera Stopped)	440
1989		3	P U Container	465

SUMMARY	1038 Sec		
	476 Sec	Dist–2547 Ft.	800 Secs/50 Cont
	529 Sec	Total Time–2478 Secs	1678 Secs/6 Cont
	84 Sec		
	188 Sec		
	163 Sec		
	2 Times		

tion pictures were used to obtain the time values for the man process time chart. However, man process time charts can be made from data collected by a sweep-second wrist watch, or even a stop watch. It is important to note that the time values are not accurate; it is important only to get general relationships among the various time values and symbols. Therefore, these other techniques for gathering the time data are quite usable.) Because the operations and activities are rather lengthy, only sections of the work are shown by these charts.

2. Assemble special switchboards

This product is made in many different sizes and styles. In most cases there is only one switchboard to be made with

Fig. 6-4. Original basic man process chart for the assembly of special switchboards.

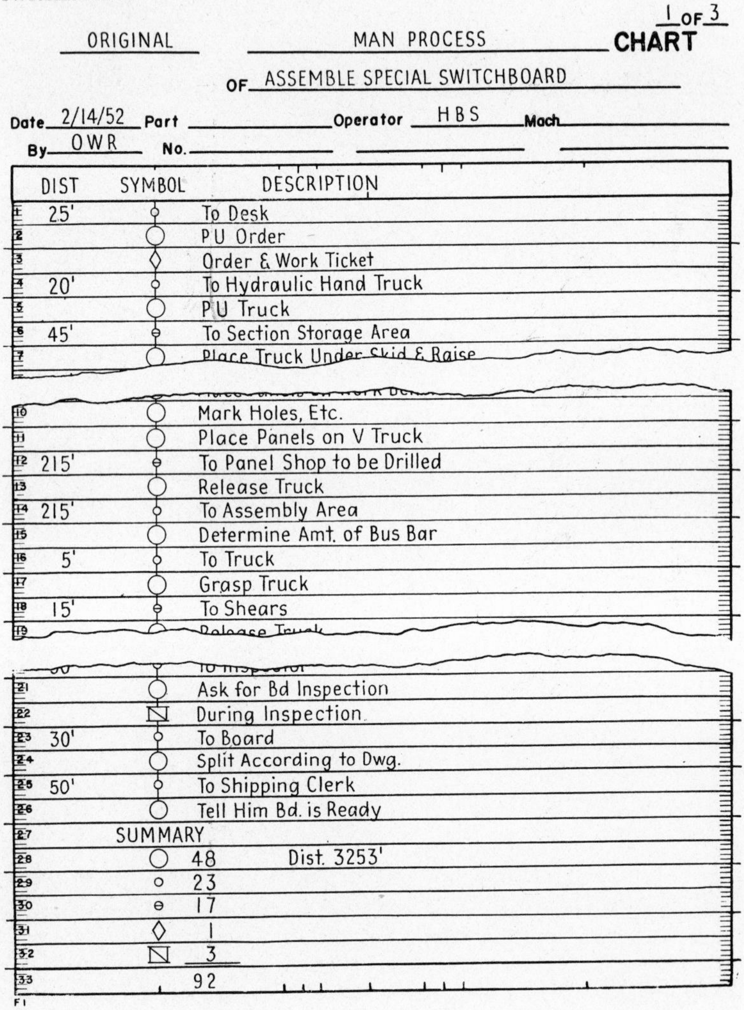

ORIGINAL _____ MAN PROCESS _____ **CHART** $\frac{1}{}$ OF 3

OF ASSEMBLE SPECIAL SWITCHBOARD _____

Date 2/14/52 Part _____ Operator H B S Mach _____

By O W R No. _____ _____ _____

DIST	SYMBOL	DESCRIPTION
1 25'	○	To Desk
2	○	P U Order
3	◇	Order & Work Ticket
4 20'	○	To Hydraulic Hand Truck
5	○	P U Truck
6 45'	○	To Section Storage Area
7	○	Place Truck Under Skid & Raise
		~~
10	○	Mark Holes, Etc.
11	○	Place Panels on V Truck
12 215'	○	To Panel Shop to be Drilled
13	○	Release Truck
14 215'	○	To Assembly Area
15	○	Determine Amt. of Bus Bar
16 5'	○	To Truck
17	○	Grasp Truck
18 15'	○	To Shears
19	○	Release Truck
		~~
21	○	Ask for Bd Inspection
22	◲	During Inspection
23 30'	○	To Board
24	○	Split According to Dwg.
25 50'	○	To Shipping Clerk
26	○	Tell Him Bd. is Ready
27	SUMMARY	
28	○ 48	Dist. 3253'
29	○ 23	
30	⊙ 17	
31	◇ 1	
32	◲ 3	
33	92	

F1

any given set of specifications. Therefore, this operation borders on the nonrepetitive type of work. There are certain general steps which are followed by an assembler. The specific goal for this operation was to save walking for the skilled assemblers. Because there was this general procedure, it was felt that a general man process chart could be made. This chart is shown in Fig. 6-4. Some of the sections of this chart have been omitted to save space. A flow diagram was made, but since it encompassed the entire plant, it is not given here. The problem of movement can be readily observed by looking at the distance column on the chart.

CHAPTER 7

OPERATION CHART

Several techniques will be presented for analyzing method. The various techniques are designed to analyze work situations with different physical characteristics. There are only two basic physical characteristics upon which all the charts are based. The charts to be presented in the following chapters are adaptations of the two basic charts (presented in Chapter 6 and the present chapter), for variations of physical characteristics.

The man process chart was used for an individual who went from one workplace to another in accomplishing his job. And the operation chart is just about the opposite. The operation chart (Op Ch) is the symbolic and systematic presentation of the method of work performed by the hands (and other body members, if used) when the work is at one workplace without the use of cycle-time controlling equipment.

Many operations studied by work simplification are performed at one workplace. This makes the operation chart a basic tool for getting facts. Many large savings have been found in a few moments with this type of chart or one of its adaptations. Many people of different backgrounds in plants are capable of making and using operation charts. For example, operation charts have been successfully taught to foremen, supervisors, presidents, vice-presidents, nurses, workers in factories, and clerks in offices.

USES OF OPERATION CHARTS

The operation chart is used to assist in gathering information and to present facts gathered about the method being used for a particular operation. It is also used for planning the method a man should use in future work when that work must be done at one workplace. Like all the other techniques, the operation chart helps sell changes. An original operation chart does this by pointing out what is wrong with the present method. In some cases, an operation chart can "sell" improvements where previously the improvement had not been accepted.

The areas where operation charts have been applied and can be applied are numerous. Making sandwiches at home, desk work in an office, assembly operations, and serving food in a restaurant are illustrations of good possibilities for operation chart analysis.

SYMBOLS

The symbols used on an operation chart are presented in Table 7-1. As with man process charts, both geometric and time symbols are shown. All the symbols listed are used to describe the activities of the hands. Alongside each symbol (name) are a series of numbers denoting the use of that symbol for other body members when needed. Basically, the operation chart is made to analyze the work and activity of two hands. In some situations, however, the other body members play an important role in the method of that operation, and they too are charted. A line of symbols should be drawn for each body member charted. There would be two lines of symbols for the two hands, three lines for two hands and one foot, etc.

The time symbols are presented for the same reason they were presented with the man process chart symbols. Operation time charts are not made frequently, but when needed

Table 7-1. Operation Chart Symbols

Geometric symbol	Time symbol	Name	Hand activity represented
◯	▪	Suboperation (1, 2, 3) *	Performing something at one work area in a workplace.
◯	▦	Movement without load (2)	Changing location without load from one work area to another work area in a workplace.
⊖	▨	Movement with load	Changing location with load from one work area to another work area in a workplace.
▽	▨	Hold	Maintaining an object in a fixed orientation to allow work on or with object.
▽	▢	Delay (1, 2, 3)	Waiting or idle.

* 1. Feet, 2. Eyes, 3. Knees

they show much information not readily available with a regular operation chart.

COLUMNS ON OPERATION CHART

For the basic chart for two hands, there are four columns on an operation chart. The four columns are the left hand symbol column, the left hand description column, the right hand symbol column, and right hand description column. The activity for each of the hands is charted so that the symbols on the same line of the chart for the two hands represent activities occurring at essentially the same time.

If other body members are charted, other columns would be placed on the chart. One other column that might be placed on the operation chart is a time column (a listing of the estimated time to perform each line on the chart). In most cases a time column is not used.

The symbol columns are placed in a vertical position. The analyst records each step of the activities of one hand, and then charts the activities of the other hand so that they match up with the first hand charted. For this reason the hand doing most of the work is usually charted first. Then it becomes easier to chart the second hand to match up the work.

WORKPLACE DIAGRAM

In keeping with the general policy of charting, the operation chart is accompanied by a diagram. In this case the diagram is called a workplace diagram. A workplace diagram shows the layout of the workplace in which the work is performed. Very seldom are the lines of movement of the body members shown. If lines of movement were shown, the diagram might become complex and hard to understand. The workplace diagram points out where the various work areas are located.

MAKING THE OPERATION CHART

The pickup or grasping of a new part is a good point at which to start an operation chart. A more complete and meaningful picture is obtained when the chart is started with the handling of a new part. The analyst then continues to chart one of the hands. The other hand is filled in after the first one is completed. It is important to make certain that the activities of each hand occurring at the same time line up on the same line of the chart.

When an analyst first starts watching the operation, he soon notices that the operator does not use exactly the same method each time a cycle is performed. Yet, it is possible to make an operation chart for such activities. The only thing that must be remembered is that the analyst must chart the *usual* activity. In some cases it is wise to chart the method which is most inefficient. The easiest way, though, is to chart what usually occurs to get a general idea of the type of activity performed. Again, one of the important concepts here is to learn to think in terms of the symbols, and this itself helps analyze work and find better ways.

When a symbol for one hand actually involves more work than one or more symbols for the other hand, the symbols should be repeated on the subsequent line opposite the activity of the other hand. This is necessary to maintain the concept of charting activities which occur at about the same time. However, to reduce the work of writing additional symbols, a vertical line connecting the bottom of the symbol for the longer activity to the top of the next symbol can be drawn. This line is much like a ditto mark, since it means that the symbol from which the line is drawn is repeated or remains the same for that number of horizontal lines on the chart. This concept of ditto marks assists in making the summary at the end of the chart meaningful. The total number of symbols for one hand must equal the total for the other hand when the summary is made. By recognizing the ditto marks as symbols, the different types of activities are represented more completely.

When the summary is made, other body member symbols, if used, should be summarized. Notice that the total number of horizontal lines used on a chart for operation chart purposes must be accounted for in the summary.

ILLUSTRATIONS

1. Packaging shoulder straps

Figure 7-1 is the operation chart for the repetitive operation of packaging shoulder straps. This illustration came

FIG. 7-1. Original basic operation chart for packaging shoulder straps.

ORIGINAL   OPERATION   1 OF 1   CHART

OF PACKAGING STRAPS

Date 1/23/50   Part SHOULDER STRAPS   Operator _____ Mach _____

By F.S.   No. 66

No.	LEFT FOOT	LH DESCRIPTION			RH DESCRIPTION
1					To Shoulder Strap
2					PU Strap
3					To LH
4		Grasp & Position (Pull Down)			Position Strap (Pull Out)
5		To Cardboard Insert			
6		PU Board			
7		To RH			
8		Place Board with Strap			Place Strap with Board
9		Board & Strap			Wrap Strap Around Board
10					To Straps
11					PU Strap
12					To Board in LH
13		Grasp 2nd Strap			Place Strap on Board
14					Wrap Strap Around Board
15		Release Board to RH			Take Board & Strap from LH
16		To Cellophane			
17		PU Piece of Cellophane			
18		To Work Area			
19		Place on Felt Pad			To Cellophane
20					Place Board on Cellophane
21		Wrap Cellophane			Wrap Cellophane
22		Slide to Sealer			Slide to Sealer
23	○	For Sealer (Depressed 3X)			For Sealer
24		Release to RH			Take Package
25		To Work Area			To Finish Stack
26					Release Package

		LH	RH	BOTH	LEFT FOOT
27		LH	RH	BOTH	LEFT FOOT
28	○	9	12	21	1
29	o	3	3	6	—
30	⊖	3	4	7	—
31	▽	7	7	14	—
32	▽	4	0	4	25
33		26	26	52	

from a plant making novelty items and consisted of many hand motions. It is one of the simple types of activities to which operation charts can be applied. Although some of the motions are involved and might be better analyzed by one of the later techniques, the operation chart does give needed information. The workplace diagram is shown in Fig. 7-2. Notice how the ditto marks and activities are lined up so that what occurs at about the same time appears on one line.

FIG. 7-2. Workplace diagram for original method of packaging shoulder straps.

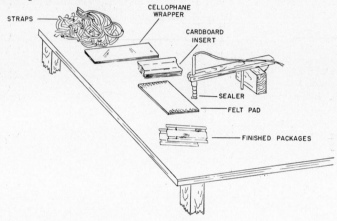

2. Center punching release-valve rods

After bending and shaping operations had been performed on a steel rod, it was necessary to drill a hole. A center punching operation had to be performed to assure a good hole. Since many different rods and a large volume of each had to have the same type of operation, this job was a good one for analysis. At first a basic operation chart was made, as shown in Fig. 7-3. The workplace diagram is shown in Fig. 7-4. Because the volume of work was large and there were many operators doing this type of job, it was decided to make an operation time chart. In this particular case, the time chart was made from motion pictures. This permitted the finer time values shown in the operation time chart of Fig. 7-5. Compare the differences in presentation of data by the two types of charts. See how the symbols take on a more significant relationship.

FIG. 7-3. Original operation chart for center-punch release-valve rods. (Only the first page of two is shown.)

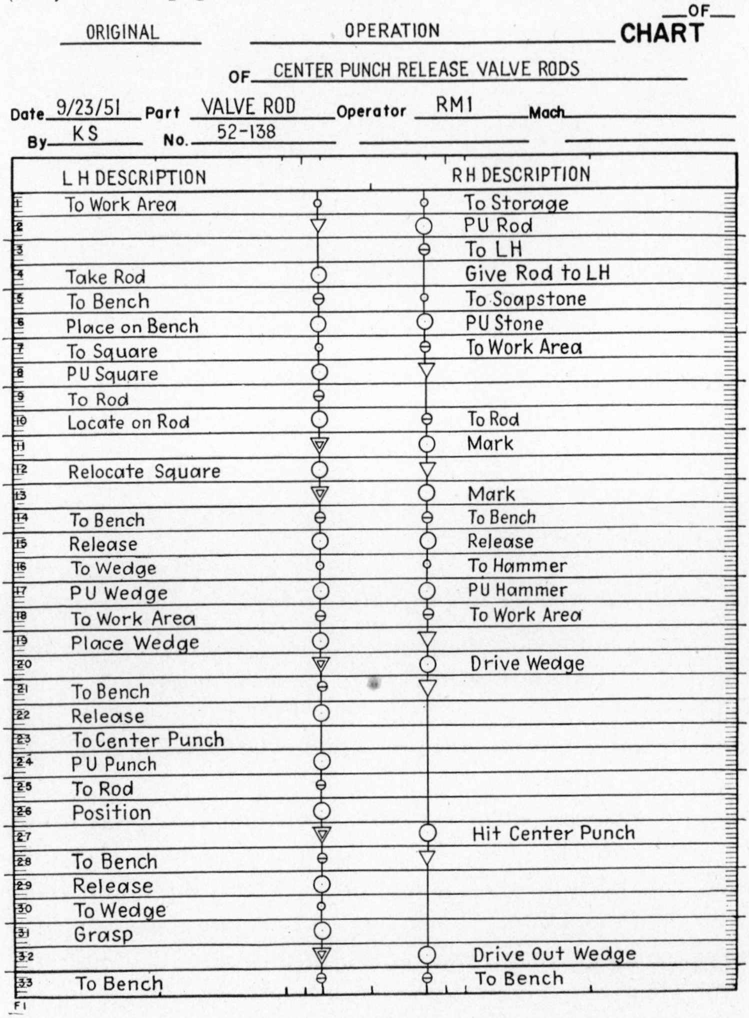

ORIGINAL   OPERATION   __OF__ CHART

OF___CENTER PUNCH RELEASE VALVE RODS___

Date_9/23/51_ Part _VALVE ROD_ Operator _RM1_ Mach_____
By__K S__ No._52-138_____

#	L H DESCRIPTION			R H DESCRIPTION
1	To Work Area			To Storage
2		▽	○	PU Rod
3			⊖	To LH
4	Take Rod	○		Give Rod to LH
5	To Bench	⊖		To Soapstone
6	Place on Bench	○	○	PU Stone
7	To Square		⊖	To Work Area
8	PU Square	○	▽	
9	To Rod	⊖		
10	Locate on Rod	○	⊖	To Rod
11		▽	○	Mark
12	Relocate Square	○	▽	
13		▽	○	Mark
14	To Bench	⊖	⊖	To Bench
15	Release	○	○	Release
16	To Wedge			To Hammer
17	PU Wedge	○	○	PU Hammer
18	To Work Area	⊖	⊖	To Work Area
19	Place Wedge	○	▽	
20		▽	○	Drive Wedge
21	To Bench	⊖	▽	
22	Release	○		
23	To Center Punch			
24	PU Punch	○		
25	To Rod	⊖		
26	Position	○		
27		▽	○	Hit Center Punch
28	To Bench	⊖	▽	
29	Release	○		
30	To Wedge			
31	Grasp	○		
32		▽	○	Drive Out Wedge
33	To Bench	⊖	⊖	To Bench

F1

Fig. 7-4. Workplace diagram for original method of center punching release-valve rods.

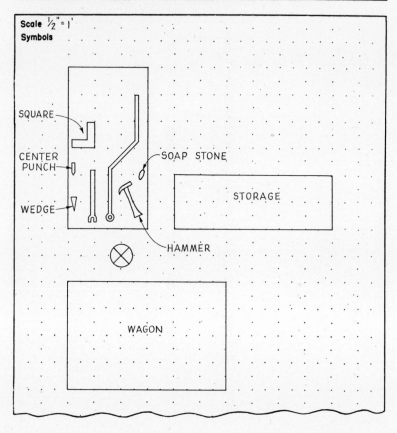

WORKPLACE **DIAGRAM** ACCOMPANYING ORIGINAL OPERATION CHART

OF CENTER PUNCH RELEASE VALVE ROD

Scale 1/2" = 1'
Symbols

SQUARE

CENTER PUNCH

WEDGE

SOAP STONE

STORAGE

HAMMER

WAGON

Fig. 7-5. Original operation time chart for center punching release-valve rods.

ACC TIME MIN.	LH DESCRIPTION			RH DESCRIPTION	FILM
					530
.05	To Work Area	.055	.065	To Storage	580
		.045	.010	PU Rod	
			.025	To L H	
.10	Take Rod	.010	.010	Give to LH	630
	To Bench	.020	.015	To Soapstone	
	Place on Bench	.010	.005	PU Stone	
.15	To Square	.015	.015	To Work Area	680
	PU Square	.010	.055		
	To Rod	.010			
	Locate on Rod	.030			
.20		.020	.005	To Rod	730
			.020	Mark	
	Relocate Square	.015	.015		
.25		.015	.015	Mark	780
	To Bench	.015	.015	To Bench	
	Release	.005	.005	Release	
	To Wedge PU Wedge	.010	.010	To Hammer PU Hammer	
.30	To Rod	.015	.015	To WA	830
	Place Wedge	.015	.015		
	To Bench	.010	.010	Drive Wedge	
.35	Release	.010			880
	To Center Punch PU Punch	.010	.065		
	To Rod	.015			
	Position Punch	.015			
.40	To Bench	.015	.015	Hit Center Punch	930
	Release	.010			
		.005			
	To Wedge	.010	.030		
	Grasp	.005	.010	Drive Out Wedge	
.45	To Bench Release	.010	.010	To Bench Release	980
	To Rod	.005	.005	To Rod	
		.010	.010		
	Grasp	.010	.010	Grasp	
.50					1030
	To Wagon	.050	.050	To Wagon	
.55	Release	.020	.020	Release	1080
.60					1130
		SUMMARY			
		.185	.145		
		.100	.095		
		.155	.135		
		.070	—		
		.045	.180		
		.555	.555		

3. Insert glue in case

To hold a hard-packed powder in place, a glue compound is placed in the end of the case. The operation chart (shown with time columns estimated from a sweep-second wrist watch) is shown in Fig. 7-6, with the workplace diagram in

FIG. 7-6. Original operation chart with time columns for inserting glue in case.

ORIGINAL OPERATION CHART 1 OF 1

OF INSERT GLUE IN CASE

Date 1/22/53 Part CASE Operator S.L.E. Mach
By W. J. W. No. 50-3

#	LH DESCRIPTION		TIME SEC.			RH DESCRIPTION
1	To Work Place	ϕ	1	1	ϕ	To Chute
2		▽	2	1	○	PU One Case
3				1	ϕ	To LH
4	Grasp Case Between Thumb & 1ST F.	○	1	1	○	Give to LH
5		▽	3	1	ϕ	To Chute
6				1	○	PU One Case
7				1	ϕ	To LH
8	Grasp Case	○	1	1	○	Give to LH
9	Perform A 4 Times					
10	To Tip of Nozzle	ϕ	1	1	ϕ	To Handle
11	Position 1ST Case	○	2	1	○	Grasp Handle
12		▽	3	4	○	Apply Pressure
13	Position Next Case	○	2	2	▽	
14		▽	3	3	○	Apply Pressure
15	Perform B 4 Times					
16	To Rack	ϕ	2	1	○	Release Handle
17	Place Cases in Rack	○	6	7	▽	
18						
19						
20						

Summary

		LH (Time)		RH (Time)		Both (Time)	
23	○	11	21	17	28	28	49
24	○	1	1	6	6	7	7
25	e	2	3	5	5	7	8
26	▽	17	27	0	0	17	27
27	▽	2	2	5	15	7	17
28		33	54 SEC.	33	54 SEC.	66	

Per 5 Cases

Fig. 7-7. Workplace diagram for original method of inserting glue in case.

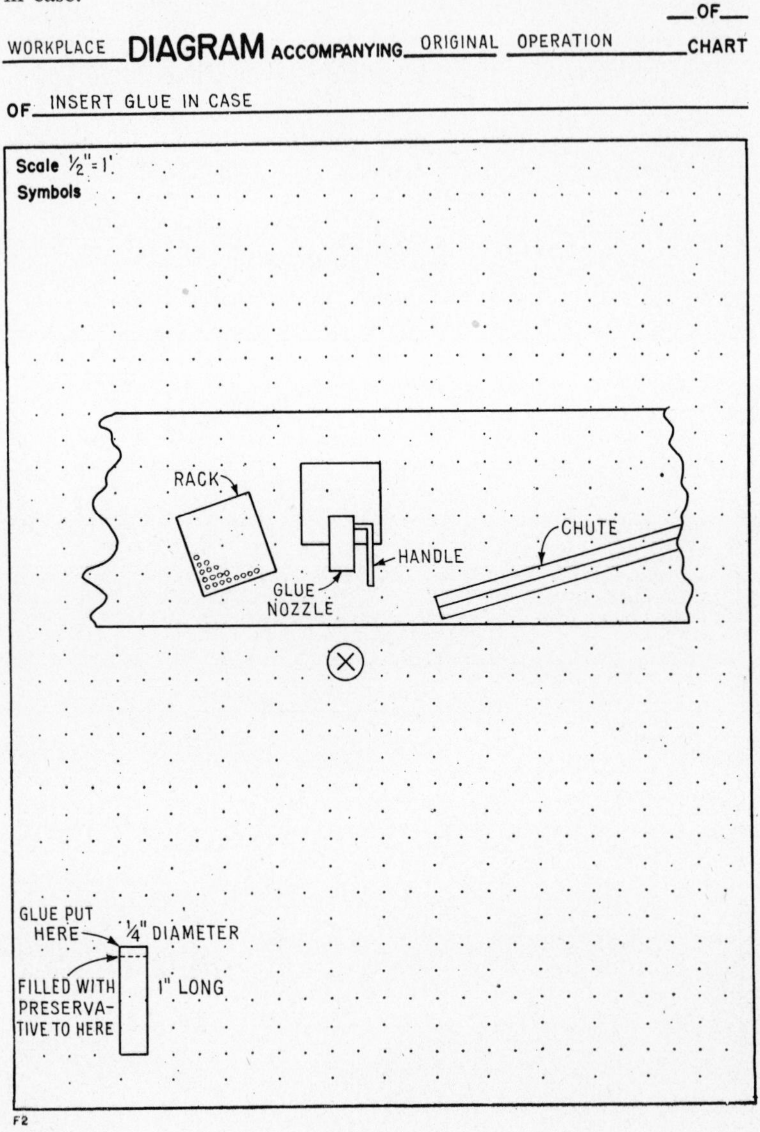

WORKPLACE __ **DIAGRAM** ACCOMPANYING __ORIGINAL   OPERATION__ __OF__
__CHART__

OF__INSERT GLUE IN CASE_____

Scale ½"=1'
Symbols

RACK

CHUTE

HANDLE

GLUE
NOZZLE

⊗

GLUE PUT
HERE — ¼" DIAMETER

FILLED WITH   1" LONG
PRESERVA-
TIVE TO HERE

F2

Fig. 7-7. With the large volume required, two operators performed this repetitive operation. The specific goal was to increase the production of the operation to avoid the necessity of placing another operator on the job. Since the individual symbols took less time than could be determined with the sweep-second wrist watch, groups of symbols were timed and the time prorated as indicated in the illustrations. For example, the first four symbols of the right hand were timed at approximately three seconds. The analyst felt that each symbol took about the same amount of time because of the nature of the part and its contents. To maintain round numbers, the analyst assigned a value of one second to each symbol. Relative values, not accuracy, are of prime importance in such cases.

CHAPTER 8

THERBLIG CHART

Two charts have been presented for analyzing sequence: product process chart and form process chart. Two charts have been presented for analyzing method: man process chart and operation chart. These latter two charts represent the analysis techniques for the basic physical characteristics of work. They do not in many cases present sufficient methods detail. This chapter and the next present techniques which are refinements of the two basic methods charts to take care of these situations.

The therblig chart (Therb Ch) is the *detailed* symbolic and systematic presentation of the method of work performed by the body members of a man, usually when his work is at one workplace. The word "usually" indicates that the activity of the operator need not be strictly limited to just one workplace. Most of the therbligs are closely related to the symbols used on operation charts; this means that they are somewhat related to work done at one workplace.

The word "therblig" was originated by Frank and Lillian Gilbreth. Therblig refers to the symbols used in making the therblig chart. This is somewhat different from the other charts presented up to this point. They have had functional titles; the name of this chart refers to the symbols.

WHEN TO MAKE A THERBLIG CHART

There are obviously certain special situations where the therblig chart would be made. Some are:

1. Large volume operations.

2. Where other analysis techniques do not give sufficient detail. If an operation method is charted according to operation chart characteristics and a suboperation, for example, does not show enough information about the actual activity, then the therblig chart can be made to give the needed information.

3. When the hand and fingers perform small and involved motions, making it difficult to specify exactly what is done by means of symbols presented previously. This indicates that the operation is relatively complex or the skills and dexterity are high.

Using therbligs means that the analyst must be able to observe and "penetrate" into work methods to determine each of the small units of accomplishment used in performing the work. These are transferred to therbligs to make the therblig chart.

USES OF THERBLIG CHARTS

The therblig chart is used to help gather information and present facts gathered about the method of work on an operation, and to help plan the work for future operations. The fact that small details of work can be recorded help immeasurably in planning future work. The many different ways the work could be performed can be analyzed in fine detail. This permits the selection of the proper method in a more accurate manner than could be done with any of the other charting techniques.

SYMBOLS

The symbols for a therblig chart, called therbligs, are presented in Table 8-1. The Gilbreths identified 18 therbligs, from which the first 17 therbligs in Table 8-1 are taken. The eighteenth has been found to coincide with some other therbligs. It has been omitted from this list. The additional

Table 8-1. Symbols for Therblig and Simo Charts

B—Indicates the point at which the hand (or other applicable body member, like foot, eye, etc.) begins the therblig
F—Indicates the basic function of the therblig
E—Indicates the point at which the hand (or other applicable body member) ends the therblig

Ther-blig symbol	Therblig name	Time (0.0001 min.)	Activity represented	Color symbol
			1. Work classification: "Do," or terminal, therbligs at one work area	
1.G	Grasp		B—First contact with object F—Placing object under control of hand (or other body member) E—Control of object established (Control depends on what is to be done with object. Control of bolt to be picked up is different from control of paper to be held on table for writing after control is gained.)	Dark red * EP745 † DP383
G1	Contact grasp	20	When merely touching object comprises control	
G2	Pinch grasp	40	Thumb opposes finger tip(s) to gain control, or control is gained by any two fingers of one hand opposing each other	
G3	Wrap grasp	60	Hand wraps around object for control	
G4	Regrasp	50	Shift of object to gain control at another point of the object or, in a few cases, taking the object from the other hand	

* EP—Eagle pencils.   † DP—Dixon pencils.

Ther-blig symbol	Therblig name	Time (0.0001 min.)	Activity represented	Color symbol
2.RL	Release load		B—Initial relaxation of control of object F—Losing control or let-ting go of object E—Control of object has ceased	Light red
RL1	Contact release load	5	Losing control by merely raising or lifting body member	
RL2	Other release loads	20	Loss of control by open-ing fingers or hand	
3.P	Position		B—First manipulation of object to align, orient, or line-up F—Manipulation of object to achieve a specific alignment, orientation, or line-up E—Object oriented for proper purpose	Dark blue EP741 DP376
P1	Cylin-drical position	30 **	Line-up when mating parts are cylindrical	 CYLINDRICAL POSITION (P1) COMBINED WITH VERTICAL POSITION (P4)
P2	Noncylin-drical position	60 **	Line-up of noncylindrical and symmetrical or nonsymmetrical mating parts	 NONCYLINDRICAL POSITION (P2) COMBINED WITH HORIZONTAL POSITION (P3)

** If two classifications occur together, average the time values.

Table 8-1. Symbols for Therblig and Simo Charts (*Continued*)

Ther-blig symbol	Therblig name	Time (0.0001 min.)	Activity represented	Color symbol
P3	Hori-zontal position	25 **	Line-up involving orien-tation of the hand (with the part) in horizontal plane	HORIZONTAL POSITION (P3) COMBINED WITH CYLIN-DRICAL POSITION (P1)
P4	Vertical position	25 **	Line-up involving orien-tation of the hand (with the part) in vertical plane	VERTICAL POSITION (P4) COMBINED WITH NONCYLINDRICAL POSITION (P2)
xP5	Turn position	0.75 ** per degree	Line-up involving turn-ing of hand and object with center line of arm and hand as axis	TURN POSITION (P5) (ILLUSTRATED IS 135P5)

Note: In place of x substitute number of degrees. P1 and P2 can occur in combination with P3, P4, and/or P5. P1 and P2 do not occur in com-bination (combination noted as P13, P245, etc.).

4.PP	Pre-position		Same as position except that line-up or orienta-tion of object is used at a later time and/or an-other place (This ther-blig is not used often. However, it could be used more frequently if it referred to line-up or orientation occurring in conjunction with TL, or one orientation preced-ing another orientation.)	Light blue

Ther-blig symbol	Therblig name	Time (0.0001 min.)	Activity represented	Color symbol
5.A	Assemble		B—First contact of mating parts or objects to be made integral F—Placing together of objects E—Objects placed together	Dark violet EP742 DP377
xA1	Loose-fit assemble	15 (0.25)	1/8 in. or above total tolerance	
xA2	Free-fit assemble	25 (0.50)	1/32 to 1/8 in. total tolerance	
xA3	Medium-fit assemble	40 (0.75)	1/100 to 1/32 in. total tolerance	
xA4	Snug-fit assemble	60 (1.00)	Less than 1/100 in. total tolerance	

First value is per inch; in parentheses, per degree.
Note: In place of x substitute number of inches (or degrees) required.

6.DA	Disas-semble		B—Initial separation of one object from mating or integral object F—Separation of objects E—Objects separated	Light violet

Table 8-1. Symbols for Therblig and Simo Charts (*Continued*)

Ther-blig symbol	Therblig name	Time (0.0001 min.)	Activity represented	Color symbol
xDA1	Loose-fit dis-assemble	10 (0.20)‡	⅛ in. or above total tolerance	
xDA2	Free-fit dis-assemble	20 (0.45)‡	⅟₃₂ to ⅛ in. total tolerance	
xDA3	Medium-fit dis-assemble	35 (0.70)‡	⅟₁₀₀ to ⅟₃₂ in. total tolerance	
xDA4	Snug-fit dis-assemble	50 (0.90)‡	Less than ⅟₁₀₀ in. total tolerance	

‡ See note under Assemble.
Note: In place of x substitute number of inches (or degrees) required.

| 7.U | Use | | B—First manipulation, activation, or pressing of control or tool
F—Manipulation, activation, or pressing of control or tool for its designed purpose
E—Completion of employment of control or tool | Purple |
| xUT | Tool use ‡‡ | | When object applied, pressed, or manipulated is free to move in all directions | |

Ther-blig symbol	Therblig name	Time (0.0001 min.)	Activity represented	Color symbol
xUC	Control use	‡‡	When object applied, pressed, or manipulated is restricted in one or more directions	

‡‡ These values must be estimated.

Note: In place of x substitute number of inches, degrees, and/or pounds required.

Investigate possibility of another therblig (like P, TL) in combination with use.

II. Work classification: Grasp-preparatory therbligs

8.SH	Search		B—Initial groping and/or hunting for object in a group of dissimilar objects F—Trying to locate an object in a group of dissimilar objects E—Sought-for object found	Black EP747 DP379
SH1	Large object search	10	Object at least twice as large as other objects in group	
SH2	Medium object search	20	Object from one to two times as large as other objects in group	
SH3	Small object search	30	Object smaller than other objects in group	

91

Table 8-1. Symbols for Therblig and Simo Charts (*Continued*)

Ther-blig symbol	Therblig name	Time (0.0001 min.)	Activity represented	Color symbol
9.ST	Select		B—Initial contact with several objects in a group of similar objects F—Picking out one object from group of similar objects E—Object located	Gray
ST1	Large object select	5	Objects over 1 in. sq.	
ST2	Medium object select	10	Objects from ⅝ in. sq. to 1 in. sq.	
ST3	Small object select	15	Objects smaller than ⅝ in. sq.	

III. Work classification: Movement therbligs

Ther-blig symbol	Therblig name	Time	Activity represented	Color symbol
10.TL	Transport loaded		B—Start of motion with object or load F—Change location of object from one work area to another E—Arrival at destination or cessation of movement	Dark green EP738 DP416
xTL1	Transport loaded to indefinite location	25 5/in.#	When disposal point of object is not fixed or the object is going to be tossed	

Ther-blig symbol	Therblig name	Time (0.0001 min.)	Activity represented	Color symbol
xTL2	Transport loaded to definite location	35 5/in.#	When disposal point is fixed or the object is going to be released carefully	

Add .75%/lb. for weight.
Note: In place of x substitute number of linear inches moved.

11.TE	Transport empty		B—Start of motion of empty hand F—Reach for object, or change in location of hand E—Cessation of free movement	Light green
xTE1	From indefinite location transport empty	15 5/in.**	When origination point varies or hand is already in motion	
xTE2	From definite location transport empty	20 5/in.**	When origination point is fixed	
xTE3	To definite location transport empty	20 5/in.**	When object moved to is at a definite point	
xTE4	To indefinite transport empty	15 5/in.**	When object moved to varies in its location, or when eyes must direct hand to its next activity	

** See note under Position.
Note: In place of x substitute number of linear inches moved. TE1 or TE2 can occur in combination with TE3 or TE4 (xTE14).

Table 8-1. Symbols for Therblig and Simo Charts (*Continued*)

Ther- blig symbol	Therblig name	Time (0.0001 min.)	Activity represented	Color symbol

IV. Work classification: Delay therbligs

12.UD	Unavoid-
	able
	delay
			B—Start of idleness
			F—Waiting, which is part
			   of method being used,
			   while another body
			   member or machine is
			   doing something
			E—Waiting ceases
				Yellow ochre
				EP736
				DP412

UDB	Balanc- ing delay	# #	Waiting for other body member or machine	
UDC	Change direction delay	10	When no G or RL occurs between movements in opposite directions	

13.AD	Avoid-
	able
	delay
		# #	B—First motion which is
			   not part of method
			   being used
			F—Any activity not
			   needed in method
			E—Activity or idleness not
			   part of method ceases
				Lemon yellow
				EP735
				DP374

\# # Use actual times or estimate.

14.H	Hold	# #	B—Start of maintaining
			   an object, controlled
			   by a body member, in
			   fixed orientation
			F—Maintaining an object
			   with a fixed orientation
			E—When fixed orientation
			   is no longer required or
			   before start of any other
			   therblig
				Gold ochre
				EP736½
				DP388

Ther-blig symbol	Therblig name	Time (0.0001 min.)	Activity represented	Color symbol
15.R	Rest	# #	B—Idleness F—Overcoming fatigue as part of every cycle E—Resuming the work of the cycle	Orange EP737 DP372

V. Work classification: Mental-activity therbligs

16.PN	Plan	# #	B—Idleness or motions which are not productive work F—Worker deciding on the next work or activity E—When next activity is determined	Brown EP746 DP378

17.I	Inspect	60 per inspected point	B—Start of examination or testing of object F—Feeling, viewing, or examining an object to determine quality E—Quality determined	Burnt ochre EP745½ DP398

VI. Work classification: Gross body movements (not included in original therbligs). Colors are not assigned to these gross therbligs since they are used mainly for the therblig chart which uses no colors.

18.W	Walk		Movement of the body from one workplace to another
xWW	Walk without load	40/ft.	

Table 8-1. Symbols for Therblig and Simo Charts (*Continued*)

Ther-blig symbol	Therblig name	Time (0.0001 min.)	Activity represented	Color symbol
xWL	Walk with load	50/ft.		

Note: In place of x substitute number of linear feet walked.

19.B	Bending		Trunk movement with hips as hinge	
BD	Bend down	150		
BU	Bend up	175		
BT	Bend and/or body turn	175		

Ther-blig symbol	Therblig name	Time (0.0001 min.)	Activity represented	Color symbol
20.SI	Sit	200		
21.SD	Stand up	250		
22.K	Kneel		Movement of the body with the knees as hinge	
KD	Kneel down	150		
KU	Arise kneel	200		
K1	One-knee kneel	150		
K2	Two-knee kneel	300		

Note: KD and KU occur in combination with K1 or K2, KD2.

therbligs listed have been found useful in the analysis of work and might be considered as necessary additions.

The symbols in Table 8-1 are presented both as the basic therbligs developed by the Gilbreths and as finer detail or condition for each of the therbligs. For example, the therblig *grasp* is defined as the Gilbreths basically established it. In addition four specific grasp conditions for finer-detail purposes are listed. A therblig chart is almost always made with finer-detail therbligs. The numbering of finer-detail therbligs is such that the therblig with the smallest number, 1, usually takes the least amount of time to perform. This is a general statement. Certain therbligs with smaller numbers may take more time than therbligs with larger numbers; for example, G2 may take more time than G3. Although this reversal is not at all unusual, a general rule is that a therblig with a smaller number represents the therblig which takes the least amount of time.

To assist the analyst, relatively general therblig times have been listed with each of the finer-detail therbligs. It should be recognized that these time values *are not accurate* and are placed in the table to provide an easier basis for analysis and evaluation. Notice that the table even lists a reversal of the kind mentioned above: G4 is listed as taking less time than G3.

Because of their fineness, each therblig is established to represent a complete concept of activity. This means that it must have a beginning point and an end point, and of course must be defined in terms of what occurs between the two points. Each basic therblig is therefore defined in terms of these three activities. There is a beginning point (noted as B) for the therblig, a function (noted as F) and an end point (noted as E). For example, the basic therblig grasp would begin whenever the hand or body member first came into contact with the object. The function of the therblig grasp would be to place the object under control of the hand or other body member. The end point of the basic therblig grasp would be when the hand or body member has gained control of the object. Each fine-detail therblig has an additional definition. This definition for the fine-detail therblig merely modifies or further clarifies the *function* of the therblig. The beginning and end points remain the same for the finer-detail therbligs, but the function is modified as indicated. For example, G1 indicates that the control being gained is only concerned with touching an object. G2 indicates that control must be gained by having the thumb opposing the fingertip(s). But in all cases the beginning and end points for the fine-detail therblig are the same.

MAKING THE THERBLIG CHART

The therblig chart, when used for analyzing the work of a person at one workplace, is made in almost the same fashion as the operation chart. Activities of the two hands occurring simultaneously are charted on the same line. In place of the geometric symbol of the operation chart, the numerical and alphabetical fine-detail therblig is substituted. Because of the finer detail, the therblig chart will be longer than the operation chart when made for identical operations. In similar fashion, the therblig chart will look more like a man process chart when made for an individual going from place to place in accomplishing his work.

It is possible to make a combination therblig chart. It would be simple to chart, for example, therbligs for the two hands and other body members until such time as the man moves from place to place. Then a single column would indicate the man's activity for his movements from place to place. After stopping at another workplace to perform some activity, it would be possible to revert to the two-handed or other body member analysis for that phase of the work.

WORKPLACE DIAGRAM AND SUMMARY

The workplace diagram illustrates the area in which the operation takes place. Some sort of presentation of the area in which the work is performed is necessary with therblig charts.

The summary at the bottom of the therblig chart follows essentially the same format as that on an operation chart. This is shown in the following illustration:

Package ring and expander

A transparent paper bag is filled with a ring and expander, as one operation of six in which a set of replacement piston rings is bagged and boxed. This repetitive operation took the longest time to perform, and the specific goal was to reduce the time needed for the assembly. The workplace diagram is shown in Fig. 8-1. The therblig chart made for the operation is shown in Fig. 8-2. Notice how any individual, even though unfamiliar with the operation, can reproduce almost exactly the method being used by the operator. All that is needed is to read each line of the chart and actually perform the motion. This shows how the greater detail of fine-detail therbligs permits a much finer analysis of work.

SIMO CHART

It is possible to make a therblig time chart if motion pictures are taken of the operation. The therblig time chart is commonly called a simo chart (simultaneous motion cycle chart). The simo chart was originally developed by the Gilbreths. The simo chart is made only when the volume of work is exceptionally large and the hand and finger motions are exceptionally complex and involved. It is not made often but is used mainly for demonstrations and selling purposes. The whole concept of using therblig symbols and the simo chart was originally called micromotion study.

Fig. 8-1. Workplace diagram for original method of packaging ring and expander.

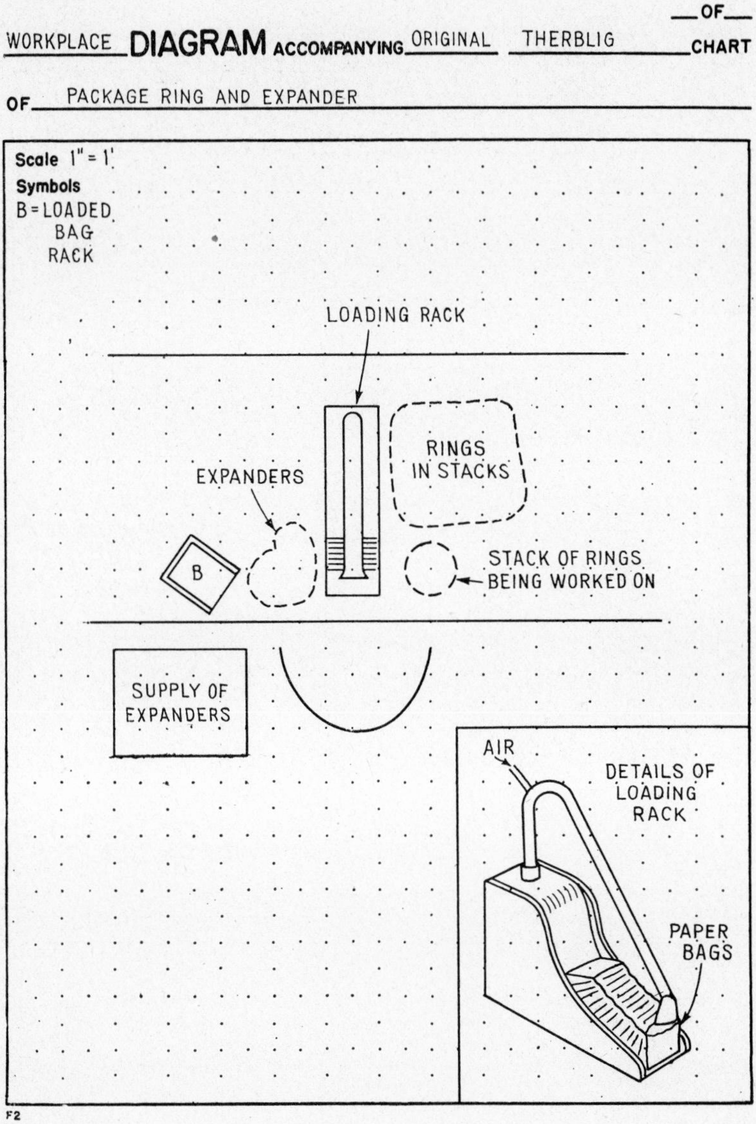

WORKPLACE **DIAGRAM** ACCOMPANYING ORIGINAL THERBLIG ___OF___ CHART

OF PACKAGE RING AND EXPANDER

Scale 1" = 1'
Symbols
B = LOADED BAG RACK

LOADING RACK

EXPANDERS

RINGS IN STACKS

B

STACK OF RINGS BEING WORKED ON

SUPPLY OF EXPANDERS

AIR

DETAILS OF LOADING RACK

PAPER BAGS

F2

FIG. 8-2. Original therblig chart for packaging ring and expander.

ORIGINAL		THERBLIG	CHART _OF_

OF **PACKAGE RING AND EXPANDER**

Date **5/31/52** Part **BAG-RINGS** Operator **MBY** Mach
By **OHC** No. **EXPANDERS L207-STD**

LH DESCRIPTION		RH DESCRIPTION	
1 Edge of Filled Bag	G2	9TE23	To Rings
2 To Bag Rack (Loaded)	15TL2	G2	Top Ring
3 For Rack	P24	9TL2	To Bag
4 In Rack	1A1	UDB	For Air to Open Bag
5 In Rack	RL2	P24	For Bag
6 To Expanders	9TE24	3A1	In Bag
7		RL2	In Bag
8 PU Expander	ST1 &	1TE23	To Edge of Bag
9	G2	G2	Edge of Bag
10		H	Open for LH
11 To Bag	6TL2		
12 For Bag	P24		
13 In Bag	3A2		
14 In Bag	RL2		
15 To Edge of Bag	1TE23	RL2	Edge of Bag
16			
17			
18		LH	RH
19	TE	2	2
20	TL	2	1
21	ST&G	3	0
22	G	2	2
23	P	2	1
24	A	2	1
25	RL	2	2
26	H	0	5
27	UD	0	1
28		15	15
29			
30			
31			
32			
33			

F1

This is the name the Gilbreths associated with the use of therbligs. Very little about micromotion study and simo charts is presented here. This technique is not used much in industry or office. When it is used, it is usually made by a staff analyst or industrial engineer who has the facilities for taking and analyzing the pictures.

If a rough simo chart is required for some selling purposes, it can be made with the information already presented. It should be reemphasized that this would be a very general and inaccurate simo chart. In place of the letters of therbligs, colors are the notation for the symbols. Colors are used in place of geometric figures and black shadings of the chart symbols presented previously. Although it is possible to devise black or gray lines as shadings for all symbols on the simo chart, they become so complex and involved that, unless an analyst has many opportunities for making simo charts, they are not desirable. The color symbols are used just as are the time symbols for man process chart and operation chart. It is possible to lengthen or shorten the symbol, depending upon the amount of time the activity takes. The format for the simo chart will be shown later.

To obtain the time values for a rough simo chart, it is possible to use the approximate therblig times given in Table 8-1. It should be reemphasized that these are general relationships, and the simo chart made with these time values is only relatively accurate. It is quite possible that the relationships among two or more of the therbligs could be completely reversed in the actual situation as compared with what would be shown with the approximate therblig times. The following illustration was made from a motion-picture record of a job, and therefore many of the time values will not agree with the approximate values given in Table 8-1. But this is to be expected. To get a complete picture of how the simo chart would look, the reader should put in the appropriate colors from Table 8-1 in the color columns of the illustration.

Assemble sprocket and packing

The sprocket assembly, a part of a control device, consists of the parts shown in Fig. 8-3. The operation was repetitive, and the specific goal was to increase production of the long-run operation. Regular motion pictures were taken of this job. The analysis in this case was made with fine-detail ther-

Fig. 8-3. Parts for sprocket assembly.

___OF___

PARTS **DIAGRAM** ACCOMPANYING ORIGINAL SIMO CHART

OF SPROCKET ASSEMBLY

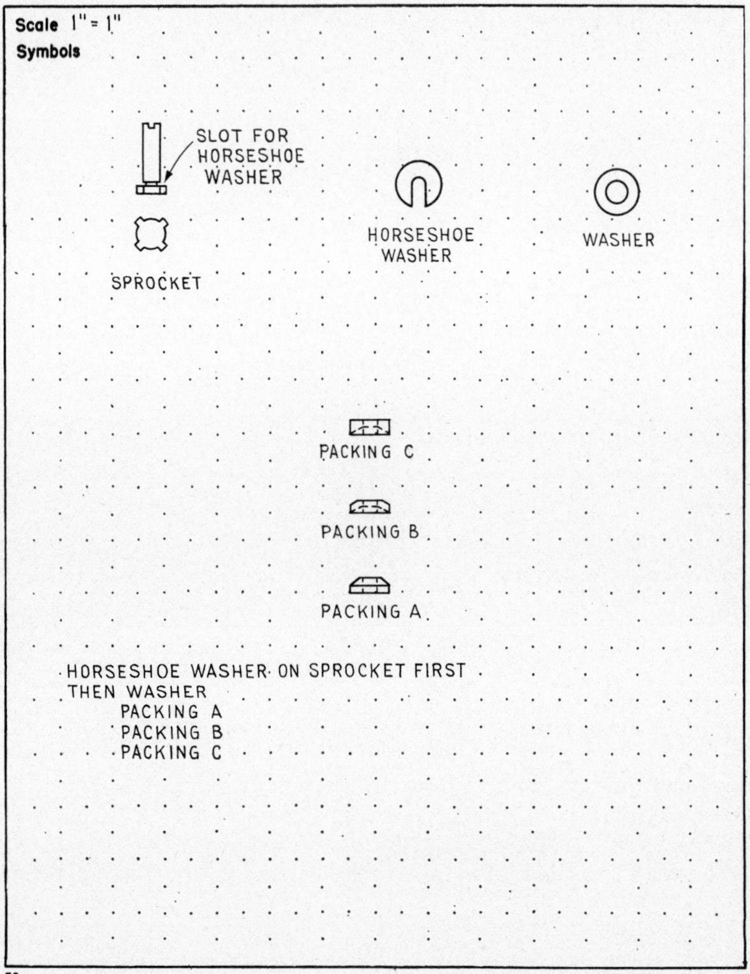

F2

Fig. 8-4. Workplace diagram for original method of assembling sprocket and packing.

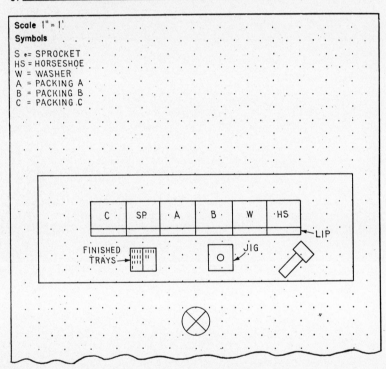

FIG. 8-5. Original simo chart for the assembly of sprocket and packing. (Fine-detail therbligs for hands.)

LH DESCRIPTION		TIME IN 1/2000 MIN			RH DESCRIPTION		CLOCK
1							
2 To A	9TE23	13	—10—	15	18TE23	To B	—260
3							
4 A	ST3	12	—20—				—270
5	& G2				ST3	B	
6			—30—	27	&		—280
7 To Jig	11TL2	15			G2		
8			—40—				—290
9 For Jig / On Jig	P13 / 1A2	3 / 2					
10 Release	RL2	1	—50—				—300
11				19	6TL2	To Jig	
12 To C	24TE23	22	—60—				—310
13				5	P13	For Jig	
14	ST3		—70—	8	1A2	On Jig	—320
15 C	& G2	6		1	RL2	Release	
16			—80—		9TE23	To W	—330
17				12			
18 To Jig	24TL2	23	—90—		ST3	W	—340
19				9	& G2		
20 For Jig	P13	4	—100—				—350
21 On Jig	RL2 1A2	3 / 1		16	9TL2	To Jig	
22			—110—				—360
23 To SP	18TE23	22		6	P13	For Jig	
24			—120—	3	1A2	On Jig	—370
25				2	RL2		
26			—130—	16	15TE23	To HS	—380
27	UDB	14					
28			—140—				—390
29 SP	ST2			12	ST3 & G2	HS	
30	& G2	13	—150—				—400
31							
32 To Jig Area	18TL1	21	—160—	23	15TL1	To Jig Area	—410
33							
F1							

FIG. 8-5 (Cont.)

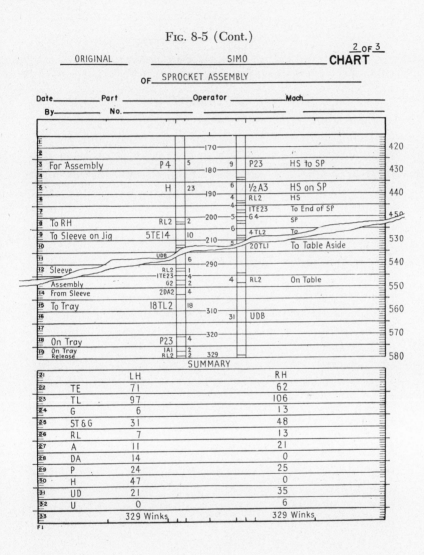

ORIGINAL   SIMO   **CHART** 2 OF 3

OF SPROCKET ASSEMBLY

Date_____ Part _____ Operator _____ Mach_____

By_____   No._____

1				-170-			420
2							
3	For Assembly	P 4	5	-180-	9	P23	HS to SP	430
4							
5		H	23	-190-	6	½ A3	HS on SP	440
6					4	RL2	HS	
7				-200-	4	ITE23	To End of SP	450
8	To RH	RL2	2		5	G 4	SP	
9	To Sleeve on Jig	5TE14	10	-210-	6	4 TL2	To	530
10					5	20TL1	To Table Aside	
11		UDB		-290-	6			540
12	Sleeve	RL2	1				
		ITE23	4		4	RL2	On Table	550
13	Assembly	G2	2				
14	From Sleeve	2DA2	4				
15	To Tray	18TL2	18	-310-			560
16					31	UDB	
17				-320-			570
18	On Tray	P23	4				
19	On Tray Release	1A1 RL2	2 2	329			580

SUMMARY

	LH	RH
TE	71	62
TL	97	106
G	6	13
ST & G	31	48
RL	7	13
A	11	21
DA	14	0
P	24	25
H	47	0
UD	21	35
U	0	6
	329 Winks	329 Winks

bligs. In some cases it may be desirable to use only basic therbligs. The workplace diagram is shown in Fig. 8-4, and the simo chart is shown in Fig. 8-5.

GENERAL APPLICABILITY OF THERBLIGS

Therbligs represent one of the best ways of developing methods consciousness. As mentioned before, it is important for every analyst and individual to penetrate into the motions of every job. It is necessary to think in terms of therbligs or symbols of some kind even though a chart might not be made. Thinking in terms of standard units of accomplishment helps tremendously in developing ways of improving work.

Everyone should know about all charts, even if they use only several of the many. This means that those people who work in heavy industries should know about therbligs even though they may never use them. In the same manner people who work in plants or activities involving fine hand and finger motions or assembly work should know about the more gross techniques, like man process charts and operation charts—just as in other fields we may know about making accurate measurements in inches (say, to $\frac{1}{100}$ of an inch) even though we might make most of our measurements in yards (or we may know about millimeters when we make most of our measurements in feet, etc.). Everyone can do a better job if he knows about more techniques than he actually uses. This is especially true of therbligs. Knowing about therbligs is very important, even though an analyst may never make a therblig chart. It helps him penetrate into the method of any operation regardless of what chart is made.

CHAPTER 9

MULTI-ACTIVITY CHART

Frequently the two basic physical characteristics of activity, man going from place to place and man working at one workplace, have complicating factors introduced which the man process chart and operation chart (and even the therblig chart) cannot easily detect. This means that insufficient information is obtained. The series of multi-activity charts have been designed to help provide a solution to this problem.

The multi-activity chart is the symbolic and systematic presentation of the method of work performed by a man when his work is coordinated with one or more cycle-time controlling devices, such as another man, a machine, or two or more machines. All multi-activity charts have a man and one or more other items charted on the same chart.

Although the word "machine" appears frequently in relation to multi-activity charts, there is another important time-controlling factor other than machines. There are process controls with which men work and for which multi-activity charts would be made. A process may not even be a machine. As a very simple illustration, take the boiling of a three-minute egg. Here is a process which is time-controlled and which is not a "machine." Similar situations exist in chemical plants, in taking temperatures in a hospital, in various housekeeping functions, etc.

TYPES OF MULTI-ACTIVITY CHARTS

No multi-activity chart, as such, is ever made. Rather there are five specific types of charts which are made and are included in the multi-activity group. These are the charts which are actually made for the specified situation.

1. Man and machine chart (M&M Ch).

2. Man and multi-machine chart (M&MM Ch), indicating that the man is working with two or more "machines" which control all or part of the cycle time.

3. Multi-man chart (MM Ch). This chart is made when the work and method of one man could not be performed exactly the same way if the other man or men were not present to do their work in relation to the first man. This is called coordinate work.

4. Multi-man and machine chart (MM&M Ch), made when a machine controlling all or part of the cycle time is used by the men working coordinately.

5. Multi-man and multi-machine chart (MM&MM Ch).

The physical characteristic which is fundamental to multi-activity charts is the showing of interrelationships of men and machines. These jobs could be performed at one workplace, or could require a man to go from place to place. Yet the additional interrelationship characteristics require the additional techniques in this chapter.

USES OF MULTI-ACTIVITY CHARTS

The various types of multi-activity charts gather information about the method being used on a particular operation. Of course, the charts are used for planning methods as well as improving methods. One of the useful results of these charts is the ability to help determine the number of machines that a man should run or the number of machines a group of men should run. Multi-activity charts help to determine the optimum cost relationship by finding the proper utilization of man and machine. The multi-activity chart, like other charts, helps sell and demonstrate proper methods design and improvements to people. With activity involving relationships between two or more items it is frequently difficult to demonstrate the method to people without charts.

SYMBOL BREAKDOWNS

Any one of the above five types of multi-activity charts may be made with one of three symbol breakdowns. These breakdowns are:
1. Multi-activity process chart
2. Multi-activity operation chart
3. Multi-activity therblig chart
The word "process" refers to man process chart symbols; the word "operation" to operation chart symbols; and the word "therblig" to therblig chart symbols.

These breakdowns represent different ways of gathering detail about the method. The man process chart symbols give gross detail. The main purpose of this chart is to find the relationships among various activities irrespective of the method being used for the individual activities. The second and third breakdowns emphasize the methods for the activities within the whole cycle, as well as give the interrelationship of all body members and machines or processes.

In a very general way, the man and machine types of chart tend to be made with the operation or therblig chart breakdowns. Likewise, the multi-man types of chart tend to be made with the man process chart breakdown. However, it is not essential to follow either of these general observations.

As the name implies, the multi-activity process, operation, and therblig charts will use the geometric or letter-abbreviation symbols presented previously. It is also possible to make the time chart version of each of these charts. As a matter of fact, the time charts are frequently more desirable and usable. There is the multi-activity process time chart, the multi-activity operation time chart, or the multi-activity therblig time chart. The therblig chart breakdown is not used often in multi-activity relationships, although it is a highly desirable technique when the detail is required. However, no illustration will be given of the multi-activity therblig chart, and the rest of the discussion will be concerned mainly with the process and operation chart breakdowns.

MAKING THE MULTI-ACTIVITY CHART

Remember: There is no such thing as an actual multi-activity chart. Rather, one of the above-mentioned five charts would be made. The number of columns on a multi-activity chart vary with the type of activity being charted.

If one man and one machine are being used in an operation, a man and machine process chart (M&MPC) will have four columns—a symbol column for the man, explanation column, distance column, and symbol column for the machine. If the same man and machine operation were to be charted with an operation chart breakdown (M&M Op Ch), then a minimum of five columns would be used—a symbol column for the machine, two symbol columns for left and right hands, and two explanation columns for the hands. The number of columns varies with the situation. There is no upper limit on the number of items or men that can be charted in a multi-activity chart.

MACHINE SYMBOLS

There are only two things that the machine can do: It can control time, or it can modify the product without controlling time. If the machine is controlling time, whether or not it is modifying the product, the large circle (operation symbol) is used to represent the activity. The large circle is used also when the machine modifies the product. Note that the use of the circle when the machine *controls time* without modifying is an important feature of the chart. If the therblig chart is being made, the large circle can likewise be used. When the machine or process is not controlling time, the single triangle (delay symbol) is used. The same symbol would be used on the therblig chart breakdown.

DIAGRAM AND SUMMARY

A multi-activity chart should be accompanied by a diagram of some sort. If the work takes place essentially at one area or workplace, then a workplace diagram would be suitable. If the man moves about in performing his duties, then a flow diagram might be more desirable.

A summary can usually be made for multi-activity charts. These are illustrated in the following examples.

ILLUSTRATIONS

Several illustrations of the different types of charts that can be made should help explain multi-activity charts.

1. Shear snubber wire to length

Two sizes of wire were sheared with the same method. One operator could not perform her method exactly the same way when she was there alone as when the two operators were present. Therefore, a multi-man operation chart (Fig. 9-1) was made to show the relationship of the operators as well as give enough detail to help meet the specific goal of reducing the costs (increase man utilization in the crew). After this chart was made, it was decided to make a time chart. The operation was repetitive, and it seemed best to have the data collected by 16-frame-per-second motion pictures. Figure 9-2 shows the workplace diagram. The multi-man operation time chart is shown in Fig. 9-3.

Notice how the time chart gives much more information about the relationships of the motions. Whereas one symbol on the geometric chart was on one line, the same symbol on

Fig. 9-1. Original basic multi-man operation chart for shearing snubber wire to length.

ORIGINAL _____ MULTI-MAN OPERATION _____ **CHART** ¹ OF ¹

OF ___ SHEAR SNUBBER WIRE TO LENGTH ___

Date 12/17/52 Part WIRE 6 FT. LENGTH Operator RS & MU Mach_____

By J G No. 20-2

	OPERATOR 1 L R		OPERATOR 2 L R		
1 Regrasp Wire ◯ ▽		Release Wire ◯ ◯		
2 To R H ◔ ◔ To L H		To Position Near #1 ◔ ▽		
3 Release ◯ ◯ Grasp Wire		▽ •		
4 ▽ ◔ To Oper. #2				
5 ◯ Give to Oper. #2		Take Wire ◯		
6 To Back of Wire ◔ ◔ To Back of Wire		Help Pull ◯		
7 Grasp Wire ◯ ◯ Grasp Wire		◔ To L H		
8 To Oper. #2 ◔ ◔ To Oper. #2		To R H ◔		
9 Position in Shear ◯ ◯ Release Wire		Release ◯ ◯ Take Wire		
10 ◔ To Handle		To Wire ◔ ◔ To Stop		
11 ◯ Grasp Handle		Grasp ◯ ◯ Position at Stop		
12 ▽ ◯ Shear Wire		▽ ▽		
13 Release Wire ◯ ◯ Release Handle		To Aside ◔ ◔ To Aside		
14				
15				

	LH	RH	BOTH	LH	RH	BOTH	TWO OPERATORS
16							
17 ◯	7	7	14	6	3	9	23
18 ○	1	3	4	2	2	4	8
19 ⊖	2	2	4	2	2	4	8
20 ▽	1	0	1	1	1	2	3
21 ▽	2	1	3	2	5	7	10
22	13	13		13	13		
23							
24							
25							
26							
27							
28							
29							
30							
31							
32							
33							

F 1

FIG. 9-2. Workplace diagram for original method of shearing snubber wire to length.

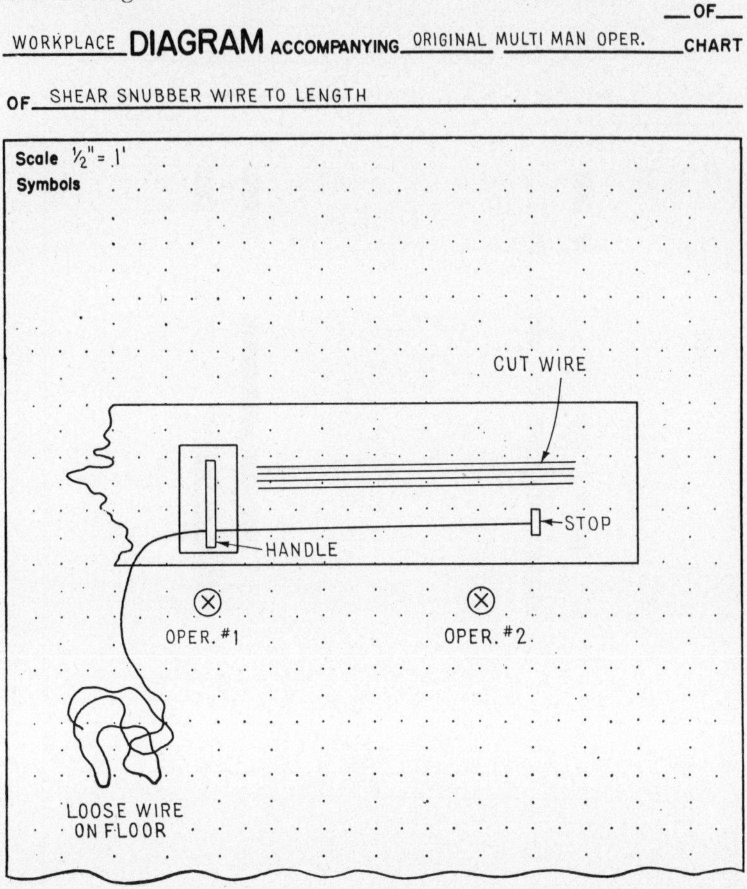

WORKPLACE **DIAGRAM** ACCOMPANYING ORIGINAL MULTI MAN OPER. __OF__ CHART

OF SHEAR SNUBBER WIRE TO LENGTH .

Scale ½" = 1'
Symbols

CUT WIRE

STOP

HANDLE

⊗
OPER. #1

⊗
OPER. #2

LOOSE WIRE
ON FLOOR

FIG. 9-3. Original multi-man operation time chart for shearing snubber wire to length.

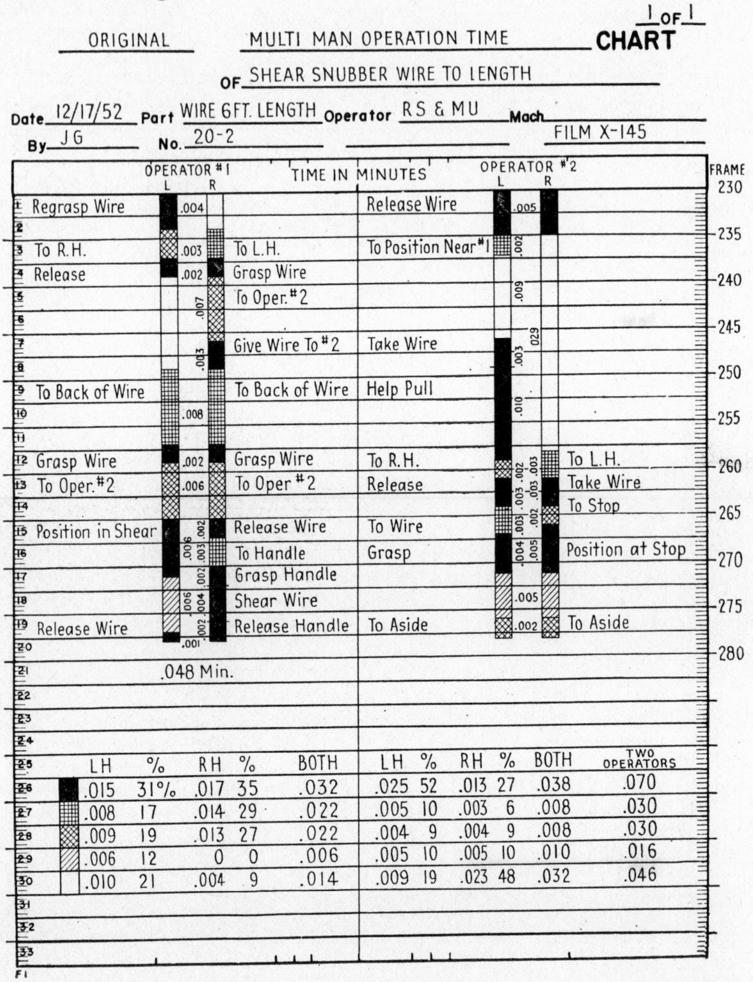

ORIGINAL   MULTI MAN OPERATION TIME   **CHART** 1 OF 1

OF SHEAR SNUBBER WIRE TO LENGTH

Date 12/17/52   Part WIRE 6FT. LENGTH   Operator RS & MU   Mach

By JG   No. 20-2   FILM X-145

OPERATOR #1 L / R	TIME IN MINUTES	OPERATOR #2 L / R	FRAME
1 Regrasp Wire .004	Release Wire .005		230
2			235
3 To R.H. .003	To L.H.	To Position Near #1 .002	
4 Release .002	Grasp Wire		240
5 .007	To Oper. #2	.009	
6			245
7 .003	Give Wire To #2	Take Wire .003 .029	
8			250
9 To Back of Wire	To Back of Wire	Help Pull .010	
10 .008			255
11			
12 Grasp Wire .002	Grasp Wire	To R.H. .003 .002	To L.H.	260
13 To Oper. #2 .006	To Oper #2	Release .003 .003 .002	Take Wire	
14		.002	To Stop	265
15 Position in Shear .002	Release Wire	To Wire .001 .005		
16 .006 .003	To Handle	Grasp .004 .005	Position at Stop	270
17 .006	Grasp Handle			
18 .006 .002	Shear Wire	.005		275
19 Release Wire .002	Release Handle	To Aside .002	To Aside	
20 .001			280
21 .048 Min.			
22			
23			
24			

	LH	%	RH	%	BOTH	LH	%	RH	%	BOTH	TWO OPERATORS
26	.015	31%	.017	35	.032	.025	52	.013	27	.038	.070
27	.008	17	.014	29	.022	.005	10	.003	6	.008	.030
28	.009	19	.013	27	.022	.004	9	.004	9	.008	.030
29	.006	12	0	0	.006	.005	10	.005	10	.010	.016
30	.010	21	.004	9	.014	.009	19	.023	48	.032	.046

Fig. 9-4. Original basic man and machine process chart for making a tensile test.

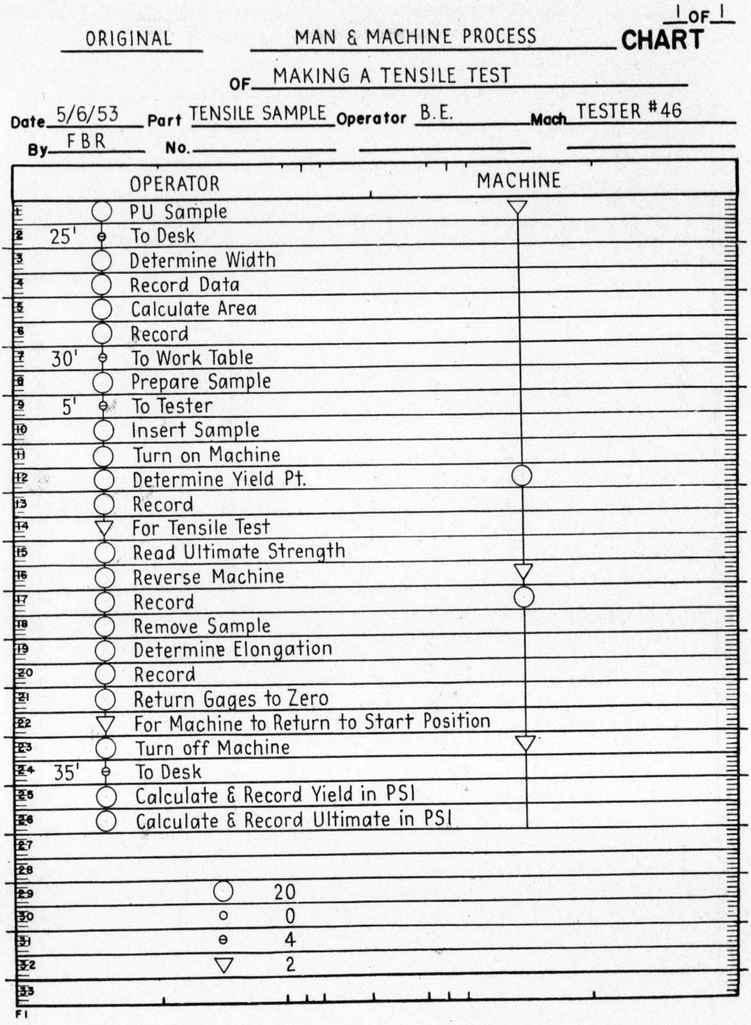

ORIGINAL	MAN & MACHINE PROCESS	CHART 1 OF 1

OF MAKING A TENSILE TEST

Date 5/6/53   Part TENSILE SAMPLE Operator B.E.   Mach TESTER #46

By FBR   No.

		OPERATOR	MACHINE
1		◯ PU Sample	▽
2	25'	⊖ To Desk	
3		◯ Determine Width	
4		◯ Record Data	
5		◯ Calculate Area	
6		◯ Record	
7	30'	⊖ To Work Table	
8		◯ Prepare Sample	
9	5'	⊖ To Tester	
10		◯ Insert Sample	
11		◯ Turn on Machine	
12		◯ Determine Yield Pt.	◯
13		◯ Record	
14		▽ For Tensile Test	
15		◯ Read Ultimate Strength	
16		◯ Reverse Machine	▽
17		◯ Record	◯
18		◯ Remove Sample	
19		◯ Determine Elongation	
20		◯ Record	
21		◯ Return Gages to Zero	
22		▽ For Machine to Return to Start Position	
23		◯ Turn off Machine	▽
24	35'	⊖ To Desk	
25		◯ Calculate & Record Yield in PSI	
26		◯ Calculate & Record Ultimate in PSI	
27			
28			
29		◯ 20	
30		○ 0	
31		⊖ 4	
32		▽ 2	
33			

FI

FIG. 9-5. Flow diagram for original method of making a tensile test.

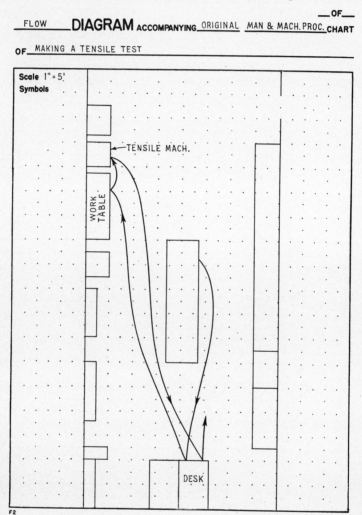

the time chart may take up more (or less) lines to show the correct relationship. Although motion pictures were used in this illustration, it is possible to use a sweep-second wrist watch, or stop watch, to obtain rough estimates of times. The approximate therblig times can provide some estimated times for motions on the chart.

2. Making a tensile test

A laboratory was going to receive a large increase in the amount of tensile testing. The specific goal was to decrease the time and skill required for this operation. Since the operator moved from place to place, the man and machine process chart of Fig. 9-4 was made. Figure 9-5 shows the flow diagram for this activity. It was desirable to get a truer relationship of activities, and the man and machine process time chart of Fig. 9-6 was prepared. Notice how the interrelationships of activity show up strikingly on the time chart.

3. Making large paper-bag containers

To maintain a reserve of empty cans, food processors keep a supply of containers packed with 200 cans per container. In the can manufacturing plant, the containers are made from large sheets of paper. The specific goal for this repetitive operation with a two-girl team was to reduce the cost of the operation. While making the multi-man and machine process chart, the analyst used a sweep-second wrist watch to get some estimates of time for the symbols. The controlling first operator (forming the bag) was timed, and the second operator's times were estimated in relation to the first operator. The obtained times were recorded as shown in the multi-man and machine process chart with time column (Fig. 9-7). The flow diagram is shown in Fig. 9-8.

Fig. 9-6. Original man and machine process time chart for making a tensile test.

ORIGINAL	MAN & MACHINE PROCESS TIME	CHART 1·OF 2

OF MAKING A TENSILE TEST

Date 5/6/53 Part TENSILE SAMPLE Operator BE Mach TESTER #46

By FBR No.

	MAN	SECS	MACHINE	FRAME
1 PU Sample To Desk	2			90
2	16			100
3 Determine Width				
4	36			120
5				140
6 Record Data	6			
7 Calculate Area		124		160
8	20			
9 Record	4			180
10 To Work Table	20			
11 Prepare Sample	12			200
12 To Tester	2			
13 Insert Sample Turn on Machine	4 2			220
14 Determine Yield Pt.	29			
15				240
16 Record	5			
17 For Tensile Test				260
18				
19				280
20				
21		206		300
22				
23				320
24	168			
25				340
26				
27				360
28				
29				380
30				
31				400
32				
33 Read Ultimate Length	4			420

FIG. 9-6 (Cont.)

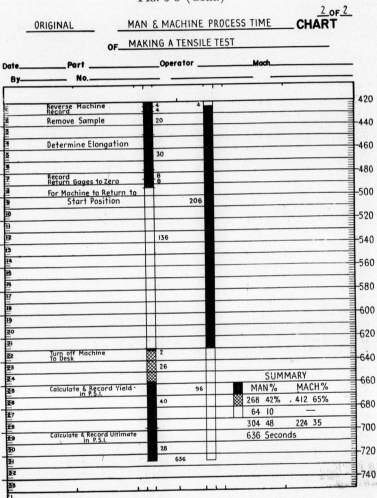

ORIGINAL   MAN & MACHINE PROCESS TIME   CHART 2 OF 2

OF MAKING A TENSILE TEST

Date_____ Part _____ Operator _____ Mach_____

By_____ No._____

FIG. 9-7. Original multi-man and machine process chart with time columns for making large paper-bag containers.

| ORIGINAL | MULTI-MAN AND MACHINE PROCESS | __OF__ CHART |

OF MAKING LARGE PAPER BAG CONTAINERS

Date 11/20/50   Part P-3 PAPER   Operator MM-EG   Mach
By S.F.C.   No. 4521

	FOLDER - 1ST OPERATOR	SECONDS	GLUER - 2ND OPERATOR	GLUE MACHINE
1	3' 4 ⊖ To Right Side of Paper	4 ◯	Remove Bag from Form	44 ▽
2	5 ◯ P U Edge	7' 5 ⊖	To Press	
3	3' 2 ⊖ To Center of Table	3 ◯	Raise Press with Foot	
4	3 ◯ Fold Side Over Form	8 ◯	Place Bag Under Press	
5	3' 1 ⊖ To Left Side			
6	2 ◯ P U Edge			
7	3' 1 ⊖ To Center of Table			
8	5 ◯ Fold Side Over Form	2 ◯	Smooth Stack	
9	7 ◯ Get Tape	2 ◯	Smooth While Lower Press	
10		2 ◯	Smooth Side of Stack	
11		6' 4 ⊖	To Base Supply	
12	3 ◯ Position Tape	9 ◯	P U Base	
13	10 ◯ Glue on Tape	3' 5 ⊖	To Glue Machine	
14	9 ◯ Fold Up Bottom	5 ▽	Other Side of Base - Glue 1st side	5 ◯
15		3 ◯	Turn Base (Rotate)	3 ▽
16	6 ◯ Fold End	5 ▽	2nd Side	5 ◯
17	4 ◯ Get Base	3 ◯	Turn Base (Rotate)	3 ▽
18	6 ◯ Insert Base	5 ▽	3rd Side	5 ◯
19		3 ◯	Turn Base (Rotate)	3 ▽
20	6 ◯ Smooth Bottom Stop	5 ▽	4th Side	5 ◯
21	8 ◯ Smooth Sides	2 ◯	Turn Base Over	9 ▽
22		4' 2 ⊖	To Table	
23		3 ◯	Move Base on Table Over, Place New	
24		3' 2 ⊖	To 1st Operator	
25				
26				
27	1ST 2ND TOTAL MACH.			
28	◯ 20 15 35 4			
29	○ 2 2 4 −			
30	⊖ 2 3 5 −			
31	▽ − 0 0 20			
32	▽ − 4 4 −			
33	24 24			

F 1

FIG. 9-8. Flow diagram for original method of making large paper-bag containers.

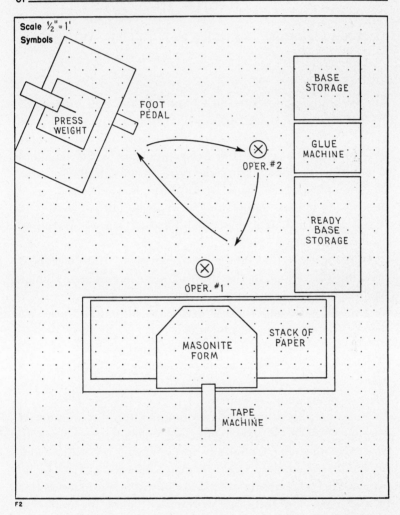

__ OF __

WORKPLACE __ **DIAGRAM** ACCOMPANYING ORIGINAL MULTI-MAN & MACH. PROC. **CHART**

OF __ MAKING LARGE PAPER BAG CONTAINERS

Scale ½"=1'
Symbols

PRESS WEIGHT

FOOT PEDAL

OPER. #2

BASE STORAGE

GLUE MACHINE

READY BASE STORAGE

OPER. #1

MASONITE FORM

STACK OF PAPER

TAPE MACHINE

F2

CHAPTER 10

ANALYZING NONREPETITIVE WORK

The techniques presented in Chapters 4 through 9 basically are for repetitive work and work with only slightly variable cycles. It is easy to understand why. Not only does it take time to make the chart, but most important is the fact that it would be impossible to make one of these charts for completely nonrepetitive work because the analyst would never be able to see the same thing over again. Repetitive work is the type to which work simplification has been mainly applied in previous years.

More work is becoming nonrepetitive. Automation is bringing this about in the form of more maintenance men, technicians, engineers, etc. Generally, nonrepetitive work is associated with supervisory activities, although there are many production operations which can be classified as nonrepetitive. Activities and operations such as those of map maker, expediter, foreman, purchasing agent, draftsman, a maid in a home, and an executive of a company are illustrations of nonrepetitive work.

Work simplification needs techniques for the analysis of nonrepetitive work. Too many inefficiencies occur in nonrepetitive jobs. The techniques for anlayzing repetitive work have sufficed to date because many operations had to be improved. Today nonrepetitive work must be designed better or improved. The techniques presented below for analyzing nonrepetitive work have been applied in industry and other work situations. Although there are one or two other major techniques used for analyzing nonrepetitive work (like 1 FPS motion pictures and past performance records), the ones listed below are the ones most widely used and most easily applied.

There is no fine dividing line between repetitive and nonrepetitive work. Many jobs are part of each. The techniques presented in this chapter are basically usable for nonrepetitive work. The analyst must select from among the various techniques presented the proper one for whatever situation he is working with. Even if the job is not completely nonrepetitive, he may choose a nonrepetitive analysis technique. Circumstances surrounding the work will dictate the use of the proper chart or technique.

1. PLACE OBSERVER WITH INDIVIDUAL(S) DOING NONREPETITIVE WORK

This procedure results in a record of all the activities and the time for each activity performed by the individual doing the nonrepetitive work. The observer merely records the starting time for each new activity or series of motions as he records a description of what is being done. Amount of time for each activity can be obtained by subtraction.

When an individual moves over great distances, from department to department or from building to building, this technique represents one of the best that can be used. (Another technique for analyzing work of this nature is presented later.) However, this obvious technique of getting information becomes at the same time an obviously expensive procedure. For example, the period of time for which the analyst would be assigned to the individual whose work is being analyzed would necessarily be short—one, two, or three days at the most in most cases. A question would then arise as to whether or not the information obtained provides a representative picture of all the activities of this individual. There would be the feeling that the study was not taken over a representative period of time. Another objection to this procedure is that only one individual or one crew was studied. What about the other crews or other individuals performing the same type of work? If only one crew or one individual is doing the nonrepetitive work, then this procedure does give good information.

Since the procedure is relatively simple, easy, and requires little or no previous knowledge of work simplification, an illustration of an analysis performed by an individual un-

FIG. 10-1. Record of the activity of a seven-man crew as obtained by an observer who followed the crew for a day.

Record of Activity of Seven-man Crew

8:34 a.m. First maintenance truck leaves city garage with two men aboard.

9:40 a.m. Truck stops at 2020 West Cullerton. One man apparently siphons gas from truck into gas can and puts it in another car.

9:57 a.m. Truck proceeds to Maplewood & Flournoy, meets five men, who drive up in own cars.

10:02 a.m. Two men put ladder against pole. Others do nothing.

10:05 a.m. One man ascends pole to attach rope at top. Others do nothing.

10:23 a.m. One man starts painting base of pole. Man on pole erects pulley arrangement to enable him to get can of paint to top of pole without carrying it.

10:29 a.m. Three men go to other car and drive off. Only one man working.

10:47 a.m. Three men come back in their car.

10:54 a.m. Cars and truck leave.

11:25 a.m. New location, School & Ravenswood.

11:26 a.m. Equipment unloaded. One man digging, others watching.

11:45 a.m. Six off for lunch. Go to tavern nearby.

12:00 a.m. Last man to lunch.

12:54 p.m. Six men return from tavern and one resumes digging.

1:03 p.m. One man ascends pole and detaches electric wire. One man digs.

1:08 p.m. One descends pole.

1:37 p.m. Two men working to remove pole.

1:49 p.m. Two men remove pole, using pulley; put in new pole.

2:02 p.m. Two men tamp dirt.

2:04 p.m. Two men go to tavern.

2:15 p.m. One man on top of pole, attaching wire.

2:21 p.m. One man on top of pole, one painting base of pole.

2:25 p.m. Man on pole working, others in truck.

2:40 p.m. One man painting pole, three in tavern, three in truck.

2:48 p.m. Man descends pole, puts ladder back in truck. Nobody working.

2:52 p.m. Another man leaves for tavern; no one working.

2:54 p.m. Last three men leave for tavern. All seven men in tavern now. Truck unattended though motor is running, as it has been all day.

3:12 p.m. Mass exodus from tavern.

3:19 p.m. Truck drives off. Other men get in cars and leave.

familiar with formal work simplification is shown in Fig. 10-1. This illustration was chosen from a report in *Time* magazine.[1] A councilman of a city studied the activities of an electrical maintenance crew of seven people. The simplicity of this procedure is obvious from the illustration. The illustration would be humorous if it were not true.

One point should be made about Fig. 10-1. Although it clearly illustrates how one man can observe the work of others and make a record of it, the observer in this case did not follow one important human relations rule: He did not tell the crew that he was studying them. Although he would not have gotten the same results if he had told them, it is most important for the morale and well-being of employees to let them know a study is being made. That the crew would in that case probably have worked differently in itself is not bad. The analyst would have had a record of what was "good" work. This would have provided a basis for comparing later work. This is an important consideration, for the major purpose of work simplification is to eliminate unnecessary activity, and if this is the way it can be done, so much the better. Those being studied should know it. Only harm can come from not telling them.

2. OPERATOR RECORDS WHAT HE DOES

Another type of nonrepetitive work involves an individual who moves to all parts of the plant and even out of the plant in performing his nonrepetitive work. Technique number 1, where the analyst stays with the man, could be used. However, this is difficult in many cases because the work and means of transportation of the individual(s) being studied becomes complicated and involved.

Therefore, it has been advisable in many cases to have the operator record on an established form for his work his activities during the day. The form gives the time of day which

[1] *Time*, vol. 60, no. 26, p. 15, Dec. 29, 1952.

is checked when performing an activity. The results of such a study cannot be treated as completely accurate. For example, it is unlikely that an individual will record with any fervor or detail the delays that occur during work or that he takes during the day. The study, however, is valuable to help report to the analyst the type of productive activity being performed and a fair approximation of the amount of time spent on each activity.

Figure 10-2 shows a form used for expediters in a large plant. Each expediter was given one of these forms every day so that he could check the activity he was performing during each 15-minute period of the day. It is possible to make the periods of day smaller, but in most situations it is not too advisable to attempt to get too much detail in such a procedure. After all the sheets have been collected, they can be grouped to obtain names of, and time for, categories of the nonrepetitive work.

3. OCCURRENCE STUDY (WORK SAMPLING)

The occurrence study is one of the most widely used new techniques for analyzing nonrepetitive work. It gets very good results, and it does not require a man to spend full time getting the results. In other words, a foreman or supervisor can use the occurrence study and still perform almost all his other functions.

The occurrence study determines the per cent of time spent (by the individual or individuals engaged in the nonrepetitive work) in relation to the various activities of the job. This is done by means of random observations. The occurrence study overcomes many of the objections to procedures 1 and 2 mentioned above. The occurrence study can be made for a short period of time or, as is usual, for a long period of time. For example, it is possible to make an occurrence study which lasts from three to five days, or for six to eight weeks and even more if required. The occurrence study can actually be used to gather information for all types

F‍ɪɢ. 10-2. Form given each expediter in a large plant to fill in daily. (Part of a study of nonrepetitive work where each operator records his own activity.)

Expediter Study

Date 3/19   Expediter   H. Peters

	7	7	8	8	8	8	2	2	2	2	3	3	3	3
	30	45	00	15	30	45	00	15	30	45	00	15	30	45
Tool crib—Picking Up Tools			✓											
Tool crib—Looking for Tools			✓									✓		
Looking for Tools 161–163														
Checking Tools 125–123														
Checking Tools, Tool Insp.			✓											
Tool Planning														
Making Tool Requests														
Making Tool Lists								✓	✓	✓				
Picking Up & Order. Viny.														
Picking Up & Order B/Prints					✓						✓			
Lost Cards & Mixed Up Parts														
Splits and Dupl. Orders				✓										
Planning Changes				✓	✓		✓							
Assisting Other Expediters														
Assist. Shop Foreman & Sb. Fore.	✓											✓		
Assist.-Disp. or Utility		✓				✓			✓	✓			✓	✓
(Sectional Duties)							✓	✓						
Checking Tool List			✓								✓	✓		
Checking Flow of Work														
Checking Misc. Lists														
Purchasing & Subcontract														

of work, repetitive or nonrepetitive. However, it is best suited for nonrepetitive work, since it would take much longer to gather the data for repetitive work by this technique than by any of the other techniques presented in the previous chapters. Even so, repetitive work, like materials handling or other long-cycle repetitive work, can be satisfactorily analyzed with the occurrence study. The occurrence study is easy to make and results in valuable and fairly accurate information. It is even useful in fields other than work simplification. For example, the results obtained are usable for making job descriptions for job evaluation and employment purposes. The occurrence study can be made on a large group of people doing the same type of nonrepetitive work as well as on one person performing nonrepetitive work.

To illustrate better how an occurrence study is made, a step-by-step procedure is outlined below with an example of how it was applied in an unusual situation.

Step 1. Determine who is to be studied

Service managers in a department store are similar to the foremen of a production department in a manufacturing plant. The service manager is in charge of the selling personnel in a number of departments on a given floor. The specific goal for studying service managers was to determine their relation to the salespeople involved. In other words, what per cent of the time was spent by the service managers in relation to salespeople.

Since there were so many service managers, it became essential to select particular people, and areas in which the service managers would be studied. Basically, it was decided to study mainly those service managers in areas affected by women shoppers. By selecting areas which are somewhat similar in nature, it is possible to reduce the total number of trips taken by the analyst through the store or plant. In many cases it may not be necessary to select areas, because the type of activity being studied does not require many people.

Then the individuals in these areas should be selected. Usually a maximum of 20 people can be included in one occurrence study of a given type of nonrepetitive work. Since occurrence studies can be, and usually are, made by people with other work to do, this limit has been found to be optimum. Obviously, if an individual can devote full time to these studies, the limit on the number of people included is determined by other factors, like distance or analyst's capabilities. In all cases, specify those people doing the similar types of work who should be included in one study. This is the important rule: Include only those people doing similar types of work in one occurrence study. If people doing different types of work are to be studied, they should be included in other occurrence studies.

Step 2. Make a list of activities

The person who is going to make the occurrence study should be familiar with the activities of the individuals being studied. The analyst should observe the work of the individuals and, at the same time, talk to them to obtain their ideas of what they do that may not be observed during the observation period. At any rate, this step allows the analyst to explain the study to the supervisors and the people. The human relations aspect is much better taken care of this way, and the way to a successful study will have been started.

The observation of work assumes great importance when it is considered that human beings will be the subjects for the study. The study can be completely biased if the initial groundwork is not properly laid. Usually the people who would be included in an occurrence study are performing some type of activity which requires some specialized skills. In most cases, the final objective of the study of nonrepetitive work is for greater utilization of the skills of the individuals. This objective appeals to the individuals and is frequently the key to gaining cooperation.

The list of activities should be placed on a form to be used during the occurrence study. Figure 10-3 shows the form used especially for the service manager's study. In this particular case, the recording of activity is divided into

FIG. 10-3. Example of filled-in observations on the service manager study form.

WEEK BEGINNING _November 2_   SERVICE MGR. _Mr. Williams_

FLOOR _4th_   DEPT. _Men's Wear_

DUTIES	Mon.	Tues.	Wed.	Thurs.	Fri.	Sat.	TOTAL
HANDLING RETURNS	1 11	1	1	1 11		1	8
ACTIVE SUPERVISION		1 11	1	11	1		7
PASSIVE SUPERVISION	1	1	1	1			4
HANDLING ADJUSTMENT	1			1			2
TALKING WITH CUSTOMER	1	11				1	4
DAILY REPORT OF SALES-PEOPLE							
RETURN STOCK							
WORK ORDERS							
WAIT ON CUSTOMER							
EXCHANGES	1					1	2
DISTRIBUTE SERVICE NOTES							
CHARGE WITHOUT PLATE			1				1
PERSONAL TIME	1		1				2
LUNCH	[1]		[1]	[1]			[3]
TELEPHONE	1			1		1	3
SIGN SHOPPERS PASSES		1		1			2
TALK TO SUPERINTENDENT						1	1
O.K. BANK CHECKS			1				1
TOTAL	1 5	4 3	4 1	1 3	3 2 3 1	1 4 1	37

three time periods of the day as well as days of the week. This was desirable, since department stores feel that business volume varies with the period of the day. That is, 9:30 to 11:30, 11:30 to 4:00, and 4:00 to 5:30. Many spaces should be left clear on the form to accommodate activity which has not been observed and listed prior to the start of the study.

It is better to obtain a finer breakdown of activities than to make a gross breakdown. After a fine-breakdown study has been completed, it is possible to combine many of the observations for activities, but it will never be possible to subdivide a gross breakdown after observations have once been obtained. Each observation was recorded in terms of the floor, the department, the service manager, the period of day, the day, and the week. This permits an analyst to make as many analyses as desired. Even though an analyst cannot foresee any value to recording information by periods of the day, and by fine breakdowns of activity, it would be desirable to record this information anyway.

Step 3. Estimate the number of observations

The occurrence study is more accurate with more observations. There are ways of determining an accurate estimate,[2] but if an analyst obtains at least 1,000 observations, he will be on fairly safe grounds.

Using the 1,000 figure, it is important to interpret what this means in view of the objectives of the study. If the purpose is to determine what all 20 service managers do, then the 1,000 observations would have to be divided among all service managers. However, if the goal was to determine what one service manager was doing, then 1,000 readings would have to be obtained on that one service manager. Since our purpose was to find out what all the service managers were doing, the 1,000 observations were divided among the service managers. The number of observations on each service manager was 1,000 divided by 20, or 50 observations

[2] G. Nadler, *Motion and Time Study*, New York: McGraw-Hill Book Company, Inc., 1955, pp. 162–163.

for each service manager. Since the analyst will usually make an observation on each service manager on each trip through the store, he will need a minimum of 50 trips. In the same way any other relationships could be obtained. For example, if we wanted the per cent of time spent in relationship to salespeople for one area of 4 service managers, 1,000 divided by 4, or 250, observations would be needed on each individual in that area.

The total length of time over which the study is taken can be lengthened or shortened as the goal and analyst dictate. All the observations can be made in a few days or week, or they can be spread over three, four, or more weeks.

Step 4. Rules for making observations

Before making any observations, it is essential that the individuals being studied do not in any way attempt to bias the study. The introductory part of the study should have been satisfactorily taken care of, and the individuals being studied should pay no attention to the analyst. Many problems can arise, and the analyst should be careful. If difficulties arise, it is usually wise to make "dry runs," so that the individuals become more familiar with the analyst and therefore less conscious of the analyst's presence. This is usually achieved after a short period of time.

Rule 1. There Must Be Random Intervals of Time between Observations. A random interval of time means that the amount of time between observations must not be a specific amount. If possible, the observations should also be randomized within the days or within the weeks, etc. The determination of random intervals can usually be accomplished by having the analyst decide when he should make a trip through the area. While he is working, he may merely decide to get up and go through the plant at any specific time. This permits him to perform other activities at the same time the study is being made. He can stop at any point in his work to make observations, regardless of how long the other work may take. However, if there is a possibility that the analyst will be careless, tables of random numbers can be used to establish the times for making observations. This would not permit the analyst to have complete freedom in performing his other work, although he can do many other things.

Rule 2. The Observations Must Be Instantaneous. The analyst must select a position, or spot, in the area in which the individual is working and not make his observation until he reaches that point. At that instant, and only at that instant, he records exactly what the individual being studied is doing. If the individual has left the area, he must ascertain where the person is and, if possible, make an instantaneous observation of what the individual is doing at his different location.

Figure 10-3 shows the record for a week's activity of a service manager. The check marks are located where the analyst put them.

Step 5. Compile results

Placing the data in final form involves three simple steps. For each individual category for which information is desired, first, determine the total number of observations for the entire study or group; second, determine the number of observations in the entire study or group for the category for which information is desired; and, third, divide the number of occurrences for each item of interest by the total number of observations for the grouping. For example, 1,455 observations were made on the service managers during the study. Of these observations, 653 were in relationship to salespeople. Dividing 653 by 1,455 and multiplying by 100 gives a percentage of 44.88 of all service managers' time in the store spent in relationship to salespeople. The same procedure is followed for other breakdowns or groupings. For example, the total number of observations for all service managers on the first floor was 433. Of this number, 240 observations were in relation to salespeople. Therefore, 55.43 per cent of the time of the first-floor service managers was spent in relation to salespeople. The summary of results grouped by floors of the department store and also grouped by the days of the week is given in Fig. 10-4.

FIG. 10-4. Summary of results of service manager occurrence study, grouped by floors and by days of the week.

Summary of Study Data Grouped by Floors

	Store	D.S.S.	First	Second	Third	Fourth	Fifth
Relation to sales-people	44.88	42.65	55.43	36.17	51.59	40.11	35.39
Relation to cus-tomers	36.38	43.88	28.07	40.66	28.59	36.30	47.77
Relation to mer-chandising	3.37	1.63	1.71	6.73	3.50	2.82	3.92
Miscellaneous	15.37	11.84	13.66	16.44	16.32	20.76	12.72

Summary of Study Data Grouped by Days of Week

	Store	Mon.	Tues.	Wed.	Thurs.	Fri.	Sat.
Relation to sales-people	44.88	43.87	41.85	47.48	45.69	45.40	45.10
Relation to cus-tomers	36.38	40.09	38.24	32.96	36.25	33.70	36.15
Relation to mer-chandising	3.37	1.89	4.47	3.07	3.56	2.96	4.24
Miscellaneous	15.37	14.15	14.57	16.48	14.50	17.94	14.51

The per cent of time spent for each individual activity can also be calculated. The results of an analysis made by floors of the store are shown for each individual activity in Fig. 10-5. Notice how valuable the detailed list of activities is.

There is a formula for checking the error in any given percentage figure. The formula is:

$$E = 2\sqrt{\frac{p(100 - p)}{N}}$$

p = per cent of time spent in the activity for which the error is being checked, N represents the total number of observations in the study (or grouping), and E = the error associated with a given per cent value. For example, if the p came out to be 20 per cent and the E was 3 per cent, then

FIG. 10-5. Complete tabulation of results of service manager occurrence study, grouped in terms of floors.

Tabulation of Data by Floors

	Store	D.S.S.	First	Second	Third	Fourth	Fifth
Relation to *Salespeople*							
Active Supervision *	25.04	21.43	25.19	24.07	26.40	26.27	25.30
Passive Supervision †	11.78	11.02	21.24	5.53	14.02	8.19	6.63
Daily Rep. of Salespeople	2.11	2.45	2.77	1.20	2.96	1.55	1.08
Sign Shoppers Passes	1.14	2.04	1.71	.90	1.20	.42	.68
Production Report	.92	.41	1.07	.30	2.52	.14	.41
Sales Summary	.76	1.63	1.07	.90	.44	.14	.68
Void Sales'Slips	.58	.61	.53	1.35	.11	.71	.41
Requisition for extras	.56	.20	.43	.15	.99	1.27	.14
Time Cards	.56	.61	.61	.60	1.20		
Schedule Lunch Hours	.40	.61	.64		.99		
Supper Money	.29	.61	.53	.45	.22		
Register Envelopes	.22	.20	.11	.45		.71	
Distribute Service Notes	.22	.41	.21	.15	.11	.56	
Yellow Sheet Analysis	.11			.15	.11	.14	.27
Schedule Days Off	.09		.21		.22		
Short Slips	.02		.11				
Plan Meetings	.02	.20			.11		
Incomplete Register Checks	.02	.20					
Total for Group	44.88	42.65	56.43	36.17	51.59	40.11	35.39
Relation to *Customers*							
Handling Returns	21.63	26.53	22.95	21.52	19.39	17.66	23.41
Talking with Customer	5.03	5.31	2.77	5.68	4.38	3.81	9.07
Exchanges	2.65	5.71	.64	2.09	.77	3.39	5.28
Complaints	1.17			5.08		.71	1.76
Handling Adjustments	1.48	1.02	.53	1.64	.99	1.55	3.38
O.K. Bank Checks	.88	1.84	.21	.60	1.10	1.27	.68
Wait on Customers	.70	1.84	.53	1.20		.99	.27
Accommodation Checks	.61	.20		.45	.33	2.54	.27
Mail Orders	.38			.15		1.98	27
Telephone Orders	.38	.41	.21	.30	.11	.71	.68
C.O.D. Sales	.18			.60		.14	.41
Work Orders	.18					.14	.95
Advanced Pay Sales	.11			.45	.22		
Nondelivery Complaints	.11	.20				.28	.27
Garage Parcel Check	.11			.15	.11	.14	.27
Charge without Plate	.09			.15	.22	.14	
Gift Wrap	.09	.20	.11	.30			
Request for Authorization	.07					.28	.14
Future Form	.07			.15	.22		
Money Mistakes	.07	.41					.14

Fig. 10-5 (Cont.)

Tabulation of Data by Floors (Cont.)

	Store D.S.S.	First	Second	Third	Fourth	Fifth
Relation to *Customers* (Cont.).						
O.K. Discount Sales	.07		.15	.22		
Bi-returns	.07	.11			.14	.14
Co-op Sales	.07		.33			
Bi-cash Sales	.04			.11		.14
Accident Report	.02					.14
Correct Cross Charge	.02				.14	
Wear Out	.02				.14	
Inclosures	.02				.14	
Wagon Pickup	.02					.14
Will Call	.02	.20				
Parcel Post	.02			.11		
Total for Group	36.38	43.88	28.07	40.66	28.59	36.30	47.77
Relation to *Merchandising*						
Return Stock	1.86	1.02	.21	4.33	2.41	1.84	1.62
Contact Buyer	.72	.41	.32	1.35		.99	1.49
Collect Want Slips & Tax Exempts	.40	.20	.43	.90	.22		.68
Arrange Stock	.18		.21	.15	.55		
Repairs on Merchandise	.16		.53		.11		.14
Orders Memos	.04				.22		
Total for Group	3.37	1.63	1.71	6.73	3.50	2.82	3.92
Miscellaneous						
Personal Time	6.93	6.33	8.00	7.17	7.89	6.78	4.74
Telephone	3.01	2.24	2.56	3.14	2.30	3.95	4.06
Watch Other Section	1.84		.53	1.49	2.30	5.37	1.08
Talk to or Look for Superintendent	1.86	1.22	1.92	2.24	2.41	1.69	1.35
Attend Meetings	.70	.61	.11	1.05	.22	1.69	.81
Order Supplies	.38	.20	.11	.60	.55	.56	.27
Fix Cash Register	.20	1.02	.32	.15			
Call or Talk to Dectective	.07	.20				.14	.14
Miscellaneous	.38		.11	.60	.66	.56	.27
Total for Group	15.37	11.84	13.66	16.44	16.32	20.76	12.72

* Active Supervision is an overt act of a supervisory nature.

† Passive Supervision includes contemplative supervision and idle time which cannot be adequately distinguished in this study.

most of the time we would expect the true value for the particular activity to be between 17 and 23 per cent.

If the errors found are satisfactory with the analyst for the purpose for which the study is to be used, the study can be ended. If the errors are too large, more observations are needed and can continue to be made until the error is reduced to the desired point.

ADVANTAGES OF OCCURRENCE STUDY

Some of the advantages of an occurrence study are:

1. A longer period of time is covered by the occurrence study, which helps obtain a more representative analysis of what the group of individuals actually does.

2. The observer or analyst can perform other work at the same time.

3. It is capable of expansion or compression to accomplish whatever needs must be met.

4. It provides valuable time-for-activity information.

5. It has all the other advantages of any procedures for analyzing nonrepetitive work.

To show another illustration of where the occurrence study has been applied, Fig. 10-6 gives the results of a study made on 12 assistant foremen in a large manufacturing plant. The goal was to determine the per cent of time spent in relationship to production workers. Notice how this occurrence study was broken down into an analysis by days of the week. Occurrence studies can be broken down in various ways, if the data are collected properly.

THE ADVANTAGES OF ANALYZING NONREPETITIVE WORK

It should be apparent that analysis techniques for nonrepetitive work are becoming essential. To summarize, some of the advantages of nonrepetitive work analysis techniques are:

Fig. 10-6. Complete tabulation of results of occurrence study made on 12 assistant foremen in a large manufacturing plant, grouped by days of the week. (Reprinted with permission from G. Nadler, "What Do Your Foremen Do?" *Mill and Factory*, vol. 53, no. 4, pp. 88–92, October, 1953.)

Tabulation of Data by Days of Week

(Total Number of Observations—1,043)

	Dept.	Mon.	Tues.	Wed.	Thurs.	Fri.
Relation to Production Workers						
Personnel problems	8.3	11.7	8.0	6.9	6.2	8.7
Explaining print	4.8	2.3	4.7	6.1	5.5	4.2
Explaining optical equip.	3.6		4.1	4.7	4.8	4.4
Active supervision (other)	2.4	0.3	1.2	6.7	2.5	1.3
Other	1.1		0.7	2.0	3.6	0.4
Total	20.2	14.3	18.7	26.4	22.6	19.0
Relation to Production Problems						
Checking supplies	5.3	4.2	5.4	4.9	5.3	6.7
Check on location of gauges	4.4	2.3	4.3	5.6	5.6	4.2
Trouble—call on line	3.0	1.2	3.3	3.8	3.7	3.0
Accident	1.4	1.3	1.6	1.4	0.7	2.0
Scrap problem	1.0		0.8	3.0		1.2
Other	1.6	0.4	1.5	2.3	3.8	
Total	16.7	9.4	16.9	21.0	19.1	17.1
Relation to Paper Work						
Schedules	20.1	26.3	18.8	18.3	17.9	21.1
Equipment requisitions	8.3	5.1	9.4	9.2	9.5	8.3
Repair requisition	4.4	4.2	4.8	3.8	5.2	4.0
Working schedules	3.8	5.9	1.9	2.7	3.8	4.6
Planning for info.	2.4	5.3	1.5	1.2	1.6	2.4
Other	2.6	5.3	0.2	2.1	0.7	2.9
Total	41.6	52.1	36.6	37.3	38.7	43.3
Relation to Other Depts.						
Tool design for info.	6.4	7.2	8.3	4.3	6.0	6.2
Conference—L.P. & E.	5.7	6.1	5.9	3.4	5.4	7.7
Check with engr.	2.2	3.4	3.2	1.1	1.3	2.0
Check with prod. cont.	1.9	3.0	3.4	0.2	1.0	1.9
Check with final assem.	0.6	0.8	2.0			0.2
Other dept. calls	0.6	0.6	2.0		0.1	0.3
Total	17.4	21.1	24.8	9.0	13.8	18.3
Miscellaneous						
Talk with foreman	1.4	1.2	1.5	2.0	0.4	1.9
Attend meetings (misc.)	1.1	0.3	0.6	2.1	2.3	0.3
Free time	0.9	0.7	0.8	1.2	1.7	0.1
Other	0.7	0.9	0.1	1.0	1.4	
Total	4.1	3.1	3.0	6.3	5.8	2.3

1. They focus attention where other work simplification or motion study techniques can be applied. Those activities involving the most time can be analyzed for simplification. Forms, paper work, manual activity can be simplified to reduce the amount of time spent in that activity.

2. They give management information for action, by giving them the tools for finding out what is done by people performing nonrepetitive work.

3. They present facts to the people studied when talking with them about their own activities. Much of the time in industry, opinions form the basis for discussing what our colleagues do. These techniques allow facts instead of opinion to dominate discussions.

4. They point out areas in which training might be necessary. Have the operators or supervisors been properly trained to fulfill a particular function?

5. They help determine "skill utilization" for groups of people or for individuals hired for their possession of certain skills. With this information regarding amounts of time for activities, it is possible to rearrange duties, responsibilities, and activities to utilize the skills of the people better.

CHAPTER 11

OTHER ANALYSIS TECHNIQUES

This chapter presents techniques which would be usable and needed by the work simplification specialist. The techniques in the previous chapters are those which can be readily used by anyone. The work simplification specialist may sometimes need some specially adapted techniques for specific situations. Even though the reader is not a work simplification specialist, he will find this chapter interesting. Learning about other techniques which are available and have been devised should make everyone more aware of the potentialities of work simplification.

Many techniques have been devised to make an analysis of work performed under repetitive and nonrepetitive, as well as other physical, conditions. The techniques previously presented are those which have found widespread and general application. However, many other techniques have been established to analyze work. When the work is performed under unusual conditions, or a special effect of analysis is desired by an analyst, these special techniques are used. Since some of the situations where one or more of these techniques can be used may arise, some of the more useful of them are described below.

1. Chronocyclegraph

An analysis technique originally developed by Frank Gilbreth has been given more emphasis recently by Anne

Shaw.[1] The chronocyclegraph was devised to study paths of movements of the hands. It is an effective device for showing the relative velocities of body members, as well as the exact path of the motion in two dimensions. The chronocyclegraph has its greatest use on highly repetitive operations, such as sewing garments, clerical work, and many assembly jobs. Generally, the chronocyclegraph would be made where the production volume makes desirable a more detailed study of an operation than an operation chart would provide, without the expense involved in taking motion pictures. In many cases, the chronocyclegraph can be considered a photograph of the workplace with the paths of movements shown. In this respect it is a valuable adjunct to other analysis techniques, such as the therblig chart.

Making a chronocyclegraph involves placing lights on the hands which then perform with their normal pattern. The lights on the hands are attached to relays which rapidly spurt the light on and then slowly reduce the electricity to the light. This gives a series of pear-shaped dots on a picture which has been taken with an open shutter on a still camera. After the dots have been recorded, the entire workplace is photographed to give the relationship of the worker and his hands to the pear-shaped dots and the workplace. Figure 11-1 shows two chronocyclegraphs (original and improved) taken on a simple assembly operation. These dots help the analyst make a more detailed analysis of motions when they are rapid and skilled, or even before an operation is in existence by having an analyst go through the motions. These graphs also help train operators for performing jobs. Perhaps the greatest value of the chronocyclegraph is for "selling" methods; it gives a complete picture of the motion pattern at a glance, permitting easy comparisons of methods.

[1] A. G. Shaw, *The Purpose and Practice of Motion Study,* Manchester: Harlequin Press Co., Ltd., 1952, chap. 4. A simplified mechanism for making chronocyclegraphs is described in G. E. Clark, "A Chronocyclegraph That Will Help You Improve Methods," *Factory Management and Maintenance,* vol. 112, no. 5, pp. 124–125, May, 1954.

FIG. 11-1. Two chronocyclegraphs showing the original and improved methods for assembling rubber tips to copper tubes. The effectiveness of the new method is readily apparent by the light pattern. Each point of light equals 0.001 minute. (From G. E. Clark, "A Chronocyclegraph That Will Help You Improve Methods," *Factory Management and Maintenance,* vol. 112, no. 5, pp. 124–125, May, 1954.)

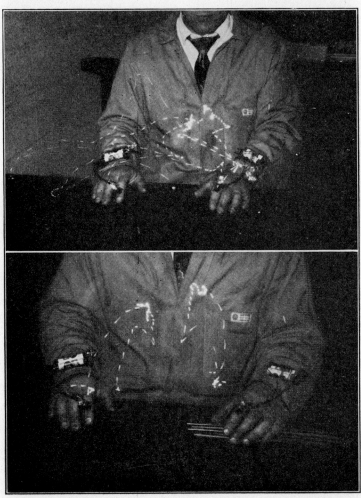

There are, however, a number of disadvantages associated with chronocyclegraphs. For example, the cycle which is studied must be of relatively short duration. If not, the dots would become too involved and complex. It would be possible, however, to make individual chronocyclegraphs for parts of an operation, but this does not present a complete picture of the work method. Also, attaching a light to the hands indicates that there might be some restriction to ordinary motion. (In most cases, if the wires are placed properly on the arm, and the operator is given sufficient time for becoming accustomed to the wires, little or no difficulty arises from this source.) The decrease in amount of light around the workplace to show up the dots might easily affect the operator's motion path. Also, the analysis of velocity and acceleration, if made, is not accurate because of the two-dimensional motion recorded. This is true even when stereoscopic pictures are taken. Special equipment is needed to create the pear-shaped dots, creating additional expense for equipment not really needed. Because the purpose of the chronocyclegraph is analysis of method rather than determination of work loads, they can be used to advantage even with these difficulties. Probably the greatest use revolves about the chronocyclegraph's ability to demonstrate the method being utilized. This assists in selling others on the inefficiency of original methods and desirability of improved methods.

2. Cyclegraph

Instead of pear-shaped dots, the cyclegraph shows the lights as a continuous line on the picture. The same advantages and disadvantages of the chronocyclegraph apply to the cyclegraph, except that velocity and acceleration information cannot be determined from the cyclegraph.

3. Motion paths from motion pictures

By projecting the frames of a motion picture one at a time on a piece of paper and placing a dot on the piece of paper upon which the film is projected, the foundation of a motion path chart is made. When all the dots are connected by a line, the result is the motion path followed by the operator's hands. Also the distance between the dots can be used to calculate velocity and acceleration information. The technique of motion pictures and dots, although not pear-shaped, on a sheet of paper represents an easy way of making an effective chronocyclegraph. However, the only disadvantage of the chronocyclegraph which remains with the motion-picture procedure is the two-dimensional aspect of the motions. Since motion-picture equipment is more likely and readily available, this procedure for making a chronocyclegraph is more desirable when and if the features of a chronocyclegraph are desired.

4. Other photographic techniques

Photography is playing a more important role every day in the areas of work simplification and measurement. The techniques above are ramifications of both still and motion pictures. Motion pictures, of course, have been mentioned in conjunction with techniques presented in previous chapters. However, still pictures are being utilized more for analysis and selling purposes. Some of the photography techniques are somewhat unusual and applicable only to special situations. For example, there is a special camera for photographing the movements of the eyes.[2] The eye camera is used mainly for visual inspection operations. In other situations, a stroboscopic camera can be used.[3] This camera provides a picture which shows the position or location of the man during the various parts of the operation. It is somewhat similar to the chronocyclegraph, except that no lights are attached to the hands and the final picture shows the entire arm and body at each position. Because of the latter, the

[2] "Eye Camera Shows How to Improve Inspection Techniques," *Factory Management and Maintenance*, vol. 111, no. 12, pp. 88–89, December, 1953.
[3] "Camera Catches Waste Motion," *Dun's Review and Modern Industry*, vol. 63, no. 2309, pp. 118–119, January, 1954.

pictures from the stroboscopic camera are usable mainly for selling purposes.

5. Time study

Because time study will be explained briefly later in this text, only a few pertinent comments concerning its utilization for work simplification will be made here.

As will be pointed out, time study is completely different from the timing which was done for the time charts. Time study determines the amount of time that should be taken on an operation or element of operation. The time charts were made to determine the interrelationships of the items being charted for a particular cycle. Because it supersedes the time charts, time study provides many clues to what might be improved. For example, in studying allowances for time study standards, the time study man frequently notices that allowances must be made for irregular occurrences (work that must be performed by the operator as part of his job) as well as for unavoidable delays. The type, number, frequency, and amount of time of irregular occurrences help determine what can be improved. This, of course, is work simplification. However, the information needed for this work study is gathered from the time study which was made on the operation.

Time studies may be made on operations which have not been improved as well as on improved operations. The time study on an unimproved operation leads to valuable information needed about the irregular occurrences and other inefficiencies. For example, in the summary of a time study shown in Fig. 11-2, much time is spent retapping holes in the cover of the duct. Because this is due to the poor quality of incoming product, work was undertaken to determine the cause and, therefore, the improvement of the poor quality of this material. The original time study, likewise, provides information on what is taking the most time in the repetitive part of the operation. Although the time charts show some of the same information as the time study, the time study

Fig. 11-2. Summary of time study made on two-man crew assembling duct. This information is valuable for helping improve methods.

Summary from Time Study on Assembling Duct

Base Time
Productive elements total	3.48 Min/Duct(6.96 Man Min/Duct)

Irregular Occurrences
Lining up screw holes in cover— includes retapping holes	1.44 Min/3 Duct
Adjusting and checking protectors	1.35 Min/5 Duct
Copper bar jamming in insulator, repair	.63 Min/8 Duct
Obtain truck	3.26 Min/30 Duct
Move skids and replace	3.04 Min/100 Duct
Relocate guides	1.76 Min/6 Duct
Miscellaneous	.54 Min/5 Duct

has the advantages of providing more representative (because of more time readings), more detailed (showing regular cycles, irregular occurrences, delays), and more accurate information than the time charts.

Some of the analysts in this field say that a time study should be made first when attempting to find an improvement for an operation. As the time study chapter indicates, times are usually obtained for elements of work, an element being a series of therbligs. It is rather difficult to make a complete time study analysis unless information has been gathered about the method of work on the operation. Therefore, it is probably wise, first, to make one or more of the charts presented previously and, second, if needed, to make a time study on the operation to gather the additional information about other than repetitive factors affecting the work. By following this procedure the analyst will know most of the motions and activities to look for before starting the time study.

6. Combination charts

Much valuable information can frequently be obtained by combining on one chart some of the other techniques already presented. It is possible, for example, to combine a man

FIG. 11-3. Combination operation and man process chart for original method of repairing a frame. (Only the first of two pages is shown.)

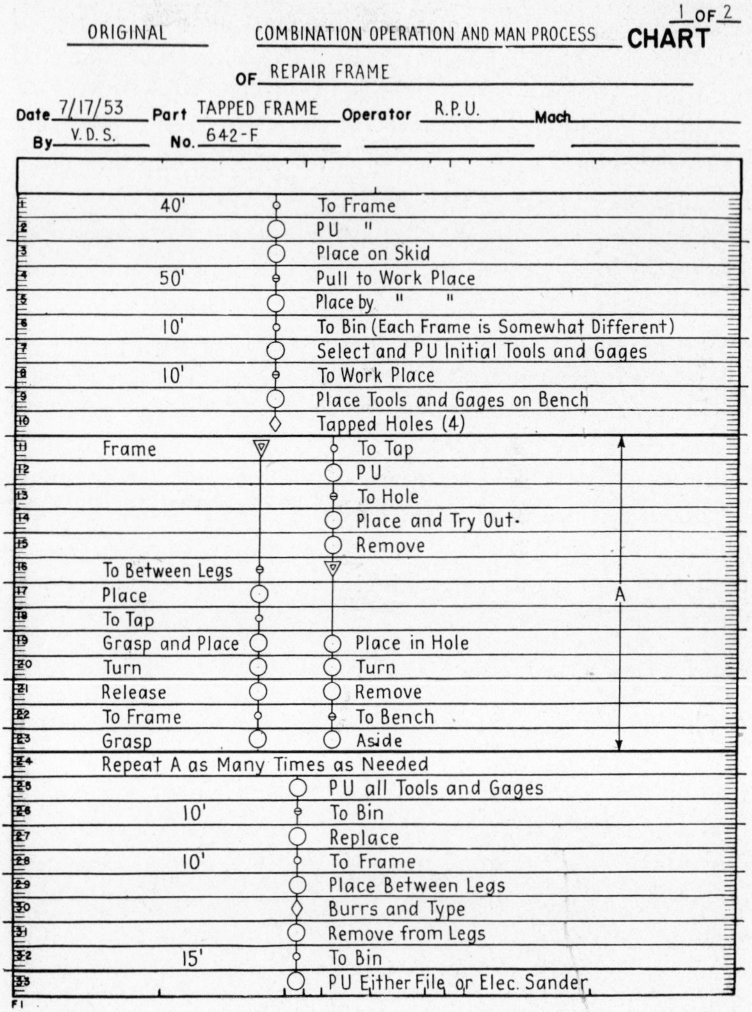

ORIGINAL   COMBINATION OPERATION AND MAN PROCESS   **CHART**   1 OF 2

OF REPAIR FRAME

Date 7/17/53   Part TAPPED FRAME   Operator R.P.U.   Mach

By V.D.S.   No. 642-F

#			
1	40'		To Frame
2			PU "
3			Place on Skid
4	50'		Pull to Work Place
5			Place by " "
6	10'		To Bin (Each Frame is Somewhat Different)
7			Select and PU Initial Tools and Gages
8	10'		To Work Place
9			Place Tools and Gages on Bench
10			Tapped Holes (4)
11	Frame		To Tap
12			PU
13			To Hole
14			Place and Try Out
15			Remove
16	To Between Legs		
17	Place		A
18	To Tap		
19	Grasp and Place		Place in Hole
20	Turn		Turn
21	Release		Remove
22	To Frame		To Bench
23	Grasp		Aside
24	Repeat A as Many Times as Needed		
25			PU all Tools and Gages
26	10'		To Bin
27			Replace
28	10'		To Frame
29			Place Between Legs
30			Burrs and Type
31			Remove from Legs
32	15'		To Bin
33			PU Either File or Elec. Sander

F 1

process chart and a form process chart whenever the man's work is being analyzed as the basis of a problem and it is found that a form with which he deals has an important bearing on his activity. It is not usual to start a form process chart and decide that a man process chart needs to be added to make the chart complete. When a combination man and form process chart is made, the activities are aligned to show simultaneous time of activity on the part of the man and the form, which is the advantage of this combination chart for analysis purposes. It is also possible to combine a man process chart and operation chart. There are work situations where the man's basic activity requires him to move from one workplace to another, indicating a man process chart analysis, but at one or more of the workplaces it might be important for the analyst to learn *how* the work is performed at that workplace. A combination man process and operation chart sometimes provides this information better than the individual charts. The first page of such a combination chart is shown in Fig. 11-3. This makes the analysis more continuous so that the analyst can better understand the operation. Of course, other combinations of charts can be made when required.

7. Special symbols

The symbols for each of the charts presented previously are for general application. However, special symbols are frequently needed for unusual situations. These special symbols usually are of a specific nature for a particular industry and plant. For example, on a man and machine operation chart, it is possible to devise a special symbol to indicate a certain activity for machine control manipulation which occurs frequently. If many analyses are made on lathe operations, a special symbol might be made to denote the activity of "start machine, run up carriage, and engage automatic feed," instead of using the ordinary series of suboperations and movements. For a large program of work simplification in a plant, special symbols devised for that plant save time, make for consistent analyses, and help find improvements which might not otherwise be feasible. An illustration of a generalized special symbol is provided by operation charts for assembly operations. On an operation chart the movement symbol is used for movement between work areas. However, the small circle could be used instead to represent a "get," or move to, pick up, and move back, activity. This is a special symbol, which, when used, makes the chart a gross analysis operation chart.

Materials handling problems are presenting a great challenge to industry today. In Chapter 4, it was suggested that the product process chart could help solve this type of problem. In many cases, the product process chart provides sufficient analysis of handling. In other cases, more information, such as type of handling equipment or storage containers, would be helpful to obtain a complete analysis. Special symbols (Table 11-1) for these pieces of equipment have been devised for addition to the product process chart in the equipment column.[4] With the quantity column, distance, and activity symbols, these symbols provide a rather complete analysis for materials handling purposes. For a particular industry, other symbols can probably be added. The new symbols are used to indicate how the product is moved, charted on the same line with the movement and/or labor cperation symbol, and in what the product is stored or moved, charted on the same line with storage symbols. Notice how the labor operation assumes a more important role with this new symbology. Figure 11-4 is the first page of a revision, with the materials handling symbols, of the product process chart presented originally in Fig. 4-3.

Because of the trend to more machines and automatic production methods, the work of the individuals involved

[4] G. Nadler and J. Goldman, "Analyzing Your Materials Handling Problems," *Mill and Factory*, vol. 55, no. 1, pp. 89–93, July, 1954. (Table 11-1 is reprinted with permission of *Mill and Factory*.)

Table 11-1. Equipment Symbols for Product Process Charts
Materials Handling Purposes

	Gravity	Powered
Roller conveyors	(R)	(R^P)
Chute conveyor	(C)	
Wheel conveyor	(W)	(W^P)
Slat conveyor		(S^P)
Apron conveyor		(A^P)
Belt conveyor		(B^P)
Trolley conveyor	(T)	(T^P)
Monorail conveyor		(M^P)
Flight conveyor		(F^P)
Carrousel conveyor	(CL)	(CL^P)
Towline conveyor		(TE^P)
Pusher bar conveyor		(P^P)
Arm elevator conveyor		(AE^P)
Bucket conveyor		(BT^P)
Pneumatic conveyor		(PC^P)

Hoist		Portable floor hoist	
Overhead traveling crane			
Yard crane		Monorail hoist crane	

Hand platform truck

Hand lift or skid jack truck

Hand lift power driven truck

Platform power driven truck   With trailers (2)

Power lift hand truck

Power lift and driven truck

  Fork   With trailers (2)

    High lift

    Low lift

  Platform   With trailers (3)

Tractor-trailer train (4)

Inverted V truck   Power   Hand

Hand truck

Man	X
Machine	M
Bench or table	T

152

Table 11-1. (Cont.)

Bag	∪		
Box	⌊ B ⌋		
Basket	⋈ B		
Carton	⌊ c ⌋		
Crate	⋈ c		
Drum	⊟		
Tote box	⌊ T B ⌋		
Pallet	▭	Place weight/pallet on top, no. of units on pallet in rectangle	3000 / 25
Skid	⌐▯	Same as above	2000 / 20
Dock	⌐		
Dolly	⊟		
Railroad car			
Box car	⊡		
Flat car	⎯o o⎯		
Highway truck	⊏⊐		
Elevator	Up ↑	Down ↓	

Symbols can be combined, i.e., a skid can be combined with a box to make a skid bin ⊢ B ⊣

will require more activity of the eyes, ears, and mind. This will become a complicating factor in the analysis of both repetitive and nonrepetitive work. Within the next 10 to 15 years, it will probably be necessary to devise special symbols for the analysis of the activity of these categories. These would help supplement the symbols now available for analysis of manipulative activity. A start has been made by trying to apply the concepts and definitions of therbligs to the eyes when making a simo chart. The inadequacies of this transfer to eyes become apparent when the nature of therbligs is considered; their definitions are almost completely limited in scope to muscular movement. Certainly all the activity of the eyes, ears, and mind in future, as well as

Fig. 11-4. Original product process chart of copper bar processing with materials handling symbols added. The chart without materials handling symbols is shown in Fig. 4-3. (Only the first of two pages is shown.)

ORIGINAL _____ PRODUCT PROCESS _____ **CHART** 1 OF 2

OF COPPER BAR PROCESSING

WITH MAT HANDLING SYMBOLS

Date_____ Part_____ Operator_____ Mach_____

By_____ No._____ SEE FIGURE 5-7

QUANT.	DIST.	SYMBOL	EXPLANATION	EQUIPMENT
1 10-12 Boxes	15'	○	From Truck to Skid	⌊B⌋ By J
2 10-12 "		▽	On Skid	6000/10
3 1 Skid		Ⓛ	Picked Up	⌐J
4 1 Skid	50'	○	To Storage Area	⌐ On J
5 1 Skid		Ⓛ	Skid Placed	⌐ By J
6 10 Skids		▽		6000/10
7 1 Skid		Ⓛ	Picked Up	⌐J
8 1 Skid	60'	○	To Bar Storage	⌐ On J
9 1 Skid		Ⓛ	Skid Placed	⌐ By J
10 10-12 Boxes		▽		6000/10
11 1 Box	Strap	Ⓜ	Strap Broken	Steel Strap Break
12 1 Box	Nails, Box	Ⓜ	Nails & Box Top Removed	
13 1 Box		▽		
14 2 Bars		Ⓛ	P U Copper Bars	X
15 2 Bars		○	To Bin	X
16 2 Bars		Ⓛ	Place	X
17 800 Bars	Box	▽	In Bin	⌊B⌋
18 2-4 Bars		Ⓛ	Picked Up	X
19 2-4 Bars	10'	○	To Press Table	X
20 2-4 Bars		Ⓛ	Placed	X
21 16-20 Bars		▽	On Press Table	
22 1 Bar		Ⓛ	Bar Placed Under Press	X
23 1 Bar		Ⓜ	Holes Punched	Punch Press
24 1 Bar		Ⓛ	Other End Placed	By X on Ⓡ
25 1 Bar		Ⓜ	Holes Punched	Punch Press
26 1 Bar		Ⓛ	Bar Picked Up	X
27 1 Bar		○	To Skid	X
28 1 Bar		Ⓛ	Bar Placed	X On ⌐
29 150 Bars		▽	On Skid	4500/150
30 150 Bars	20'	○	To Degreaser	By X On ⌐
31 150 Bars		▽	By Degreaser	⌐
32 1 Bar		Ⓛ	Bar Picked Up	X
33 1 Bar	4'	○	To Degreaser	X

F1

present, work will have to be analyzed, just as the problems of nonrepetitive work have created some techniques for analysis.

8. Gathering information about operating performance

To analyze completely a given situation, an analyst must frequently resort to procedures which cannot be specifically categorized. In most cases the additional information must be gathered by some measurement of physical facilities or operating conditions. The illustrations below provide some indication of the type of fact gathering that might be utilized in some work simplification problems.

a. Waste Control Experimentation.[5] An industrial engineer, assigned to reduce costs in a corn processing plant, found that good corn was being wasted in the various operations. In most cases, the food processors called this "normal waste." However, it was felt that this normal waste could be reduced to show a net gain when balanced against the cost of the changes. To determine what changes would be economical, it was necessary to know how much usable waste was being lost. A waste control experiment was established to determine by examination the amount of usable waste. The results of the experiment are shown in Fig. 11-5. Quite a bit of good corn was being lost, and the resultant dollar determination allowed proper economical changes to be made to save virtually all good product.

b. String Diagrams. Flow diagrams for product and man process charts can become rather complicated if the material or man moves over long or complex routes. String diagrams [6] (Fig. 11-6) provide a means for simplifying and clarifying the flow diagram. With pins representing work stations on a plan view of a plant, thread is strung around the pins to

[5] G. Nadler, "Measuring, Preventing Canners' Normal Waste," *The Food Packer*, part 1, vol. 30, no. 7, pp. 29–30, June, 1949; part 2, *The Food Packer*, vol. 30, no. 8, pp. 38–46, July, 1949.

[6] "String Diagrams," *Modern Materials Handling*, vol. 8, no. 8, pp. 67–71, August, 1953.

FIG. 11-5. Calculations to determine value of good corn being wasted in processing plant. These values were determined after a study of actual waste was made by sampling from the plant system. (Reprinted with permission from G. Nadler, "Measuring, Preventing Canners' Normal Waste," *Food Packer*, vol. 30, no. 8, pp. 38–46, July, 1949.)

Ensilage Waste Control Experiment

1. Total incoming corn to plant............................ 188.2 tons
2. Av. weight of waste per trailer load..................... 1,850 lb
3. Number of trailer loads of waste........................ 134
4. Total weight of waste carried by trailers = $\dfrac{1,850 \times 134}{2,000}$ .... 123.95 tons
5. Total weight of ensilage sold to farmers.................. 28.34 tons
6. Total weight of waste.................................. 152.29 tons
7. Total weight of sample loads of waste.................... 44,600 lb
8. Number of samples..................................... 24
9. Weight of usable ears (in terms of husked ears)............
   Unhusked... 68.00 lb
   Partially husked.................................. 101.25 lb
   Husked... 77.75 lb
10. Total weight of usable ears............................ 247.00 lb
11. Total pounds of usable ears in all waste
    $= \dfrac{247 \times 152.29 \times 2,000}{44,600}$ .... 1,687 lb
12. 60% of usable ears are kernel
    16 pounds of kernels per case of corn
13. $\dfrac{1,687 \times .60}{16} = 63.3$ cases per 8 hours of canning

or

142.4 cases per 18-hour canning day

indicate the flow. The string diagram has the additional advantage of helping sell new and revised layouts.

c. Warehousing and Distribution. Another area presenting a challenge to industry today is warehousing and distribution. Certainly these areas represent an addition to the cost of an item without an increase in the intrinsic value. Methods improvement usually can be of great help by the application of the techniques of previous chapters. However, more information is usually needed in the form of physical operating conditions data. A procedure [7] has been recom-

[7] W. W. Phillips, "How to Control Your Warehouse Space," *Modern Materials Handling*, vol. 8, no. 7, pp. 51–54, July, 1953.

Fig. 11-6. String diagram of flow of product in a plant. This is similar to a flow diagram but is somewhat more graphic because it does not become as complex as a flow diagram.

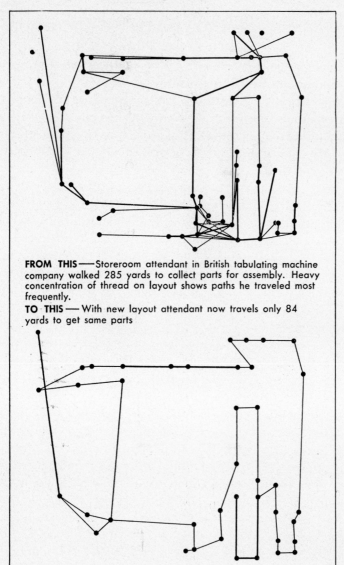

FROM THIS——Storeroom attendant in British tabulating machine company walked 285 yards to collect parts for assembly. Heavy concentration of thread on layout shows paths he traveled most frequently.

TO THIS — With new layout attendant now travels only 84 yards to get same parts mended (1) to determine the net usable cubic area of existing or planned warehousing for over-all information and (2) to determine space utilization monthly by means of a space inventory. These procedures gather some of the information necessary to making proper designs and improvements. The procedure is merely a listing of items that must be checked and measured, and also a way of relating the data to obtain the proper indices.

d. Statistical Analysis of Data. Operating performance data in their raw form are frequently usable for designing and improving methods. However, the raw data are frequently greatly enhanced by statistical and mathematical treatment. Today some people are starting to call this treatment of collected data "operations research." Included in this new term, however, is the concept of using people from different disciplines to help gather, analyze, and evaluate the data. A frequent result of this work is a mathematical model to show the relationships among all the factors affecting the problem. The model can be used for predicting both future performances under the same conditions and future performances under the changed conditions of good methods design.

This is a valuable approach and one which will probably be used more in the future of work study. For example, it may be possible to relate motions of individuals and operations and the time for a motion within a mathematical model to help determine the method to be used on an operation before it is in production. A simple example of the application of statistical analysis will demonstrate the usefulness of this approach to cost reduction and motion and time study.

A department store wanted a better way of predicting the number of salespeople that should be present on a given day. The present method utilized the predicted sales as the basic criterion which individual sales managers used, along with their individual judgment, to predict the number of salespeople for their department. Before the method of predicting the number of salespeople could be improved, a complete analysis had to be made of past records of the number of transactions, dollar volume, what a salesgirl did during the day, etc., in order to find the relationship among these factors and predicted sales. Typical statistical analysis techniques, such as time-series analysis (trends, cycles), correlation, variance, etc., were used to determine this relationship. The results were placed in mathematical model form, into which predicted sales could be inserted and the number of required salespeople, both full time and part time (those working only during the busiest part of the day), could be predicted.

One of the statistical techniques which holds great promise in the work study field for analyzing work is the sampling concept. Based on the laws of probability, this concept permits the data of a small part of much information to be analyzed for drawing conclusions concerning all the information. In many cases, such an analysis is used in conjunction with other charts. For example, an operation in an office, involving work on invoices to be mailed to customers, was being studied to find a more productive method. A form process chart was made for the forms involved, and a man and machine operation chart was made for the variable operation method. However, an important factor affecting the work, and the possible improvement, was the invoice content itself. There were many differences from invoice to invoice in number of items listed, prices, quantities, addresses, number of lines, number of pages, etc. To design the improved method properly, it should be arranged to save the most time for the type of invoice which occurs most frequently. Because there were over one thousand invoices a month, it would have taken a long time to complete a thorough analysis. However, correct sampling procedures permitted an analysis of less than 10 per cent of a year's invoices to obtain the necessary accurate information.

Other statistical techniques, like binomial distributions, poisson distributions, and tables of random numbers, probably can be adapted to many situations where more information is needed concerning operating procedures. Certainly, this approach should be used more in industry, and it will be one of the fundamental tools in industrial engineering and work simplification in future years.

9. UNOPAR

The chronocyclegraph and motion paths from motion pictures provided a possibility for determining very roughly the velocity and acceleration of body motions. Such information is desirable, and will be needed even more in future work simplification and measurement.

Electronics has entered the picture to give accurate measurements for any motion of time, velocity, acceleration, deceleration, position in space, and distance. A device called the UNOPAR (universal operator performance analyzer and recorder) provides these data.[8] With such exact data, many new insights into work will be available. Because of the newness of UNOPAR, no application illustrations can be provided. However, experiments indicate the availability of new and changed concepts for the future in the work simplification field.

USING THE ANALYSIS-OF-WORK TECHNIQUES

The purpose of the second step, getting the facts, is to gather the information about the operation or problem being worked on. This section presented various techniques and procedures for gathering and presenting this information in usable form. Obviously, each technique will not be used for every problem. The analyst must be familiar enough with the techniques presented and with the typical characteristics of the job to select the proper technique required for the situation.

[8] G. Nadler, "Electronics in Work Measurement," *Proceedings,* Sixth Annual Conference, American Institute of Industrial Engineers, May, 1955; J. Goldman and G. Nadler, "Electronics for Measuring Human Motions," *Science,* vol. 124, no. 3226, pp. 807–810, October 26, 1956.

In most cases a product process chart or form process chart will be made first in the analysis step. In some situations it might be advisable to apply the principles of methods design (see the next chapter) to the product process chart or form process chart, to learn if the operation is necessary, before making any of the other charts. However, in many situations, a complete and clear picture of the problem being studied would not be obtained by making only the product or form process chart. Another chart or charts, analyzing the method, would have to be made, which is also desirable from a "selling" aspect. Along with the information gathered by charts, the analyst would also have details concerning the material used and the way it is received, the design of the product being worked on, and the tools, equipment, and workplace at which the operation is performed. With this information obtained, the second step of the procedure for methods design is accomplished.

CHAPTER 12

GETTING IDEAS

Much information about the work being studied is available at this point. The previous chapters showed how to gather information about sequence and method, and the analyst will have gathered information about equipment, design of product, and materials. He now has all the facts about the problem; in other words, he has completed step 2.

The purpose of the next step (step 3) is to get ideas, ideas, ideas—as many ideas as possible about how the work can be designed or improved. We know much about work now. We have been able to see work as we have never seen it before. Work takes on a different light, and we should be able to penetrate the most complex inefficiencies. The analysis alone has probably produced many ideas, because a natural reaction is to ask "Why?" as we chart. "Why" is one of the most important questions in step 2.

But even if ideas were obtained during the process of charting, we have no way of knowing whether or not all possible ideas have been obtained, or even if the operation is necessary, or if the best possible idea is included. These are the purposes of step 3. Trying to get ideas is not easy, but there is a systematic approach.

Every field has some general principles. These principles are the laws or general rules by which the field operates. Mechanical engineering has its principles. Real estate practice has its rules. Chemistry has its laws. And so forth. Principles are collected as the result of application, experimentation, and theoretical research in the field. In effect, these principles represent the guides and objectives of the engineer when designing or improving the equipment or activity of his field.

However, the basic principles of any field are expressed in general terms. For example, a principle of work simplification is that, wherever feasible, hand activities should be performed with a simultaneous symmetrical hand pattern. To be useful, the analyst must see if this principle can be "applied" to the problem under study. The analyst, in effect, tries to determine the specific way the activity could be performed if the principle were used. That is, he tries to see if the operation can be performed with the simultaneous symmetrical hand pattern. This requires concentration and ingenuity on the part of the analyst. In a similar way, the analyst reviews each principle to determine if it is "applicable" to the situation.

Because of the breadth and depth of most of the principles in a field, it is obvious that all the principles are not applicable to each problem. The principles of a field tend to group themselves into their various areas of applicability. For example, there are principles governing hand pattern. There are principles governing flow of work. There are principles governing materials handling. There are principles governing design of equipment for effective use by the human being. Even a series of principles in a particular area of a field may not be applicable to each problem. The analyst usually reviews a complete series of principles in the particular area to make certain that all possible ideas that could affect his design have been developed.

Although the principles are stated in general terms, it is desirable to try to state them more specifically as a person becomes more familiar with the particular industry. In this way, the principles might take on different wordings and become somewhat more specific. For example, a principle might say, "The hands should not have idle or hold time." For a specific plant or industry, however, this might be converted into saying that it might be desirable to use portable vises, or some other such arrangement, to eliminate holding. A principle must be examined completely in the light of the purpose of the study and the facts that have been gathered about it. The analyst, through his ability, then tries to find a specific idea.

APPLICATION TO FUTURE WORK

It is never too late to reemphasize the fact that the best application of any principle of work simplification is to work which has not yet been performed. This is the easiest way, also. It is simply a matter of trying to figure out what improvement could be made over the way that a process or operation might have been performed had it gone into operation without work simplification. In this way, many human obstacles and cost factors will be avoided, thereby increasing the possible savings. However, these principles can be applied to both present and future work, and most of the illustrations in this book will be shown in relation to present work.

GENERAL PRINCIPLES

In Chapter 3, the five items affecting work (material, design, sequence, equipment, method) were discussed. We found it was important to get information about these five items as they affected the problem. In attempting to design the work to meet our objectives, it seems logical to start in a general way by questioning the conditions in each of these areas. In this way five general principles of work simplification can be stated. These general principles must be recognized as being inadequate for specific designs but rather as representing an initial approach to eliminate some of the more obvious methods errors. The five basic, general principles are:

1. Change the material being used or planned to help meet the objective for the operation being studied.

2. *Change the present or planned design of product to help meet the objective for the work being studied.*

3. *Change the present or planned sequence of modification on the product or material to help meet the objective for the work being studied.*

4. *Change the equipment being used or planned to help meet the objective for the work being studied.*

5. *Change the method or hand pattern used or planned for the operation to help meet the objective for the work being studied.*

What is "change"?

To understand these principles, it is important to define what is meant by "change." The most important concept involves the elimination of all work that can be removed. Elimination of unnecessary work (reduction of skills) is the prime objective of any approach for improvement of, or methods design for, a work situation. Trying to eliminate all possible activities should be uppermost in the minds of all work simplification men. Likewise, the word "change" includes emphasis on the arrangement of whatever work remains in the best order possible (better utilization of skills). In general, then, the word "change" can mean elimination, simplification, combination, rearrangement, or anything that can be done to help meet the objective for the work being studied. In place of the word "change" we should use the words "elimination," or "simplification." For example, instead of saying, "Can the material be changed?" we should say, "Can the material be eliminated?" "Can the material be simplified?"

Graphical picture of how five items affecting work are related

Figure 3-2 showed the way the five items affecting work are interrelated. The very same picture can be converted to show how the five basic principles are applied. This is shown in Fig. 12-1. In all cases, a change in one of the five

Fig. 12-1. Graphical presentation of procedure used for performing any type of work. The areas of the five basic principles are likewise illustrated. Material enters hopper where certain sequence of modification, equipment, and methods is used to produce the final product leaving the plant or organization.

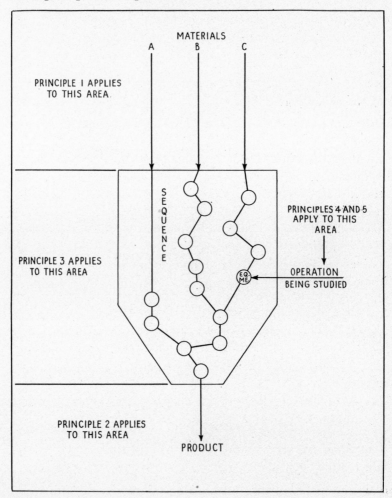

areas refers to the work originally studied. Notice that principle 1 applies to any material entering the organization—materials to be eliminated, specifications to be changed, packaging for receiving to be changed, etc.

Notice where principle 2 applies. This means that anything changed in the product leaving the organization, or service leaving the organization, can be considered a design change. This could be a change in the size, internal specifications, shape of the product, packaging, or the way the product looks.

Notice where sequence change principles apply. A sequence change could be any type of improvement or design where the sequence of modification is altered. This can be done by adding, eliminating, combining, or changing order of operations, or by making changes affecting operations other than the one under study to meet the objective.

Notice where principle 4, or equipment change, is applied. These changes refer to any designs or improvements where the equipment, machinery, tools, jigs, workplace, etc., are changed or altered. This could be done by eliminating, combining, simplifying, adding, rearranging, changing materials handling, changing layout, etc., to help meet the objective.

Notice that methods changes apply to the work under study. This refers to any change in the body motions or hand motions of the job. The change could involve elimination, combination, addition, simplification, or rearrangement of the therbligs, or motions, or motion paths, or body activities.

ILLUSTRATIONS OF DESIGN OR IMPROVEMENT IN EACH BASIC PRINCIPLE AREA

Additional understanding of what is meant by the five basic principles is provided by the following illustrations. They show what changes were actually made on operations and why they indicate that a change was made in a specific principle area.

Material change illustration: cleaning metal sheets

Original Method. The operation involved cleaning the front of a stainless steel chrome-plated sheet, Fig. 12-2. The

FIG. 12-2. Formed and punched stainless steel sheet metal with glue and paper still stuck to the sheet.

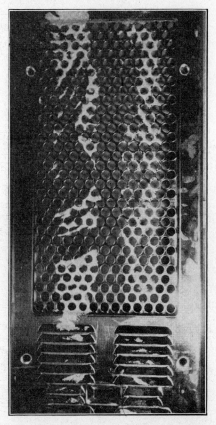

cleaning was done to remove protective glue which had been placed on the piece of metal by the manufacturer of the sheets. It took approximately three to five minutes to clean one of the sheets. The piece of metal was approximately 12 by 24 inches. This operation was difficult because the cleaner fluid had to be forced into the various grooves and punched holes on the sheet. Therefore, the specific goal for this operation was to reduce the amount of time necessary for cleaning the front of the sheet.

Improved Method. The protective glue had been placed on the sheet metal by the manufacturer because the manufacturer thought the glue with a piece of paper over the sheet was used as protection by the fabricator when forming and punching. However, the fabricator thought that the manufacturer put on the paper with protective glue to avoid scratches on the chrome-plated surface during shipment and, therefore, to avoid returns. The fabricator ripped off the paper before actually forming the metal. Therefore, the improved method involved eliminating the glued paper by the manufacturer and, instead, inserting only tissue paper between the sheets when shipping. This change involved not only the complete elimination of the operation of cleaning the protective glue from the sheet but also the saving of 2 cents per square foot of sheet metal by the elimination of the protective glue. This is a material change because the specifications of the material entering the plant were changed. In this case the design of the final product was not changed at all. However, the sequence of modification on the product was changed, the equipment of the original operation was changed by elimination, and the method was changed by the elimination of the entire hand and body pattern for the operation under study.

Design change illustration: assembling quick-match

Original Method. The operator had great difficulty in the assembly of a piece of quick-match (fast-burning, explosive fuse line), $1\frac{1}{4}$ inches in length and $\frac{1}{16}$ inch in diameter, in a hole in $\frac{1}{4}$-inch-diameter, 13-inch piece of time fuse (slow burning) to be used for an ordnance project. It took a lengthy period of time to make certain that the quick-match was placed into the hole, after which it was found that 25 per cent were rejected for poor assembly. The quick-match ends were frayed when they were put through the hole.

The specific goal was to reduce the complexity of the assembly and to reduce the percentage of rejects.

Improved Method. The ends of the quick-match were cut at an angle rather than cut square. The hole in the time fuse was enlarged slightly to provide for a better assembly. The improved method reduced the amount of time for this assembly by one-third and also virtually eliminated all rejects. Since this was a large-volume product, the savings were extensive. This was a design change because the final product leaving the plant was changed in specifications, even though the change was not visible to the consumer. The sequence was changed because the cutting operation jig had to be changed to help meet the goal for this job. The equipment and method for the operation of assembly were changed by partial elimination and simplification.

Sequence change illustration: gluing insulation in channel

Original Method. This operation involved the operator's pulling apart strips of felt with a sticky glued backside after they had been dumped into a large cardboard box. The pieces of felt, about 12 inches long by 1 inch wide, were cut to length on a punch press and thrown into a box. Originally the felt had a backing, which was removed when the pieces were cut to length. The operator would separate 12 or 15 strips and then place 2 strips in each channel, Fig. 12-3. The specific goal for this operation was to reduce the time necessary for separating the pieces of felt.

Improved Method. The improved method involved placing the roll of felt tape at the workplace where it was used. A cutter was provided to allow the operator, as she needed a piece of felt, to pull it through the cutter to the proper length. (The length was indicated by a mark on the table.) The backing would pull off at the same time that the piece of felt was pulled through the cutter. The cutter was foot-pedal operated. This is a sequence change because two operations were combined. Actually the operation with

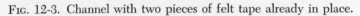

FIG. 12-3. Channel with two pieces of felt tape already in place.

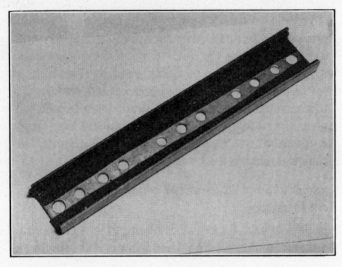

which the study started was eliminated. Notice that the equipment for the studied operation was changed and that the method used for the operation was eliminated completely. Since two pieces of felt were required for each assembly and there were approximately five thousand assemblies a year, this saving was appreciable in terms of dollars as well as in terms of morale of employees who felt that it was unnecessary to have to separate the pieces of felt in the box.

Equipment change illustration: spinning pin onto arm

Original Method. Before production started on a new product, the industrial engineers were reviewing the methods to be used in the assembly of some of the parts. The specific operation under consideration was spinning a pin onto an arm. The actual spinning part of the operation takes a certain amount of time because of the machine control. The industrial engineers felt that, if the spinning operation were used as originally planned, this operation would become a bottleneck. Therefore, the specific goal for this operation, even before production began, was to increase the productivity.

Improved Method. In place of spinning one pin onto an arm at a time, it was decided to rivet these pins onto the arm so that one machine could be used to rivet four parts. In this way the production was almost tripled, and the bottleneck was eliminated even before production began. This is an equipment change because the equipment contemplated for the operation was changed. The method planned for the operation was changed as well.

Equipment change illustration: moving dresses from finishers to draper

Original Method. Part of one operation in a garment plant involved getting dresses from the finishers and bringing them

Fig. 12-4. Original layout of area in which finishers and draper in garment plant perform their work. All materials handling is performed by the operators three or four units at a time.

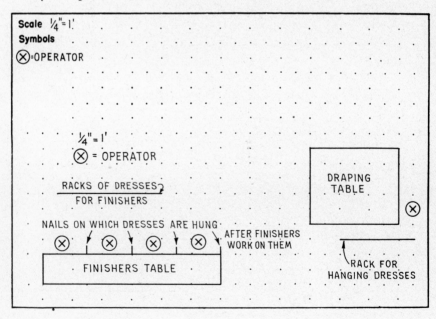

to the draper's table. The draper, who moved the dresses, was one of the more highly paid operators in the plant. An occurrence study showed that about 20 per cent of the draper's time was spent in moving dresses from the finishers' tables to her table. There were four finishers, and they were arranged and located as shown in Fig. 12-4. They had to get their dresses and take some dresses that were finished to the draper, as well. The specific goal for the operation of draper was to reduce the amount of time and effort spent by the draper in walking back and forth from her table to the finishers' tables. Since the draper was working overtime, this operation had become a bottleneck.

Improved Method. The new layout for this operation is shown in Fig. 12-5. In this case an overhead pipe rack was

Fig. 12-5. Improved layout of area for finishers and draper. One hundred or more dresses can be moved at one time by sliding them on overhead rails.

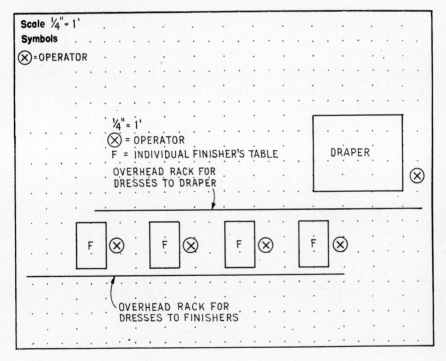

built along the side of each finisher's bench, leading to the draper's table. When dresses were needed by the draper, either one of the finishers or the draper could push all the dresses to the draper's table. The amount of time spent in moving dresses by the draper was reduced to about 2 per cent. All overtime was eliminated. The finishers had their time saved with a rack along their bench to bring them dresses. This is an equipment change because the equipment involved in the operation was changed. The method for moving (materials handling) the dresses was changed as well.

Methods change illustration: punching holes in 10-foot copper bars

Original Method. In punching holes in each end of a ¼-inch by 2-inch by 10-foot copper bar, the original procedure was performed at the layout shown in Fig. 12-6. Three men

Fig. 12-6. Original workplace diagram for punching holes in 10-foot copper bars with three-man crew.

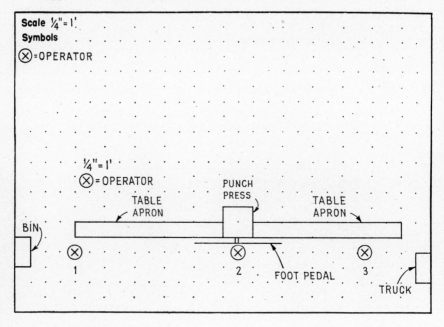

performed the operation. The first man picked up a copper bar from the bin and placed it on the apron. The end of the bar was shoved against a guide. When it was properly located, the second man depressed the pedal of the punch press. The pedal was actually a long rod that had been placed on top of the original single foot pedal. Then the bar was shoved to the third man, who placed the punched hole on a pilot, and the second man depressed the punch again, making the second hole on the other end. The third man lifted the bar off the apron to a truck while, at the same time, the first man was placing another bar on the apron on the other side. The specific goal in this operation was to reduce the cost of the operation.

Improved Method. The location of the two men needed is shown in Fig. 12-7. The first man positioned the copper bar against the guide and depressed the punch by pressing the end of the long rod with his foot. He then shoved the bar to the second man, who placed it on the pilot and depressed the punch on his side of the rod. As the second man was

Fig. 12-7. Improved workplace diagram for punching holes in 10-foot copper bars with two-man crew.

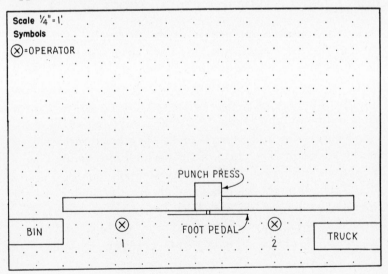

doing his work, the first man was getting another copper bar and lining it up ready for punching. When the first man was punching his end, the second man was placing the finished copper bar aside. The productivity per man hour of this group was only slightly less than in the original method. However, the cost per unit was reduced by the elimination of the third man on the operation. This is a methods change because the only change in the operation concerned the motions and motion or body pattern utilized by the men for performing the work of the operation.

"BEST" METHOD FOR CONDITIONS

Although the above methods designs represented changes which were actually made on industrial operations it is possible that some of these improved methods would not be the "best" in other situations or plants. The above methods designs and improvements represent the "best" solutions under the conditions and situations surrounding the operation as found in the actual plant.

CHECK LIST OF PRINCIPLES OF METHODS DESIGN

To facilitate the application of the principles of methods design, the five basic principles have been subdivided into many smaller items or principles. These principles have been placed in the form of questions which should be asked about the operation under study. The check list, or series of questions, is presented in Table 12-1. One complete section of the check list is devoted to each of the five basic principles of methods design. The check list is divided into general types of activity as represented by the symbols on the various charts which might have been made for the analysis of the operation. Group A on the check list refers to activity performed at one workplace or work area (terminal activities); Group B, to moves or movements between workplaces or work areas; Group C, to storages (mainly for product and form process chart), because it is important to reduce the number of these symbols, which should reduce the amount of in-process inventory; Group D, to holding activity wherever it may appear; Group E, to all types of delays; and Group F, to verification activities. Many of the principles are repeated in various categories on the check list. It is probably better to duplicate asking a question than not ask the question at all.

The basic principles for material, design, and sequence are listed first, because it is in these areas that most analysts fail to make thorough investigations. Usually, more effective changes can be found in these areas than in the method and equipment areas. When a change is made in a material area, it is usual for changes to be made in the other areas to complete the proposed method.

PRINCIPLES OF MOTION ECONOMY

Two of the basic principles, for equipment and for methods, deal with the specific workplace. A famous set of prin-

Table 12-2. Principles of Motion Economy

1. Simultaneous symmetrical hand pattern.
2. No idle or hold time.
3. Fewest number of therbligs.
4. Give work to jigs, vises, fixtures, instead of hands.
5. Preposition tools and parts.
6. Smooth continuous motions.
7. Lowest classification of body members.
8. Use momentum and ballistic motions.
9. Few number of eye fixations.
10. Use normal work areas.
11. Proper workplace height for standing or sitting.
12. Fewest number of muscle groupings.
13. Use gravity.
14. Keep points of joint work close together.
15. Reduce skills.

ciples, principles of motion economy, deals with the same areas. Many of these principles are included in the check list shown in Table 12-1. The Gilbreths developed the principles of motion economy, and although they have been changed, added to, and modified, they still represent a good listing for review. The principles of motion economy are listed in Table 12-2. These principles cannot be considered complete. There are probably many other principles which may be found by additional application and research. The order of presentation of the motion economy principles does not necessarily indicate the order (if any) of importance.

NORMAL WORK AREAS

Normal working areas and spheres are presented in Fig. 12-8. The inner curve or sphere supposedly represents the space in which the lower arm can reach easily when the upper arm is kept stationary by the body and the lower-arm movements pivot around the stationary elbow. The outer curve or sphere represents the space in which the extended arm can reach easily when the movements pivot around the stationary shoulder. (The dimensions presented are approximations from measurements of 10 industrial operators selected at random.) The statements are not exactly true all the time. For example, with the upper arm held stationary at the side of the body, it is almost impossible for the lower arm to pivot itself about the elbow beyond 30 degrees (indicated by lines on the workplace—see Fig. 12-8) on either side away from the perpendicular at each arm, to the front of the operator. The only way the operator could move farther than 30 degrees would be for the elbow to move backward and/or sideward to allow the hand and lower arm to move to the side required. It is desirable to have the height of the workplace arranged to allow the operator to sit or stand with the workplace 2 or 3 inches below the level of the elbow when the upper arm is stationary alongside the body.

FIG. 12-8. Normal working areas and spheres.

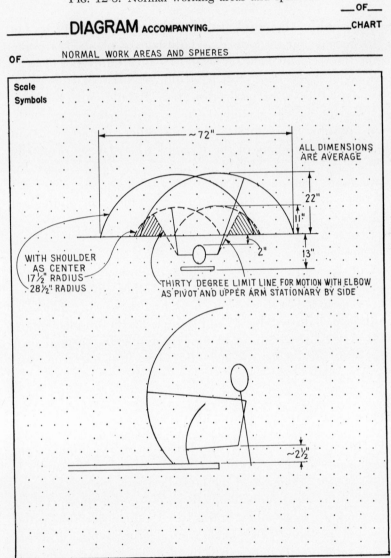

ADDING TO THE PRINCIPLES

Obviously, the check list given here is not complete, nor is it too specific for individual industries or plants. For example, the garment industry would have certain types of principles or basic ideas which would be different from some principles in sheet-metal fabrication. By adding to the principles, the industrial engineer helps provide for better methods design and improvements on other operations. As a matter of fact many of the principles listed were originally conceived and developed in this way. Another source for obtaining principles and ideas to be added to the check list is the literature in the industry in which the individual analyst works.

There are other check lists which can be used for trying to find better ways. For example, there are check lists for plant layout, materials handling, maintenance, inventory control. Some of the items on these other check lists have been included in the master check lists shown in Table 12-1. But each industry should add those from the supplementary check lists which are more directly applicable to their own type of work. This will make the check list more complete and usable.

PROBLEMS OF APPLYING PRINCIPLES

The application of the check lists in work simplification represents a difficult problem. One purpose of the application of the principles of methods design is to find as many ideas concerning probable methods design for the operation under study as possible. In this way the final selection of the feasible method will be made from a large number of ideas. This solution, therefore, will more likely represent the one which is best for the conditions of the situation.

Another problem is that many analysts fail to record all the ideas obtained by the application. Many ideas are thought of in the course of working on an operation, but many are also lost because the analyst fails to record the ideas systematically. Therefore, the application of the principles of methods design should result in a suggestion list.

SUGGESTION LIST

A suggestion list is the written presentation of all the ideas obtained for meeting the goal for the operation under study. The suggestion list is usually made on the chart form used throughout the book, or on a blank piece of paper.

USING OTHER PEOPLE TO APPLY PRINCIPLES

An analyst soon learns that he must rely on other people's experiences and information to do an effective job of applying what he knows about work simplification. Therefore the analyst should get other people, concerned with the operation under study, to offer ideas by reviewing with them the various principles of methods design. Some of the people might include the foreman of the operation, the superintendent of the foreman, the worker on the operation, the toolmaker, or other foremen.[1] Volume, total labor cost, equipment costs, etc., will affect the number of people contacted. Generally, the greater the possible savings, the greater the number of people consulted.

PROCEDURES FOR APPLYING THE CHECK LISTS

Generally, the application of the principles may be made in three ways:

[1] Many people feel this close cooperation with plant personnel is not needed if the company has a suggestion system in effect. They feel this will provide the means for obtaining the ideas of the plant people. In effect, it is felt that this is an almost automatic way of "supervising" the elimination of production and cost bottlenecks, which can reduce the amount of time management has to spend on such problems. Although suggestion systems are worthwhile and provide many good ideas if they *really* give *high* cash

1. Over-all application

In this part the analyst applies only the five basic principles with their subdivisions of elimination, combination, simplification, and rearrangement to the operation under study. This first approach should be used for all problems, regardless of whether or not much time can be allotted to the problem. The application of the principles in this part would be made to the over-all chart or charts constructed and on the basis of summaries of activity performed. For example, looking at a specific product process chart, the analyst might ask generally, "What part of the sequence could be eliminated to help meet the goal for this operation?" The analyst would then review and question the sequence of modification on the chart and other information gathered in the analysis of the work to see if some ideas related to the question asked and the goal for the operation occur to him. Even though an idea is not the result of the question asked, it should be recorded anyway.

It is good practice to record ideas that may sound ridiculous and silly or too costly. This is a sound procedure, since it frequently leads to better suggestions and ideas for this and other operations at a later date. Although reasons can be presented against a given idea, it is wise to record it anyway. For example, a punch press used for special work in several departments is centrally located. For an operation in one of the departments, the analyst should record the suggestion of moving the punch press to the operation under study, even though he knows other departments use it. He may find later that the operation under study uses the press the majority of the time, thereby effecting an over-all savings by the installation of this idea.

After asking the first question concerning material elimination, the analyst would proceed to material combination,

payments, management analysts and industrial engineers should always seek better methods on their own and better relations and cooperation with the plant personnel.

then through the remaining general questions. As each question is asked, the information gathered in the analysis of work should be reviewed to determine if there is some possibility of utilizing the concept of the question for the solution of the problem. Each question will not necessarily yield an idea for solving the problem, because all principles are not applicable to every operation. Yet this does not mean that an analyst should move too fast in trying to find ideas from a specific principle. He should, instead, review each principle as thoroughly as possible to obtain ideas.

The above procedure then would be followed for all five basic principles with each of the four categories in each principle.

2. Over-all application plus application of motion economy principles

Frequently, an analyst will have only enough time to make a cursory or over-all application of principles in all areas with just enough time to make a more detailed application of principles in the equipment and methods areas. In such a case, the analyst would review the principles of motion economy in relation to the operation after following procedure 1 above. In effect the analyst would use the motion economy principles as questions concerning the equipment and methods, as was done above. In most cases this adds additional ideas to the suggestion list.

3. Complete application of principles

This is the most detailed application of principles. The concept of asking questions is the same as the over-all application. Instead of general and motion economy principles, each check item listed for each type of activity in each general principle area would be reviewed for the operation. The activity taking the most time or present most frequently would be questioned by looking under the specific category of activity for each basic principle and reviewing each of the check items in that category for ideas to meet the goal for the operation. If suboperations occur most frequently on an operation chart (as indicated by the summary), then the items under the suboperation (or large circle) category of *each* principle would be reviewed carefully to obtain ideas.

If two or more analysts of the same caliber work separately on the same operation, there will probably be differences in detail for some of the suggestions, but basically their suggestion lists will be about the same. Obviously, because of the engineering nature of the principles, the engineer with the most ingenuity and intelligence will develop a suggestion list more complete and far reaching than the "average" engineer.

GENERAL OBJECTIVES OF APPLICATION OF PRINCIPLES

At all times when applying principles of methods design, the analyst should try to meet the basic objective of work simplification: *Eliminate unnecessary work.* Every attempt should be made to explore the necessity of having every therblig, group of therbligs, operation, storage, movement, etc. At the same time (because it is frequently impossible to eliminate an operation, or there may be no time to do so), the analyst will find it useful to find all ideas related to *simplifying the operation,* or arranging the work in the best order possible. Actually these concepts should be used by everyone in simplifying any work they perform or supervise.

USING THE PRINCIPLES FOR NONREPETITIVE WORK

The check list was originally designed for application to repetitive or slightly varied work. However, much nonrepetitive work occurs, and some of the analysis techniques were designed for nonrepetitive work. The check list can be used for nonrepetitive work as well. The principles of methods design can be applied to these techniques by selecting the items or areas which provide the greatest trouble or which take the most time, and applying the principles to these items or areas. In some cases it may be possible and/or necessary to make one of the repetitive work analysis charts for the item which takes the most time. If so, this should be done and then the principles applied as discussed above. However, many of the items in a nonrepetitive work analysis cannot be further analyzed by one of the charting techniques. If so, the only feasible approach would be, first, to use the over-all application and, secondly, to scan roughly the individual check items for possible suggestions. The information gathered by nonrepetitive analysis techniques usually can be divided into categories of activity somewhat similar to some categories of activity on the check list.

The illustrations referred to below should indicate how the suggestion list is made. It is difficult to show the exact thought process for arriving at the various suggestions. However, the suggestion lists here were developed in the plant or situation where the operation took place.

HOW MANY SUGGESTIONS?

A frequent question about suggestion lists concerns how an analyst is to know when enough suggestions have been obtained. A corollary question asks how an analyst is to know whether or not the "best" suggestion is included. There are no answers to these questions, because if there were, there would be no need for the remaining steps of the work simplification procedure; the correct answer would be known without going through the next step. However, there are practical limits which tend to restrict the number of suggestions obtained. The analyst himself is one of the most important limiting factors. A particularly ingenious analyst can develop more ideas than an average one. Of course, the amount of time which can be spent on a problem would produce limitations on the number of suggestions.

The general experience and familiarity of the analyst with the plant or industry is a factor. Perhaps the most important aspect of these questions is the implication that as many suggestions as possible should be found. This can be done best by following the detailed instructions on how to apply the principles.

ILLUSTRATIONS

Two suggestion lists are shown below for some of the operations and work presented previously. The reader should try to reconstruct the application of the principles to see how some of these suggestions may have been arrived at.

1. Policy writing

For the form process chart problem presented in Chapter 5, Figs. 5-2 and 5-3, the suggestion list is shown in Fig. 12-9.

2. Insert glue in case

For the operation chart problem presented in Chapter 7, Figs. 7-6 and 7-7, the suggestion list is shown in Fig. 12-10.

FIG. 12-9. Suggestion list for policy writing (FPC: Figs. 5-2 and 5-3).

SUGGESTION LIST ___OF___ CHART

OF POLICY WRITING

Date 5-'53 Part _____ Operator _____ Mach_____
By F.M.D.   No. SPECIFIC GOAL- REDUCE TIME FOR TYPING POLICY

SUG. NO.	PRINCIPLE NO.	SUGGESTION
1	3	Eliminate Backtracing - Rearrange Dep
2	1	Use Photostat Process - Elim. Typing
3	5	Retrain Typist with New Method & Layout
4	2	Redesign all Forms to Make Transfer
5		of Info Easier
5	1	Overlay Carbon Form for Easier Typing
6	3	Eliminate Checking
7	3	Eliminate Double Handling by Unit
9		Supervisor
10		
12		

Fig. 12-10. Suggestion list for inserting glue in case (Op Ch: Figs. 7-6 and 7-7).

		SUGGESTION LIST	_OF_ CHART

OF INSERT GLUE IN CASE

Date JAN '53 Part _____ Operator _____ Mach _____

By W.J.W. No. SPECIFIC GOAL - INCREASE PRODUCTIVITY _____

SUG. NO.	PRINCIPLE NO.	SUGGESTION
1	4	Attach Foot Pedal to Handle
2	5	P U Two at a Time
3	4	Make Multi-Nozzle
4	5	Place Cases in Each Hand for Filling
5	5	Simultaneous-Symmetrical Hand Pattern
		When Foot Pedal Used
6	1	Use Tight Fit Seal Instead of Glue
7	4	Move the End of the Chute Next to Nozzle
8	4	Make Racks in Which Case Can be Placed
9	3	Have Preceding Operation Place Cases in
		Rack to Make Glue Placing Easier

BASIC CONCEPTS ABOUT WAYS OF DOING WORK

Whenever principles are being applied to work, it is important to have in mind a basic concept of how the work should be performed. This can be stated simply: The material or products coming in the organization should be handled and processed without ever putting it down, storing it, or rehandling it.

Of course, it will not be possible to do this with all products or services. There are great differences in product types, volume, cycle times, and other factors. But this should be the basic objective with which work should be approached. There are many ways that these things can be accomplished if an analyst puts his mind to it. There are chutes, levers, arms, hoppers, and so forth which can be used. When an analyst starts with this approach, then it is possible to modify it slightly to suit the situation. At least, with this concept of never handling or storing the product, it is more likely that better ways of doing the work will be developed. Backing down from the ideal rather than building up from the worst type of production can result in better procedures. As you can recognize, this is the approach to automation.

Applying the principles of methods design is one of the most important steps in the procedure for solving work simplification problems. The analyst tries to get as many ideas as possible. This is different from the procedure which says that intuition is the best way of getting answers. With intuition there is usually only one possibility, which the person assumes is the "best" answer. However, this step requires thought and ingenuity. To arrive at specific ideas for the problem, the analyst must be systematic in his approach with the use of principles.

The knowledge of other people should be used in applying principles. This helps ideas, and is in accordance with the general principles of human relations. It is important to get the ideas and suggestions of other persons concerned with the activity. By applying principles and talking with other people, almost anyone can get many ideas for designing or improving the work problem.

Throughout the check list for each basic principle some of the more common basic questions are scattered. These are all related to the basic question "Why?" "Why do it at all?" "Why have the person doing it do it?" "Why is it done where it is?" "Why is it done when it is?" "Why is it done the way it is?" These "why" questions relate to the basic questioning attitude. These comments are not placed in any particular order in the check list but merely as reminders of the questioning attitude. Remember: Ask the question "Why?" in relation to "What is done?" "Who does it?" "Where is it done?" "When is it done?" "How is it done?" This is essential.

CHAPTER 13

SELECTING THE "BEST" METHOD

The third step has now provided a sufficient number of ideas from which to select the solution for the work. Now, step 4 determines the idea or ideas which will be the most feasible for the work and the conditions under which it is performed. Because many ideas are collected on the list, it is frequently possible to install many of them at one time. By installing many ideas at the same time, the analyst avoids many problems caused by human relations factors; those associated with the work are disturbed frequently with individual changes.

When selecting the most feasible solution, several factors must be considered. The importance of the various factors depends on the situation. For many situations, the economic considerations (greatest savings) are most important. For many home and office situations, physiological factors, or reduction of effort, are most important. There is no way of knowing which factor will be most important for any given situation; the analyst must place most emphasis on the factor determined in the first step, "State the problem."

WHAT FACTORS AFFECT "BEST" METHOD?

Each suggestion on the suggestion list should be evaluated to select the best one or combination for the work. The definition for the word "best" would have to be made in terms of the factors which affect the solution. These factors are the ones which must be evaluated in selecting a feasible solution. These factors also help find new and different ideas or combinations of ideas which are sometimes better than some on the suggestion list.

For example, when determining the cost of installation of a particular suggestion, a single item may be causing most of the cost. This single item might then be analyzed to arrive at an idea which will make the suggestion more feasible.

Four factors must be evaluated to select the most feasible solution. Again, there is no one factor which is most important. The factors vary in importance in relation to the work being studied. However, many situations place the most importance on the first factor.

1. Economic
2. Hazard
3. Control
4. Psychological

1. Economic factor

The evaluation of the economic factor can be divided into two parts. Each suggestion must be evaluated to determine, first, "How much does it cost?" and, second, "How much does it save?" The objective is to find the suggestion (or group of suggestions) which costs the least and saves the most.

a. How Much Does It Cost? There are many items contributing to the cost of a suggestion. A general listing of the types of items is shown in the upper half of Fig. 13-2.

The form shown in Fig. 13-2 is called the evaluation worksheet. This makes the evaluation of ideas more systematic. Notice that the economic factor takes up most of the space. There is space to evaluate each suggestion; it is usually not possible to know what suggestion will be desirable until a complete evaluation is made.

The evaluation worksheet is a general guide for tabulating cost figures. Each of the cost items, in most cases, includes more than one cost. However, the items listed in

Fig. 13-2 give broad classifications for an analyst to evaluate all factors in the cost picture of a suggestion. Some changes in the worksheet might be made in the way overhead charges are evaluated. Some companies may want to subtract a certain percentage of the cost instead of total cost from yearly savings.

A company should place the general information of Fig. 13-2 in whatever specific format is desired, by changing, adding, or eliminating. Using an evaluation worksheet is usually good practice.

b. How Much Does It Save? The savings of a suggestion must balance the cost. However, some situations may require the savings to be calculated in terms other than dollars and cents. For example, the objective may require that an operation be less tiring, or involve less skill. The savings would be physiological or psychological in nature and would be difficult to evaluate as part of the economic factor. However, this type of suggestion should, in most cases, cost no more than the possible monetary savings.

One of the most important items in the determination of savings is the amount of time the original and proposed operations take. In most cases the original operation time is known. The big problem, therefore, is to determine the amount of time the operation would take if the particular suggestion were installed. This would permit savings to be calculated. To obtain time values for the operation with the suggestion included requires estimates on the part of the analyst. Frequently, some of the ideas must be detailed to get information about what its cost or time will be. Of necessity, this information is relatively rough at this point.

There is little likelihood that each suggestion would actually be evaluated. Rather there seems to be a process of, first, eliminating those suggestions which are apparently ineffective, and, second, combining several of the ideas which seem to go together. This is better than trying to evaluate them separately. For example, one idea might be to use a drop chute for removal of the part. Another idea might be to have a simultaneous symmetrical hand pattern. In most cases it would be wise to combine these two ideas and evaluate them together. This process of combining ideas for eventual evaluation is one that requires the analyst's judgment. It is done quite frequently, though, to reduce the number of actual evaluations that will be made.

Some of the ways of obtaining time estimates are as follows:

1. If some type of time chart has been made for the original method, a synthetic time chart permits a somewhat close comparison of methods. The proposed time chart would be made by using the time values of identical activity as they appear on the original chart, by using other time charts of similar activity, by going through the hand motions, or by estimating time for certain activities by using its relationship to present data. Even a synthetic geometric symbol chart can help obtain rough estimates of time, by comparison of the synthetic chart with known time and activity on the original chart.

2. The time can be estimated by using elemental standard data values from time studies, if the organization has such information. Therbligs form an excellent basis for determining any time estimates for proposed work. The estimates of time in Table 8-1 would be used with a synthetic therblig chart. The approximate time values of Table 8-1 should not be used in any way related to setting accurate standards or work loads on operations. It is not necessary to have made an original therblig chart for the job. A synthetic therblig chart can be made in this step to evaluate an idea for ease in using the therbligs times. (Other systems of predetermined motion times can be used, like Motion-Time-Analysis, Methods-Time-Measurement, Work-Factor, Basic Motion-Timestudy, or Dimensional-Motion-Times.) The admonition about the inaccuracies of these time values is true for all systems of predetermined times. If the circumstances indicate that a time value is too small or large for a specific therblig, the analyst should change it accord-

ingly. This can be done readily, because this step requires only estimates. Probably the main advantage of using therblig times is that it forces the analyst to detail the complete method, motion by motion.

3. Another way of obtaining time for the method including the proposed suggestion would be to make a mockup. Then some individual can go through the proposed hand pattern, and, with a wrist watch or stop watch, another person can obtain a time estimate. Another variation is to have the analyst go through the hand pattern without the mockup. Some other person, and even in some cases the person going through the motions, can time that procedure.

4. The flow diagram is helpful for evaluating various suggestions. For example, in evaluating the work of a housewife, a flow diagram would be one of the most useful techniques. Here it would be possible to compare walking in the original method with the flow diagram for the proposed method. Taking fewer steps would show up easily to help in evaluation. Materials handling activities frequently can be analyzed and evaluated effectively with flow diagrams. However, flow diagrams should be used as a supplement, rather than as the sole technique for analyzing any suggestion.

5. And, of course, the last procedure which can be used is the out-and-out guess. The experience of the analyst plays an important role in determining the guess. If the analyst does not have too much experience, it would be advisable to obtain the estimate in conjunction with other people who are more familiar with the type of activity. Obviously, this procedure has been put last because the analyst should in most cases attempt to use other procedures for determining estimated time. (There are some situations where the other techniques will help only slightly. Forms systems, some plant layout and materials handling suggestions, and production control suggestions are some examples.)

With the time information for original and synthetic methods, it is possible to estimate the monetary values needed for determining the savings. This information is put on the evaluation worksheet in the space indicated.

The procedures of your own organization should be used for calculating machine rates, overhead, and burden charges. There are many different ways of utilizing these values in calculating savings.

In general, much information should be sought and obtained from other sources within the company when evaluating the economic factor. For example, it is possible for engineering, tooling, maintenance, accounting, purchasing, and development to be brought into the picture on any given suggestion for work study. This should result in greater accuracy and more information about the various suggestions. In addition, better relationships between work simplification functions and other branches of the organization should ensue.

2. Hazard factor

There are many methods and suggestions which would help design an operation better but which, however, would involve definite hazards to the worker. The purpose of the safety or hazard factor in evaluation of suggestions is to force the analyst to look into the various components of the suggestion to make certain that the individual worker does not have any more hazards introduced into his operation than the normal level in the plant. The work simplification man should always try to *eliminate* hazardous features of the operations on which he works.

The goal of the analyst in reviewing a suggestion in the hazard factor is to make certain that the operation does as much as possible to safeguard the worker, or create conditions which would be better than the present level of hazard in the plant. The hazard factor may easily eliminate a suggestion, although it follows the best principles of design and might save the most money, if some safeguards are not provided.

The hazard factor is needed in evaluation of methods to

protect the people in the organization. When visualizing
new methods the analyst should try to eliminate the hazards
that might exist or creep into the new method. Space is provided on the evaluation worksheet for some comments on
hazard, in relation to each suggestion.

3. Control factor

Certain controls of quality and quantity usually are placed
on a process or procedure. The control factor in the selection
of feasible solution attempts to determine whether the suggestion will violate or change (even increasing the amount
of control) some of the basic considerations of control as set
up by management. There is nothing that states the controls
instituted are proper or actually do what they should. The
control factor concerns *any* specifications of material, design, and equipment; the information needed for this factor
must answer the questions: How does the suggested change
affect these specifications? Does it make for better product
quality or quantity control?

Many operations have controls inherently built in. Therefore, the suggestions for those operations must be concerned
with whether or not the controls as desired or required are
being met or being violated. An increase in quality on an
operation may not be desirable because of cost. In other
cases, a quality betterment may even be the goal for the
operation.

In many cases the control factor question cannot be answered by the analyst alone. In certain operations the analyst should discuss with other people in the organization
the factors of control and what is desired in all ramifications.
Since every operation has a specific function, there are certain quality and quantity characteristics of product or work
which are expected from the operation. *The suggestion's
effect on these control characteristics is what must be determined in the control factor.*

Some suggestions do not present any problem as far as
the control factor is concerned. For example, a suggestion to

move parts or bins closer to the work area does not, in almost all cases, involve a problem of control.

4. Psychological factor

This factor is sometimes the most underrated of all the factors involved in the selection of a feasible solution. It is sometimes the most difficult to understand. All operations and methods, of course, deal with human beings. This includes not only the operator but other people in the organization from whom authority and information must be obtained. There are different personality characteristics with which the analyst must cope. This can in many cases affect the actual solution regardless of whether or not it is the "best" method as determined by the other factors, especially if "peculiar" characteristics are present on the management side.

There are two components to the psychological factor:

1. What personalities will affect the adoption of any specific suggestions? Will one individual be opposed to a specific type of suggestion, or will another type of individual overwhelmingly support certain ideas? It is important to evaluate the level of acceptance and cooperation of the people with whom the analyst is dealing. For example, the analyst may know that certain types of suggestions are not acceptable to the person who must approve it. In this way, some doubt about the suggestion could affect its selection.

2. What approach should be used to "sell" (to the people involved) the desirability of using the particular suggestion?

The psychological aspects of the worker must be taken into consideration. In some cases people do not object to the entire motion study activity but to methods changes which affect them only. Therefore, it might be advisable to install a method which changes the equipment but does not save as much as a change in the method might have saved. (Of course, it would be advisable to take care of the human relations problem in a better manner, but in some cases a change must be made immediately.) The training situation might cause one method to be used instead of another requiring special training. For example, the absence of a training department might easily persuade the analyst to select a method with which the foreman could help train the operator.

Frequently, when operator participation is utilized, a method may be suggested by the operator which is not quite as good as one found by the analyst or engineer. (This could probably be avoided by the proper approach, as outlined in Chapter 2, but even then this situation does occur.) In such situations it is probably better to use the employee's method and perhaps, later, it may be possible to change. In some cases the employee's method, though technically not the "best," may be better in total production because a well-motivated employee using his own fairly good method can frequently outproduce a poorly motivated employee using the "best" method. Likewise, it would be advisable to use a supervisor's idea even though it is not as good as the engineer's idea. A highly motivated supervisor, supervising his own fairly good method, can frequently arrive at higher production through better supervision on the operation than could a poorly motivated supervisor using the "best" method. Certainly, the above statements should not cause an analyst to neglect trying to use the proper approach to the operator (Chapter 2).

Psychologically speaking, the other departments in an organization must be taken into consideration when evaluating some suggestions. For example, one suggestion involved the changing of specifications on a particular material. Depending upon the personalities involved in the engineering department, the suggestion may be received in disgust or in a spirit of cooperation. In the same way, the sales department or purchasing department may have a voice in the selection of a feasible solution. When an analyst knows of some of these psychological problems, he will and should take them into consideration in evaluating suggestions.

USING THE EVALUATION WORKSHEET

To select a feasible solution, the analyst should review each suggestion in terms of each factor and place on the evaluation worksheet some information concerning that suggestion for each factor, so that a final selection can be made. When a suggestion is evaluated, the cost and savings for the suggestion should include *all* possible savings which will be realized from other operations, products, sequences, etc., as well as from the operation or sequence under study. Frequently an idea will not be worthwhile (economical) for one operation only, but will be exceptionally profitable if installed for several operations. This permits the analyst to review each suggestion, first, to determine if certain ideas can be eliminated as being nonfeasible and, secondly, to help determine which one or combination of the ideas is better for the conditions. Even though the evaluation worksheet gives specific information, some judgment will have to be used in selecting the feasible solution. Consideration of the effect of the suggested change on personnel problems is important: What will the operator do with the extra time? Is there more work coming that he might do? What will be done with workers removed from operations? Company policies and executive judgment usually play an important role in decisions involving these problems.

Even though all the work of an operator or employee (secretary, etc.) will not be eliminated by a suggestion and therefore the employee must remain, the suggestion should be evaluated in terms of dollars or time saved. This is usually done because other functions may be assigned to the employee, or he will be available for other functions, which in the long run will reduce the number of employees required and prevent hiring unnecessary personnel. Ordinarily it is important to do this even for operations where the operator already has idle time; the same reasons are applicable here.

Selection and judgment

After all factors have been evaluated and considered, the analyst should select one or more of the suggestions as being feasible. Because of the nonquantitative factors, the analyst should utilize the advice and suggestions of other people. How all the factors are to be weighted is a matter of judgment in relation to the operation and its basic objectives. The key is that the final ideas selected must be correct for the conditions. Even with all the information obtained the element of judgment is never eliminated. However, judgment becomes better when influenced by the collected facts.

Basis of reports to management

The evaluation worksheet is valuable in selling the finally selected solution. The evaluation worksheet permits a person from whom authority must be obtained not only to check on various suggestions but also to compare the original method with the proposed solution. The evaluation worksheet with the project chart and analysis charts can easily form the basis for the reports to management on individual problems. It may also help to prove the desirability and the necessity of the work simplification function. The worksheet also allows an analyst to start checking the various dollars-and-cents figures obtained for calculating cost savings. For example, an overhead cost from accounting might seem out of line. A salvage figure from the maintenance department might seem out of line. The analyst might start an investigation of work in the various sections reporting certain cost figures in an attempt to improve or simplify their procedures.

EVALUATION WORKSHEET ILLUSTRATIONS

The evaluation and selection information in this chapter does not necessarily represent the best procedure for an operation in an organization other than the one in which the operation actually took place. If an operation similar to any presented here is performed in another plant, that plant should evaluate the suggestions for its own situation. Obviously, the psychological factor can easily affect the method which is considered "best" when the same operation is performed in different plants.

The length of time taken to evaluate a suggestion list varies from one extreme to another. For example, Fig. 13-1 illustrates a simple multi-man operation performed in a plant. This operation was improved by making a suggestion list and subsequently evaluating it. The evaluation, however, took only a few minutes. As a matter of fact, the analyst had recorded about three suggestions when he had the idea which was finally used. The other extreme of many days or weeks for a usable suggestion to emerge does not occur too frequently either.

Figure 13-1 includes the notes made at the time of analysis, which indicate that although a better method of performing the operation could be determined easily, the improved method shown was the most *feasible* for the conditions. Similarly, the reader may find that an idea other than the one selected in the following illustrations seems more feasible. The illustration, however, gives the solution determined in a practical situation.

Evaluation worksheets for the two operations described before in Chapter 12 are now presented below. As much detail as is feasible to include for textbook purposes is given with the evaluation of each suggestion. Not all the synthetic charts needed for the evaluation of some suggestions are presented. The one synthetic chart shown, however, should help illustrate how they are made and the purpose they serve. In almost all cases, the synthetic chart made to assist in the evaluation is rough, not made with the care and detail recommended when the charts were first presented or needed when the final proposal is charted.

FIG. 13-1. Original and improved multi-man process chart for shear screen. The notes help to indicate that the evaluation of suggestions for this operation took a short amount of time, while for other operations it may take a long time.

ORIGINAL _____ MULTI-MAN PROCESS ____ **CHART** —OF—

OF SHEAR SCREEN

Date 4/2/53 Part SCREEN   Operator _____ Mach HAND SHEAR

By 1 B   No. _____

MAN 1	MAN 2
○ PU Part	▽ At Shear
↓ To Shear	
○ Feed Part Through	○ Pump Shear Handle
↓ To Finished Area	▽ At Shear
○ Place Screen	
○ To New Part	

	MAN 1	MAN 2	
○	3	1	
○	1	0	Per 1 Part
●	2	0	
▽	0	5	

Notes:- This operation is a fill-in for the men involved. The hand shear is used for many other operations. No jig or fixture could be attached because of this. It would even be difficult to attach a foot pedal which would help many of the operations. Using one man instead of two would waste more time because of walking. Since these two men become idle on their work at the same time, it is desirable to keep them both busy. Therefore the following method was selected as feasible and installed.

Improved Multi-Man Chart

MAN 1	MAN 2
○ PU Part	↓ To Finished Area
↓ To Shear	○ Place Screen
○ Feed Part Through	↓ To New Part
○ Pump Shear Handle	○ PU Part
↓ To Finished Area	↓ To Shear
○ Place Screen	○ Feed Part Through
○ To New Part	○ Pump Shear Handle

	MAN 1	MAN 2	
○	4	4	
○	1	1	Per 2 Parts
●	2	2	

1. Policy writing (Suggestion List, Fig. 12-9)

The evaluation worksheet is shown in Fig. 13-2. This worksheet shows a few suggestions that would save money, and yet they are not used because other ideas are better. This will occur in many situations when evaluating ideas.

FIG. 13-2. Evaluation worksheet for policy writing (suggestion list: Fig. 12-9).

SELECTION OF FEASIBLE SOLUTION
Evaluation Worksheet

Operation: *POLICY WRITING*   Analyst: *F. M. D.*
Spec. Goal: *REDUCE TYPING TIME*   Date: *5-53*
Dept: *ORDER DEPT.*

	Suggestion No. *1*	Suggestion No. *2*	Suggestion No. *3*	Suggestion No. *4*
How much cost 1 New machines		$ 700 ⁰⁰		
2 New tools a Matl b Labor				
3 New designs		*FORM CHANGES* $ 75 ⁰⁰		$ 75 ⁰⁰
4 Installation				
5 Overhead				
6 Scrap of ma- chinery, tools & materials		$100 ⁰⁰ (OLD FORMS)		(WAIT UNTIL ALL PRESENT FORMS USED)
7 Misc (loss of production, wages, etc.)				
8 New cost 9 Less salvage				
10 Total cost	0.00	$ 875 ⁰⁰	0.00	$ 75.00
How much savings 11 Present method a Labor	60 FT. X 40 = 2400 MIN/TRIP 1.50/HR. X 10/DAY 200/YR. =	$ 3000 ⁰⁰	30/DAY	$.40/POLICY
b Material				
c Machine rate				
d Overhead & misc. 12 Total	$ 12 ⁰⁰ (8 HRS/YR)	$ 3000 ⁰⁰		$.40/POLICY
13 Proposed method a Labor	30 FT. X 40 = 1200 MIN/TRIP X 1.50 X 10 X 200 = $ 6 ⁰⁰	(PRESENT ORDER CLERK CAN TAKE PHOTOSTAT DUTIES) $400⁰⁰ ADD FOR MATERIAL	EST. 32/DAY (SINCE TYPIST MUST REMAIN. ONLY CHANGE WOULD BE VOLUME HANDLED)	EST. $375/POLICY
b Material				
c Machine rate				
d Overhead & misc 14 Total	(4 HRS /YR)	$ 400 ⁰⁰		
15 Expected volume 10 TRIPS per yr DAY		30/DAY		6000/YR.
16 Savings per yr 10 Less cost	$6 ⁰⁰ (4 HRS/YR)	$ 2600 ⁰⁰ $ 875 ⁰⁰	2/DAY OR· 400/YR.	$ 150 ⁰⁰ 75 ⁰⁰
17 Savings 1st yr	$6 ⁰⁰ (4 HR/YR)	$ 1725 ⁰⁰	2/DAY OR 400/YR	$ 75 ⁰⁰
18 Hazard factor	———	PROPERLY VENT- ILATE AREA	——	——
19 Control factor	NO CHANGE	AGENTS MUST ASSUME GREATER CONTROL IN FIL- LING OUT FORM	——	BETTER CONTROL
20 Psychological factor	PEOPLE HAVE IN- DICATED DISLIKE OF COMBINING ORDER CLERK & CHECKER	GEN. MGR. MUST BE CONVINCED HE IS MAJOR OBSTACLE	MIGHT BE DIF- FICULT TO CONVINCE TYPIST	
	STILL NEED TWO PEOPLE	FEASIBLE		THIS IS FEASIBLE IF SUG. 2 IS NOT ADOPTED

FIG. 13-2 (Cont.)

SELECTION OF FEASIBLE SOLUTION
Evaluation Worksheet

Operation: Analyst:
Spec. Goal: Date:
Dept:

	Suggestion No. 6	Suggestion No. 7	Suggestion No.	Suggestion No.
How much cost				
1 New machines				
2 New tools				
a Matl				
b Labor				
3 New designs				
4 Installation				
5 Overhead				
6 Scrap of machinery, tools & materials				
7 Misc (loss of production, wages, etc.				
8 New cost				
9 Less salvage				
10 Total cost	0.00	0.00		
How much savings				
11 Present method				
a Labor	$2800 (FOR CHECKER)	$1200/YR (SEE SUG.1)		
b Material		10 MIN./POLICY 600 MIN./YR.		
c Machine rate		10 HR./YR. @ $2 50/+ 12 = $37 00		
d Overhead & misc.				
12 Total				
13 Proposed method	TYPIST $10 ADD/ POLICY			
a Labor	ORDER CLERK $10 ADD/POLICY	$6 00		
b Material	$20/POLICY			
c Machine rate				
d Overhead & misc	$1200 00	$6 00		
14 Total				
15 Expected volume _____ per yr	6000/YR			
16 Savings per yr	$1400 LESS OVER TIME	$31 00		
10 Less cost				
17 Savings 1st yr	APPROX. $700	$31 00		
18 Hazard factor	—	—		
19 Control factor	ASSUMES ORDER CLERK & TYPIST CAN DO CHECKING -REDUCE THEIR LOAD	MANAGEMENT INSISTS ON PRESENT CONTROLS		
20 Psychological factor	MAY NEED OVER- TIME. INCREASES WORK OF TYPIST & ORDER CLERK			
	SUG.5 COMPLETELY ELIMINATED-TOO COSTLY FOR POSSIBLE SAVINGS	POSSIBLY FEASIBLE IF SUG. 2 IS NOT ADOPTED. THIS CAN BE COMBINED WITH SUG.4		

This worksheet also shows how suggestions can be listed in order of preference. As indicated, suggestion 2 is probably the most feasible. However, the analyst recognized that it might be difficult to install that idea because of psychological reasons. Therefore, suggestions 4 and 6 are indicated as next choice for this problem.

2. Inserting glue in case (Suggestion List, Fig. 12-10)

The evaluation worksheet is shown in Fig. 13-3. To evaluate some of these suggestions properly, they had to be combined. When suggestions 1, 2, 4, and 5 were combined, there were two possible methods that could be used. To distinguish the methods and determine their relative worth, synthetic operation charts, shown in Fig. 13-4, were made for the two methods. The synthetic charts are presented here in two ways: (a) with geometric symbols and (b) with rough time values as estimated from the times on the original operation chart, Fig. 7-6.

(a) If no symbol times were determined on the original chart, the geometric chart symbols could have been utilized in the evaluation. For example, it took 6.6 symbols per hand in the original method (Fig. 7-6) to produce one case, 4.5 symbols for method A (Fig. 13-4), and 3.3 symbols for method B. Since the total cycle time for the original method is either known or very easily obtained, using the proportions indicated by the above symbol summaries will provide estimated times for method A and method B. For example, the original cycle time per case was estimated as 11 seconds. The above procedure would give a time 4.5/6.6 of 11, or 7.5 seconds for method A, and 3.3/6.6 of 11, or 5.5 seconds for method B. Notice that this procedure did not use individual symbol times at all.

(b) The second approach presented involves estimating times for individual symbols. Although it is possible to use the times from Table 8-1 for such on operation, the times in Fig. 13-4 were estimated from the times on the original chart, and by going through the hand pattern. The original

FIG. 13-3. Evaluation worksheet for inserting glue in case (suggestion list: Fig. 12-10).

SELECTION OF FEASIBLE SOLUTION
Evaluation Worksheet

Operation: *INSERT GLUE IN CASE* Analyst: *W.J.W.*
Spec. Goal: *INCREASE PRODUCTIVITY* Date: *JAN. '53*
Dept: *SEALING*

		Suggestion No. *1,2,4,5*	Suggestion No. *1,2,4,5*	Suggestion No. *3 WITH B*	Suggestion No. *6*
	How much cost				
1	New machines	*METHOD A*	*METHOD B*	*$ 150.00*	*$ 300.00*
2	New tools				
a	Matl	*$15.00*			
b	Labor	*5.00*		*FOOT PEDAL 25°°*	*25.00*
3	New designs				*ENG. EST. 100°°*
4	Installation	*5.00*		*10°°*	*50°°*
5	Overhead				
6	Scrap of machinery, tools & materials				*50°°*
7	Misc (loss of production, wages, etc.				*SPEC. PARTS 25°°*
8	New cost				*550°°*
9	Less salvage				*10°°*
10	Total cost	*$ 25.00*	*$25.00*	*$185.00*	*540°°*
	How much savings				
11	Present method				
a	Labor	*$\frac{11}{60} \times \frac{150}{60} = .46¢/CASE$*	*.46¢/CASE*	*.46¢/CASE*	*.46*
b	Material				
c	Machine rate				
d	Overhead & misc.				
12	Total				
13	Proposed method			*USING B BASICALLY*	
a	Labor	*$\frac{6.5 \times 150}{3600} \times 27¢/CASE$*	*$\frac{5.5 \times 150}{3600} = .23$*	*$\frac{4.5 \times 150}{3600} = .19$*	*.27*
b	Material		*100% INCREASE IN PRODUCTION*		
c	Machine rate	*$\frac{11-6.5}{6.5} \times 100 =$*	*$\frac{11-5.5}{11} \times 100 =$*		
d	Overhead & misc	*69% INCREASE*	*50% DECREASE*		
14	Total	*19¢/CASE*	*IN TIME*		
15	Expected volume *1,200,000* per yr		*.23¢/CASE*	*.27¢/CASE*	*.19¢/CASE*
16	Savings per yr	*$2,280°°*	*$2760°°*	*$3240°°*	*2280°°*
10	Less cost	*25°°*	*25*	*185*	*540°°*
17	Savings 1st. yr	*$2,255°°*	*$2735°°*	*$3055°°*	*$1740°°*
18	Hazard factor				
19	Control factor	*NO CHANGE*	*NO CHANGE*	*VERY DIFFICULT TO OBTAIN EXACT QUALITY FOR BOTH CASES*	*SEAL DIFFICULT TO CONTROL WHEN VARIATION IN CASE DEPTH OCCURS*
20	Psychological factor	*FOREMAN SOMEWHAT SKEPTICAL- CAN BE CONVINCED*	*FOREMAN SKEPTICAL- CAN BE CONVINCED ✓ FEASIBLE*	*FOREMAN AND SUPERINTENDENT DO NOT THINK IT CAN WORK*	*ENGINEERING DEPT. SKEPTICAL*

SUG. 7 - NO GOOD CHUTE AS CLOSE AS POSSIBLE

205

FIG. 13-3 (Cont.)

SELECTION OF FEASIBLE SOLUTION
Evaluation Worksheet

Operation: Analyst:
Spec. Goal: Date:
Dept:

		Suggestion No. 8	Suggestion No. 9	Suggestion No.	Suggestion No.
	How much cost				
1	New machines				
2	New tools	150^{00}			
a	Matl				
b	Labor				
3	New designs				
4	Installation	10^{00}			
5	Overhead				
6	Scrap of machinery, tools & materials	100^{00}			
7	Misc (loss of production, wages, etc.				
8	New cost				
9	Less salvage				
10	Total cost	$\$260^{00}$	0.00		
	How much savings				
11	Present method				
a	Labor	.46	.46		
b	Material				
c	Machine rate				
d	Overhead & misc.				
12	Total				
13	Proposed method	$\dfrac{10.5 \times 150}{3600}=.44$	$\dfrac{10 \times 150}{3600}=.42$		
a	Labor				
b	Material				
c	Machine rate				
d	Overhead & misc				
14	Total				
15	Expected volume ____ per yr	.02	.04		
16	Savings per yr	$\$240.00$	$\$480.00$		
10	Less cost	260.00			
17	Savings 1st yr	$-\$20.00$	$\$480.00$		
18	Hazard factor	———	———		
19	Control factor	———	———		
20	Psychological factor	———	———		
			✓ FEASIBLE		

Fig. 13-4. Synthetic operation charts for two possible methods of utilizing the same suggestions for inserting glue in case.

SYNTHETIC	OPERATION	CHART —OF—
FOR SUGGESTIONS 1,2,4,5	OF INSERT GLUE IN CASE	

Date JAN/53 Part _____ Operator _____ Mach. _____
By WJW No. _____

TIME	LH	METHOD A	RH
1	To Case	○ ○	To Case
1	PU One Case	◯ ◯	PU One Case
1	To Tip of Nozzle	◐ ◐	To Tip of Nozzle
1	Until RH Case is Filled	▽ ◯	Position Under Nozzle
3		▽	For Filling
1	Position Case	◯ ◐	To Aside
3	For Filling	▽ ▽	Until LH Case is Filled
1	To Aside Rack	◐ ◐	To Aside Rack
1	Place Case	◯ ◯	Place Case
13		LH RH Both	
	◯	3 3 6	
	○	1 1 2	
	⊖	2 3 5	
	▽	3 2 5	
		9 9 Per 2 Cases	

		METHOD B	
1	To Cases	○ ○	To Cases
2	PU 2 Cases	◯ ◯	PU 2 Cases
1	To Tip of Nozzle	◐ ◐	
1	Until RH Cases Filled	▽ ◯	Position One Case
3		▽	For Filling
1		◯	Position Two Case
3		▽	For Filling
1	Position One Case	◯ ◐	To Aside
3	For Filling	▽ ▽	
1	Position Two Case	◯	LH RH B
3	For Filling	▽	◯ 4 4 8
1	To Aside Rack	◐ ◐	To Aside Rack ○ 1 1 2
1	Aside Cases	◯ ◯	Aside Cases ⊖ 2 3 5
22			▽ 6 5 11
			13 13
			Per 4 Cases

time per case was 11 seconds, and the estimated time for method *A* was 6.5 seconds, and for method *B*, 5.5 seconds. Although the times from geometric symbol evaluation and from time estimation evaluation are not exactly alike, their relationship is more than adequate for purposes of evaluation, since the *exact* times cannot be determined with any present techniques. Also of interest on the worksheet is the evaluation of suggestion 3. Although the indicated possible savings were greater than any other suggestion, this suggestion was not adopted because of the control factor.

DIFFICULTIES OF EVALUATING SUGGESTIONS FOR NONREPETITIVE WORK

The basic approach of evaluation demonstrated above is likewise applicable to all the techniques of analysis presented. For example, the suggestion list for the occurrence study, or any other nonrepetitive work analysis technique, can be evaluated in exactly the same way as any other repetitive work chart. There will be probably more difficulty in obtaining some information which is to be used for the evaluation. For example, volume or number of times the activity is to be performed may be difficult to determine. Estimates of time or savings of proposed methods may be likewise difficult to establish. Although guessing becomes more prevalent, the guesses can be more reliable if more people concerned with the activity assist in the estimating.

CHAPTER 14

DESIGNING THE PROPOSED METHOD

Although the proposed method, equipment, sequence, design, and material have been thought through to some extent, the amount of detail used in evaluating suggestions is nowhere near the requirements for the actual design of the work situation. Even though a simplified chart may have been made, more detail is needed to put the proposed method into operation.

PURPOSE OF DETAILING PROPOSED METHOD

This step usually involves the charting and/or statement, with flow or workplace diagram, of the proposed procedures for the work situation. The proposed method need not be placed in chart form but can be stated as a procedure to be followed. This is the case with forms procedures. It is almost always the case when an occurrence study or other nonrepetitive work analysis is made. The essential function of this step is to prepare adequately the information and detail to assure proper performance of the proposed method. All possible errors and difficulties should be eliminated before the installation is made. If done properly, the formulation of the proposed method is a guide to performance for the foreman or supervisor and operator. Certainly, the information from, and the method of presentation of, the detailing step are important to other functions of an organization, like tooling, purchasing, and engineering, as well as to the succeeding steps of the work simplification approach.

WHEN MENTAL DETAILING CAN BE USED

Although detailing can entail much work, this step, like all other steps of the logical approach to work simplification problems, may not involve much work or written material at all. Frequently an analyst studies an operation where the better methods design must be placed in use immediately. Such situations occur when a new work activity is to be started almost immediately, and the supervisor has an opportunity to look it over only briefly before starting. Generally, the first step, "State the problem," indicates the amount of detail required for each step of the procedure. If minimum or gross details are indicated, the analyst relies on his experience, first, to apply principles more or less mentally; second, to evaluate the ideas mentally; and, third, to formulate the proposed methods for the most part mentally. However, an analyst can usually do a better job if he performs each step with some recording procedure.

PARTS OF DETAILING STEP

The detailing step consists of three parts:

1. Visualization

The analyst must visualize the material, product design, sequence, equipment, and methods for the possible solution to the particular problem. In the last two steps, it is permissible to say that a small holding device will be satisfactory for a particular suggestion. In the detailing step, it is necessary to design the exact specifications of the holding device, where the clamping device will be placed, how far apart various components should be, etc. The analyst should expand the ideas for the work to include all improvements that might arise through the process of detailing itself. As the analyst forms his mental image, he would record the details in chart form, by jig or fixture designs, with product design specification changes, etc.

2. Design of tools, equipment, and other material items

This part requires the changes in the material, product design, and equipment areas to be exactly specified. The better the specifications and sketches and the greater the detail, the better the possibility for a good installation. If equipment is supposed to be purchased, then the analyst need not design the equipment but can use specifications provided by the manufacturer. It is not necessary to be a tool designer, or mechanically inclined as far as drawing goes; rather the analyst should be able to indicate by his sketch the general tool, equipment, or specifications desired. Then a tool designer or someone more experienced in drawing specifications can take over. Changes in layout of workplace or plant will require a proposed workplace or flow diagram.

The analyst should roughly design the changes which involve material entering the plant and the product leaving the plant or organization. This type of design requires care, but any analyst should suggest and work on it.

3. Design of the proposed method and/or sequence

Visualization usually includes two types of mental images. One concerns the design of the material, product, and equipment, and the other concerns the sequence and hand or motion pattern which the operator will have to use with the proposals of the other areas. In most cases, the procedure for recording the information necessary in this part is to make a proposed chart which is of the same type as the original chart and which incorporates the visualized solution. However, the type of chart made for the original method need not be of the same type as the one made for the proposed method. For example, an operation chart may have been constructed to analyze the original method, and a machine may be required in the selected suggestion. Therefore, the proposed chart would be a man and machine operation chart.

In most cases, some form of chart is a good way of expressing the proposed procedure. These charts also permit the design of the proper method for an operation which may be performed under varying conditions. For example, if one man in a three-man crew is absent one day, it may not be possible to assign anyone else to the crew. However, the proper method for a two-man crew can be designed before such a situation occurs with the assistance of the charts presented previously. Also, the changing conditions of labor and machine costs might indicate that another method should be used. Varying conditions or the volume of production might indicate that different methods should be used.

The basic principles of methods design are applicable to nonrepetitive work. It is difficult to design nonrepetitive work completely. Basically, changes are made in nonrepetitive work by such things as additional training of personnel in a particular area, reassignment of duties in the classification of work, or having another person perform some of the activities.

The actual designing of a method does not always completely involve the one-two-three approach indicated above. The analyst moves back and forth among the steps. For example, it might be possible to visualize and then design certain parts before completing the visualization for other sections of the work. Other situations will require other arrangements.

SUBMITTING PROPOSALS FOR APPROVAL

Frequently, after the proposed method has been designed, the method must be submitted for approval. In such situations a proposal sheet, or summary sheet, should be enclosed to state the objectives and changes of the operation.

The two most important items to be included on the summary or proposal sheet are a list of the changes necessary to install the method and their costs, and a recapitulation of the original and proposed methods with the savings noted in terms of chart symbols as well as time and dollar savings. In most cases the summary, or proposal sheet, would not be made until after the next two steps of the logical approach have been completed. However, the proposal sheet may have to be submitted after the formulation, so that someone else actually performs the *review* step. Since the evaluation worksheets are usually included in the report with the proposal sheet, the cost information on the proposal sheet need only be a brief summary. A sample proposal sheet, Fig. 14-2, is shown with the first proposed chart illustration (Fig. 14-1).

TYPE OF DESIGN FOR EACH CHART

Each chart tries to analyze some certain physical characteristic. Because of this, there are many specific principles which tend to be more important with certain charts. In presenting some of the proposed charts below, the specific type of design always to look for on that type of chart will be presented.

Product process chart

In trying to design the best sequence and layout for a product, the most important concept is: "Once you have picked up a product to start work on it, don't put it down." This is the key to automation. This includes such important concepts as eliminating backtracking, or simplifying double handling, or reducing storage space. Of course, this is not always possible with every product. But again, if we use this as the ideal and constantly strive for this situation, we are more likely to arrive at the "best" sequence and layout for our conditions. This basic concept applies only after the work has been found to be necessary.

Handling Hoppers on Unloading Platform. The original product process chart was shown in Fig. 4-2 and the original flow diagram in Fig. 1-4. The proposed product process chart is shown in Fig. 14-1, and the proposed flow diagram is shown in Fig. 1-5. The changes were simple and are ex-

FIG. 14-1. Proposed product process chart for handling hoppers on unloading platform (original PPC: Fig. 4-1).

	QUANT.	DIST.	SYMBOL	EXPLANATION	EQUIP.
1	6		▽	On Truck	
2	1	30'	○	To Position Near Tenderometer Shack	
3	25	Sample of Peas	▽	At Shack	
4		Grade Paddle			
5	1	40'	○	To Front of Dumper	
6	20	Paddle	▽	For Dumping	
7	1	20'	○	To Dumper	
8	1	Peas	Ⓜ	Peas Dumped	Dumper
9	1	5'	○	Backed Out	
10	1		Ⓛ	Turned Around	
11	1	25'	○	To Washer	
12	1		Ⓜ	Washed	Spray
13	1	50'	○	To Storage	
14	35		▽	Until Needed	
15	1	20'	○	To Truck	
16	6		▽	On Truck	
17					
18					
19			Summary		
20			Ⓜ 2		
21			Ⓛ 1		
22			○ 7		
23			▽ 5		
24			Dist. 190'		
25					
26					
27					
28					
29					
30					
31					
32					
33					

PROPOSED ____ PRODUCT PROCESS ___OF___ CHART

OF HOPPERS ON UNLOADING PLATFORM

Date 7/29/48 Part HOPPERS Operator _____ Mach ____

By E.D. No. _____

NADER

plained easily by the reference to the proposed chart and flow diagram. A sample proposal sheet for this problem is shown in Fig. 14-2. Notice how backtracking and confusion are eliminated by this arrangement. Unnecessary work is eliminated, even though it is still not the ideal stated.

FIG. 14-2. Proposal sheet used as a cover for submission to management for approval of the proposed method for handling hoppers on unloading platform.

PROPOSAL SHEET _____ **CHART** __OF__

OF_HOPPERS ON UNLOADING PLATFORM_

Date_7/29/48_ Part _____Operator _____Mach_____

By_E.D._ No._____

LIST OF CHANGES :-
1 – Move Tenderometer Shack Four Feet From Wall
2 – Have Trucks Unload and Load at Present Pre-Grade Area
3 – Level Ground By Dock to Three Heights
4 – Retrain Tenderometer Operators to Follow Standard Procedure
Advantages:-
1 – Avoid Confusion on Dock
2 – Eliminate Delay in Movement of Hoppers
3 – Eliminate Lifting and Lowering Hoppers
4 Eliminate One Man in Crew
Savings Per Year at Present Volume – $ 464.00
Cost of Installation   –   51.00
Savings in First Year   –   413.00
Product Process Chart Recap

		Orig.	Proposed	Savings
	Ⓜ	2	2	0
	Ⓛ	4	1	3
	o	9	7	2
	▽	5	5	0
	Dist.	222'	190'	32'

References Attached:
Statement and Goal of Problem
Orig. Product Process Chart and Flow Diagram–
Proposed Product Process Chart and Flow Diagram–
Suggestion List–
Evaluation Work Sheet–

Form process chart

The application of work simplification to form systems and procedures is relatively new. It is difficult to say that there is one general principle applicable to this type of work. But if there were one, it would be of this type:

After deciding that the work is necessary, no information should be copied or written more than once. This is similar to "Once a product is picked up, it should not be put down." In forms, once the material or information is originally written, it should not be copied again. In addition to this, there are many other principles slowly taking shape in relation to the design of forms when forms have to be handled by people. (Obviously, the basic principle stated above relates to greater use of automatic data processing equipment.)

Order Form. The original form process chart was shown in Fig. 5-1. The proposed form process chart is shown in Fig. 14-3. The form design was changed, and the original and new forms are shown in Figs. 14-4 and 14-5. The number of spaces on the new form have been reduced from 15 to 10. A study revealed that this was the maximum required for almost every case. The number of copies was reduced from seven to six. The original accordion-folded form was replaced by a snap-out form. Colored sheets rather than colored ink were used to identify copies. Light inks on some of the original forms were hard to read. The heading was changed to allow four departments instead of one to utilize the form. Columns, spacings, and wordings were changed to allow for better use of equipment. The sequence of copies was changed to permit removal of copies in proper order. The savings on the forms alone was $200 per year. The proposed chart showed the handlings reduced by about half, by eliminating stapling, pinning, removals, etc. Even with these changes, there are some improvements that can be found in the improved method. The tab stops are not lined

Fig. 14-3. Proposed form process chart for order form (original FPC: Fig. 5-1).

PROPOSED _____ FORM PROCESS _____ __OF__ CHART

OF ORDER FORM

Date 1/10/52 Part ORDER FORM Operator _____ Mach_____
By A.E.S. No. 1880 REV

ORDER DEPT.	FACTORY	SUPPLY ORDER FILLING	CENTRAL SUPPLY	PURCHASING DEPT.
1 ⑥ Info Typed				
2 ◯ Copies Separated				
3 ◇ 12345			12345	
4 ◇ To Factory	6		▽ In Basket	
5	◇ With Orig. Order		◯ Add Lot No. Quant. Unit. Unit Value	
6	◇ To File		← Quant. Deducted From Stock Records	
7	▽		▽ In Basket	
8	◇ Out After #5 Rec'd.		◇ To Order Filling	
9	⊠ Destroyed	▽ In Basket		
10		◇ To Stockroom		
11		→● Order Filled		
12		◇ To Packer		
13		◯ Separated		
14	5	5 ◇ With Matl. ◇ 1,2,3,4		
15	◇ With Items Rec'd.		▽	
16	◇ To Rec. File		◯ Date, B/L No., Route Added	
17	▽ I ▽		◯ Separated	
18	◇ ◇		12 ◯ To Billing 3 ◇ To File 4 ◇	
19	⊠ ▽		▽	▽ In Basket
20	→● Billing Added		◯ Extensions Entered	◇ With Tables
21	To Monthly Cost St m.		◯ Separated	◇ To File
22	▽		1 ◇ 2 ◇ To File	▽
23	◇ To File		▽	
24	▽	Summary (6 Copies)		
25		Orig.	Proposed	Savings
26	◯	15	7	8
27	○	20	17	3
28	▽	10	9	1
29	▽	7	6	1
30	◇	4	5	-1
31	→●	5	3	2
32	⊠	1	2	-1
33				

F 1

FIG. 14-4. Original form for order-form problem: accordion-folded, seven copies, 15 lines, etc.

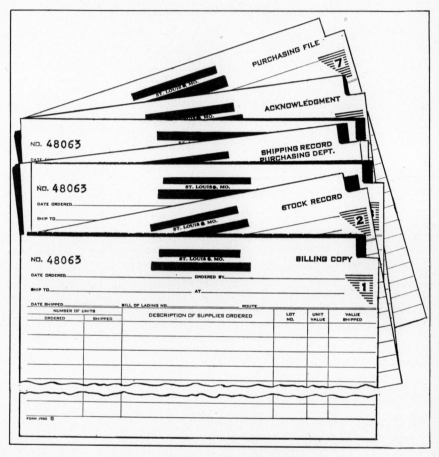

Fig. 14-5. New form for order-form problem: snap-out, six copies, 10 lines, etc.

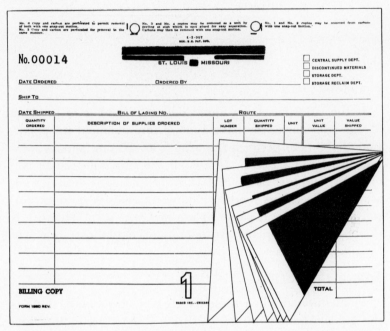

up for easy use of the typewriter. Obviously, forms design plays an important role in designing and improving systems.

Man process chart

The essential principle for designing activity for a man moving from place to place is relatively straightforward. If it has been found that the work is necessary, then the man should not go to the same place more than once in a cycle. Of course, it is good to get rid of the walking altogether. Frequently it will be found that men will go to the same place several times within a cycle, as in going to a tool crib, or the desk of an associate. The housewife is a good illustration of this. She should not go to the same place more than once if at all possible in performing her work, as in clearing off the dishes after dinner. The ideal situation

would be to take all the dishes off the table at one time. If
this can be done, with a tray or other means, then this is
the way it should be done. But at least she should make as
few trips as possible to the table for dishes. The same principle would apply in dusting, or getting ready to go to work
in the morning.

Operation chart

If the work has been found necessary and is to be done
at one workplace, the basic type of improvement for operation charts is to perform the work with a simultaneous symmetrical hand pattern. Almost all the principles in motion
economy apply here, but if this one principle is followed,
many of the others tend to follow suit. This is quite an important principle, because of the fact that so much work is
done at one workplace. An operation chart illustration will
be given in the next category.

Multi-activity charts

As mentioned when these charts were presented, there is
the basic problem of interrelating activity to reduce idle
time. But much of this depends on the specific objective.
For multi-man situations, the general objective is to reduce
the idle time for the individuals and equipment. If a machine or machines are involved, the operator should do as
much as possible during the machine time. But the work
should be simplified first. These principles are mainly applicable after it has been found that the work is necessary.

Shear Snubber Wire to Length. The original multi-man
operation chart was shown in Fig. 9-1. The original workplace diagram was shown in Fig. 9-2, and the original multi-
man operation time chart in Fig. 9-3. Since the proposed
method utilized only one operator, the proposed operation
chart is shown in Fig. 14-6 and the proposed workplace diagram in Fig. 14-7. The decision to reduce the number of
operators in this crew was made in relation to the specific
objective for the problem. In this case the goal was to reduce

Fig. 14-6. Proposed operation chart for shearing snubber wire to length. The original method involved a two-man instead of the proposed one-man crew (original multi-man operation chart: Fig. 9-1; original MM Op T Ch: Fig. 9-3).

PROPOSED   OPERATION   —OF—
                                                  CHART
                    OF SHEAR SNUBBER WIRE TO LENGTH

Date JAN. 29 '53 Part _____ Operator _____ Mach. _____
By____J. G.____ No. _____

LEFT FOOT	LH DESCRIPTION			RH DESCRIPTION
		▽		To Ends of Wire
			○	Grasp Heavy and Light Wires
▽	To RH			To LH
	Take Heavy Wire	○	○	Give Heavy Wire to LH
	To Heavy Wire Stop			To Light Wire Stop
	Place Against Stop	○	○	Place Against Stop
○	For Shearing	▽	▽	For Shearing
	To Aside			To Aside
	Place Wire		○	Place Wire
	To End of Wire By Shear			To End of Wire by Shear
	PU Wire	○	○	PU Wire
	To Aside			To Aside
	Place Wire	○	○	Place Wire

	Original (2 Operators Combined)			Proposed			Savings		
	LH	RH	Both	LH	RH	Both	LH	RH	Both
○	13	10	23	5	6	11	8	4	12
○	3	5	8	2	2	4	1	3	4
●	4	4	8	3	4	7	1	0	1
▽	2	1	3	1	1	2	1	0	1
▽	4	6	10	2	0	2	2	6	8
	26	26		13	13				

costs. The objective was met, since the number of man-minutes per unit was reduced 0.096 less 0.0335 (minute per wire), or 0.0625 minute per unit, or by 65 per cent. If, on the other hand, it was important to increase the number of heavy wires sheared per hour, this method would not accomplish the objective because one heavy wire is cut in 0.067 minute, compared to 0.048 per wire in the original method. (Of course, it would be possible to attain this latter goal by cutting two heavy wires at the same time instead of one light and one heavy wire, or making duplicate setups for two operators, if the cost of new equipment were warranted.) In any case the charts provide a procedure for testing the

FIG. 14-7. Workplace diagram for proposed method of shearing snubber wire to length (original workplace diagram: Fig. 9-2).

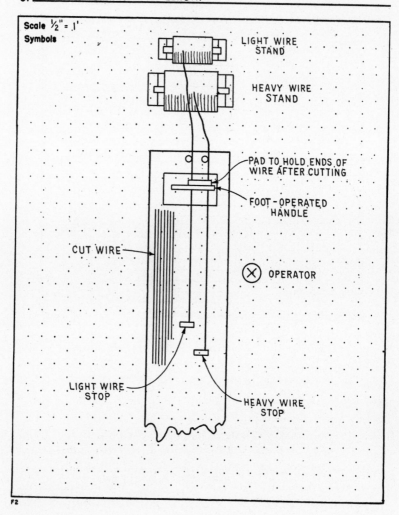

WORKPLACE **DIAGRAM** ACCOMPANYING PROPOSED OPERATION

___OF___ CHART

OF SHEAR SNUBBER WIRE TO LENGTH

Scale ½" = 1'
Symbols

LIGHT WIRE STAND

HEAVY WIRE STAND

PAD TO HOLD ENDS OF WIRE AFTER CUTTING

FOOT - OPERATED HANDLE

CUT WIRE

⊗ OPERATOR

LIGHT WIRE STOP

HEAVY WIRE STOP

F2

feasibility of methods, just as the evaluation worksheet is the procedure for selecting the most desirable solution. For the specific goal and conditions of this problem, the solution presented in Figs. 14-6 and 14-7 represents the "better" answer.

Therblig chart

The same concepts that applied to the operation chart and, in some cases, to multi-activity charts apply here.

Package Ring and Expander. The original therblig chart was shown in Fig. 8-2, and the original workplace diagram in Fig. 8-1. The proposed therblig chart is shown in Fig. 14-8 and the proposed workplace diagram in Fig. 14-9. A duplicate setup was made to permit a simultaneous symmetrical hand pattern. Time values for therbligs from Table 8-1 were used to estimate the amount of time for both the original and proposed methods. All the changes could be made by the maintenance department. For such simple and relatively inexpensive changes, the benefits were rather large, since the basic idea could be applied to three other similar operations. An inverted piece of T-shaped iron was used to hold and position the rings directly above the open bag. The end of the iron was shaped to permit one ring at a time to be removed with slight pressure.

REMINDER WHEN DESIGNING METHODS

Even though the proposed method is supposed to have been selected, and in this step the improved method is to be designed, the analyst should never forget two things:

1. It is never too late to start thinking about eliminating work, even though you are trying to design or improve the method for the work.

2. Even though the improvement is being designed, it is never too late to add new ideas or improvements, in this step or in any other step. It is desirable to make as many changes as possible at one time.

FIG. 14-8. Proposed therblig chart for packaging ring and expander (original therblig chart: Fig. 8-2).

PROPOSED   THERBLIG   CHART —OF—

OF PACKAGE RING AND EXPANDER

Date 6/7/52   Part BAG RINGS   Operator _____   Mach _____
By O.H.C.   No. EXPANDERS

LH DESCRIPTION		TIME IN .0001 MIN.	RH DESCRIPTION
To Expanders	6TE23	50	S
Expander	STI	5	A
Expander (T&IST F)	G2	40	M
To Top of Ring Rack	8TL2	75	E
Expander in Ring	P1	30	
Grasp Ring (H Expander)	G2	40	A
Pull Ring Off	1/4DA3	9	S
To Open Bag	6TL2	65	
Ring & Expander to Bag	P23	85	LEFT
Ring & Expander in Bag	3AI	45	
Pull Bag Toward Self	2TL2	45	HAND
Ring and Expander	RL2	20	
		509	

Time Values for Original Method					Original		Proposed		Savings	
Left Hand		Right Hand			LH	RH	LH	RH	LH	RH
G2	40	65	9TE23	TE	90	90	50	50	40	40
15TL2	110	40	G2	TL	175	80	185	185	-10	-105
P24	85	80	9TL2	ST&G	45	0	45	45	0	-45
IAI	15	30	UDB	G	40	80	40	40	0	40
RL2	20	85	P24	P	170	85	115	115	55	-30
9TE24	65	45	3AI	A	90	45	45	45	45	0
		20	RL2	RL	40	40	20	20	20	20
STI&	45	25	ITE23	H	0	200	0	0	0	200
G2		40	62	UD	0	30	0	0	0	30
		200	H	DA	0	0	9	9	-9	-9
6TL2	65				650	650	509	509	141	141
P24	85			X2	X2				650	650
3A2	75				1300	1300			791	791
RL2	20									
ITE23	25	20	RL2	% Decrease in Time = $\frac{791}{1300} \times 100 = 61\%$						
	650	650		% Increase in Production = $\frac{791}{509} \times 100 = 155\%$						

FIG. 14-9. Workplace diagram for proposed method of packaging ring and expander (original workplace diagram: Fig. 8-1).

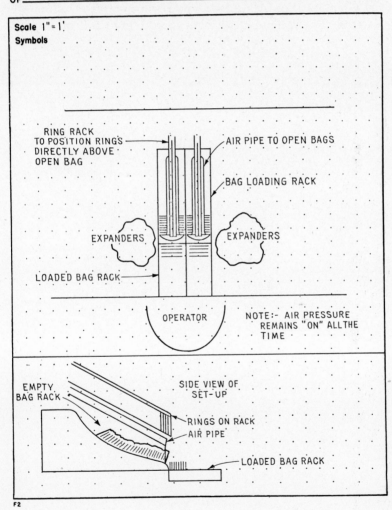

WORKPLACE **DIAGRAM** ACCOMPANYING PROPOSED THERBLIG ___OF___ **CHART**

OF PACKAGE RING AND EXPANDER

Another advantage of following the logical approach to work simplification problems, and especially in designing the proposed methods with these charts, is that it helps the analyst thoroughly think through the proposal he is going to make. This means that most of the bugs will be ironed out before the final proposal is submitted. In this way, the analyst is submitting facts for his proposal instead of opinions. "It is always easier to sell facts than it is to sell opinions."

CHAPTER 15

REVIEWING AND TESTING

Completing the detailing step does not relieve the analyst of further responsibility concerning the proposed method. There are many things that should be done after the initial design is completed.

REVIEWING THE METHOD

In many cases, work problems are complex and frequently need additional follow-up, as in almost every other field. The doctor does not pronounce his diagnosis until he has reviewed his case carefully. The engineer will not construct his bridge until he has reviewed his design. The review step of the logical approach to solving problems is quite important.

The purposes of the review step in work simplification are:

1. To determine if all possible improvements, better designs, or principles of proper methods design are incorporated in the design

2. To make certain all the details necessary for the actual installation of the method or procedure are included in the design

3. To plan the approach for getting the personnel concerned to use the methods design properly

1. Are all possible good design principles included?

This question is important for economical reasons, as well as psychological reasons to be discussed later. Money can be saved by asking the question early. Frequently a new fixture is needed and made for the new method. In such a case, if additional thought about the operation and the situation under which it is performed had been given, certain important cost-saving features might very possibly have been included. For example, a simultaneous symmetrical hand pattern method had been devised for the assembly of four parts. A new jig was required and made. After the jig was made, it occurred to the analyst that there were six additional intermittent assembly jobs with parts somewhat similar to the first but differing in size and some design features. Fortunately, the necessary changes in the jig to make it applicable to all the similar jobs could be made, because it had been designed for one of the larger sizes. In many other cases the jig could not have been changed, requiring either a series of jigs to accomplish what one could have done or scrapping the jig in favor of the properly designed jig. After a new device is made, it becomes difficult and expensive to make changes, compared to the cost for the device designed and built properly from the start.

From the employee's point of view, including as many good design features as possible at one time is important. This refers to those directly affected by the change who must be convinced of the advantages and reasons for the change. It is somewhat disheartening and bothersome to these people if after a short period of time the analyst appears again to install some additional small changes for the work. Their reaction tends to force them to ask the question, "Why didn't he install this change at the same time that he made the other changes?"

But even worse from a work simplification point of view is the likelihood that the analyst will not try to improve further an operation if he has already studied it. The tendency is to assume that no further study is needed because "the job was just improved." Although this tendency avoids the employee reaction mentioned above, it is not a good idea to have an analyst overlook possible changes in work.

How to Accomplish the First Purpose. The analyst should use his resources as well as possible. The two most frequently used resources are (1) the foreman or supervisor and other people involved with the change and (2) the check list of principles of methods design. The first resource represents one of the best ways of accomplishing this step. The people directly concerned with the jobs know them best. Also, by consulting the people, the correct psychological approach is being used. It should be assumed that the people involved with the change have been consulted and talked with before this step. The analyst should, however, discuss with the supervisor and other personnel the changes suggested for the work to stimulate them to think of still more ideas. Many refinements can be found in this way.

A review of the check list for principles of methods design is another help for this step. The check list offers much to an analyst who works by himself. There are many small items of improvement frequently overlooked in methods design. Sometimes the analyst does not look at all aspects of a good idea; he tends to drop smaller items of improvement in his enthusiasm for the one good idea. These smaller but highly profitable changes should not be ignored or lost through enthusiasm.

The use of the check list in the review step can be accomplished by simply looking over the list to determine if any of the items might be applied to the proposed methods design. In some cases where the operation is costly, the analyst might construct another suggestion list for the proposed method. This suggestion list would assume that the proposed method is actually the "original." This helps eliminate many inefficiencies in the proposed design.

2. Are all needed details included?

The problems in this part are again economical and psychological. Many details are overlooked because of enthusiasm. In this case, the analyst becomes enthusiastic about his major suggestion, and then forgets to take into full consideration the effect of the suggestion on the whole operation. For example, one analyst designed a method for spot welding with an indexing jig to accommodate eight parts, and then had the indexing jig made. The analyst, however, completely forgot to allow time or provide a method for removing the parts from the indexing jig. This was a most serious oversight, because it was difficult to add such equipment. Of course, removal should have been considered before the fixture was made. In this case, the problem was solved by providing for a longer cycle time. This reduced the estimated value of the jig. This type of error should not occur, and this part of the step requires the analyst to review all details to make certain the proposal is workable.

The psychological aspect relates to the position or standing of the analyst in the organization. What could be more embarrassing and ego-deflating than to design a proposed method, have a new jig made and installed, and then find it does not work because of some detail omitted in the design? This concept applies to all areas in which designs are made. A foreman or analyst should not permit his worth to the company to deteriorate because he has not taken the time to check details of a proposed design. Foremen and supervisors especially cannot afford to have such situations occur. More careful probing of the design can frequently avoid this.

3. Planning the approach to the people

Supposedly the analyst has been following all the concepts of good human relations mentioned in Chapter 2. He has also presumably been using the proper approach to the individuals with the various techniques. If such has been the case, then much of the planning of this part has been done. Even then, thought should be given to plan how the people involved will be notified of the change, trained, etc. Many ways of introducing a methods change are available. Motion pictures, bulletin-board announcements, group meetings, and plant newspaper, are some. Proper planning should make for a minimum of opposition to the changes.

As many people as possible should review the proposed methods. If the methods design must be submitted to someone else for approval, this frequently becomes the "review step." If an analyst hopes to make an impression on those involved, he should review the method by himself and/or with others in the company to include all possible changes and details for functioning. If a situation exists where an analyst cannot obtain assistance, he should, carefully and in detail, review the check list to make certain that all improvements are included. He should be exceptionally careful of the details needed to ensure proper functioning of his methods design. In addition, he must plan the approach to the people.

TESTING THE METHOD

Even after the review step, several problems still confront the analyst. Will the proposal actually work in the operating situation? Nothing in the review step guarantees this. An analyst with much experience will have less doubt about the workability of one of his ideas than will an analyst with only a little experience. Although some positive statements concerning details of the method can be made, there are questions concerning the workability of a particular idea. Generally, these are:

1. Can the human being do what is required or specified according to the methods design?

Are the mental and physical dexterity requirements reasonable? Frequently small parts are handled in such a way that it is difficult to do what the method says, or large parts cannot be handled in certain ways. The review step would probably not answer this question, and therefore this step might help solve it.

2. Will the jig or fixture perform as specified?

Although the jig might be made accurately, it does not necessarily mean the jig will function as desired. Variations in material, temperatures, etc., greatly affect the operation of some mechanical devices. Again, the review step could not answer these questions, leaving many of them for the test step.

3. Will the part(s) worked with perform as expected in the methods design?

Some hand patterns are dependent upon the way certain parts act when handled or worked with. The previous steps assumed a certain action which may not be the case. Such situations arise especially with small parts, springs, other unusual shapes and materials. In many cases no principles, detailing, or review procedures can give answers to these questions. Testing is about the only way.

Testing helps clarify some problems which have arisen in previous steps. In this step, it is possible that a suggestion or idea may be discarded because it is found to be unworkable. This is the important reason for following the detailing and review with still another check. This is even more important for work not yet in production. If the selected method is not workable, the analyst will go back to the fourth step to select another suggestion. Of course, the test step helps to modify and correct methods designs. The test step is the final check before installation. This should avoid costly errors and provide for a still better method.

Testing procedures

There are various ways in which a test can be conducted:

1. *Model.* For "large" problems, like materials handling or

plant layout, a model is an extremely useful device. A model is the reduced-scale version of the actual situation. A model does not work; it is only pictorial. Of course, this requires facilities to permit such an analysis. The model is an excellent way to permit examination of different layouts to determine possible defects, and the seemingly best arrangement. Usually, the best model is three-dimensional, which permits better visualization and easier changing of requirements. Two-dimensional layouts with cutouts or templates can also help clarify procedures. Two-dimensional models are less expensive. The three-dimensional models are used most frequently for selling. Models are valuable because they permit testing of many types of ideas.

2. *Workplace Mock-up.* Making an inexpensive mock-up from wood is usually an easy test method. Sometimes a rough mock-up might be made in the fourth step, selecting the best idea. A test with a mock-up gives much valuable information and is a close approach to getting information from actual operating conditions. Designing a mock-up should be done within the limits of low cost and ease of construction.

Figure 15-1 shows a mock-up made for the job of stamping numbers in metal tags. The proposed method included a tag hopper, a pickup arm, and a drop chute to line up the tags for inserting a wire. The mock-up was made up from wood and scrap sheet metal. Although rough, it showed that the basic ideas were sound and that a properly made jig would be feasible.

3. *Make an Actual Jig or Workplace Setup.* When an operation requires a number of operators, or the operation will involve work expected to be performed for a long time, it might be desirable to make the actual jig, if the cost is not too high. Made exactly as planned with correct materials, the device provides a test under actual operating conditions. Corrections can be made, if needed. If it is completely unworkable, it should not cost too much to scrap the jig. Frequently, the devices can be made by buying some equip-

F<small>IG</small>. 15-1. Mock-up of workplace for proposed method of stamping tags.

ment of a general-purpose nature which can be used elsewhere if the jig is not workable.

4. Make Simple Methods Changes. Often the proposed method involves nothing more than a slight rearrangement of equipment, tables, or workbenches, or simple methods changes within the operation workplace. If such is the case, and a test is needed, it can usually be made by simply making the changes suggested. Although this might be construed as an actual installation, it is really a test, because the equipment can be moved back to its original location if the method does not work. In some cases the new method, or a part of the method, can be tested by the analyst's going through the hand pattern, or by having an operator from the plant go through the hand pattern. If these tests are performed with the actual parts, more conclusive answers can be obtained.

5. New Machinery. When new machinery is required, such equipment cannot usually be borrowed and then tested for a particular operation. Usually, machinery has to be purchased before full knowledge of the operating characteristics becomes available. However, there are some ways of "testing" methods utilizing machinery planned for the method but not available in the plant. For example, it would be possible to use manufacturer's data on performance to determine certain operating factors. This is subject to errors of interpretation as well as to exaggerated claims. Another "test" procedure would involve visiting other plants which might have the machinery. It would be possible to learn about actual operating characteristics, and the advantages and disadvantages of the equipment. Incidentally, visiting other plants should be encouraged for all people in this field.

Of course, it may be impossible to test some new machinery, get enough manufacturer's data, or see the same machinery in other companies. In such situations, the problem becomes more acute. There might be some arrangements for the return of the equipment if it does not work. This is unlikely. Even if such an arrangement is made, it is still overly expensive. Obviously, a methods design involving new machinery is difficult to test.

6. *No Tests Possible.* There are many reasons why an analyst might be unable to test a methods design. Sometimes there is just not enough time to make a test. Sometimes the procedure being designed does not lend itself to testing. For example, some forms or procedure systems are usually not easily tested in their entirety. Most of the work of testing must be done in the review step by mentally manipulating situations and conditions to arrive at a confirmation of reasonable methods design. Sometimes there is no money available for testing.

If at all possible, testing should be done. If and when a test cannot be made for a particular methods design, it becomes imperative to perform the detailing and review steps in greater detail. Taken as a whole, the detailing, review, and test steps are procedures designed to assure the analyst and the company of good results.

CHAPTER 16

INSTALLING THE NEW METHOD

Now that we have gone through seven steps of the logical procedure, it should be assumed that the proposed method is desirable and should be used for the work situation. Since by going through seven steps the work problems have been solved, step 8 concerns the problems of installing the proposed method.

PROBLEMS OF INSTALLATION

In many cases this step can prove to be the biggest stumbling block in the entire procedure. Unusual problems can develop. The analyst must be concerned with the installation and its problems, because the work done to this point can amount to nothing if the method is not installed properly. In some cases, everyone contacted through step 7 might approve of the method, yet when it comes to installing the method, there might be some difficulty in getting the changes made. For example, one company found that a particular methods change concerning punch presses was approved by everyone including the man in charge of maintenance. After the material was ordered and delivered, this man "could not find the manpower necessary, because of other work, to install the equipment." What caused this man to change was unknown. In effect, he now opposed the change. He was an employee with long service, highly respected, and it was not felt advisable to attempt to convince him, with any enthusiasm at this stage, of the desirability of making the change. After he retired, the changes were made.

Certainly, this points to the need for more human relations activities at every step of the approach. However, this chapter has another purpose. It is to present what must be done, in a general way, when installing the new method. The obstacles in a particular plant must be eliminated on the basis of the situation.

Some functions mentioned in this chapter will sound familiar to you as part of other activities in an organization. You may even feel that these are not necessarily an analyst's function. However, the analyst should recognize what has to be done to install the proposed method properly. At one extreme the analyst may have the complete responsibility for all parts of the installation. At the other extreme the analyst may do nothing but give other departments the design and specifications for the new method to allow them to proceed with the installation. In either case the analyst should know the parts of the installation step to plan properly the work which must be done.

APPROACH TO SUPERVISOR AND EMPLOYEE

If the analyst is a supervisor, he should have been working in cooperation with the employees. If not, cooperation should have been developed. If this has been done, the installation need not include much activity on "selling." But some situations might not have permitted the analyst to do this. In such cases the first thing to be done is to give the explanation of, and the reasons for, the proposed method to those involved. Following the procedures given in Chapter 2, the analyst should be able to overcome the obstacles of the human being. Generally, it might even be wise for the analyst to review, step by step, the logical approach for solving problems. In this way almost all the information can be given to the person involved. It might even be possible to develop a better idea at this point.

PARTS OF INSTALLATION

The procedure to be used in the three parts of installation will vary not only from plant to plant but from one project to another within one plant. The three parts are presented as activities to be accomplished, but it would be virtually impossible to list all the ramifications of the procedure to be used in completing the requirements of each part. The three parts are:

1. Make the mechanical changes.
2. Train the operators and others involved.
3. Follow up to check on use of the method.

1. Make the mechanical changes

This part involves obtaining the necessary authorization to complete the changes suggested, or to complete the design of material, product, sequence equipment, and method for operations not yet in production. This part might be accomplished by placing an order for desired equipment, giving drawing designs for tools to the toolmaker, having the purchasing department order the newly specified material, requesting the engineering department to make changes on a particular product, etc. There are any number of ways of putting this part into effect. In other words, since so much work has been done in designing methods and other material factors, this part merely says, "Get the thing started by installing it."

There are some cases where it might not be desirable to install a new method even though it has been found. It might be desirable to wait until all operations in the whole department or area have been studied and improved or designed. Then the complete working area can be arranged in a suitable layout with proper materials handling or communications, to save even more and make the work require less effort and time. An important aspect in installing is to avoid losses in production. For simple changes it is not serious. For more extensive changes, the problem has other aspects. Here it is important to get the changes made with the least difficulty in production and to get them made in relation to change orders for material, parts, etc. The installation must be planned well to avoid problems and difficulties.

2. Train the operators and others involved

New methods, whether improvements or new designs, usually involve training people. There are many ways of training. It may range all the way from just a simple word or two to the employee to extensive training programs in the plant. The employee may be given written instructions about what is expected. It may be necessary to have someone spend two or three hours with the employee reviewing the method. It may be necessary to take the operator from his production job for a period of one, two, or more days to the training department, where he would be given specialized training in certain procedures and skills.

Obviously, the techniques for training are varied. A spoken word might be completely satisfactory for conveying training information for some situations. In other cases it might be necessary to have someone perform the operation hand pattern for demonstration purposes. Motion pictures can be used either with slow motion or regular projection close-up to show the operator how to do the job. Still photographs are frequently employed. Bins and tools and other workplace materials can be color-coded to assist in training. Even closed-circuit television has been employed to help train operators.

A convenient and easy means of training operators, providing them with a constant reference and also providing supervisors with a means of checking and controlling methods, is the written standard procedure (WSP), sometimes called operator instruction sheet or even standard operating procedure. The WSP outlines in simple, direct terms the method to be used by the employee. The WSP should not be confused with the operation *sheet,* or the list of operations for modifying the product. The WSP outlines how each of the operations in a modification sequence is to be performed. No symbols are used, nor are any of the technical abbreviations, such as therbligs, used on the WSP. Ordinarily the foreman as well as the employee gets a copy of the WSP. If any difficulties arise, the foreman can check the conditions surrounding the operations, as well as the method, for sources of trouble.

The WSP usually consists of three general classes of information:

The first is the general conditions and tools needed for the work. If the work is intermittent and is being set up anew frequently, the WSP can be used to determine the complete list of equipment to be obtained.

The second class of information is the description of the desired method. Varying amounts of detail can be used. For example, if the operation is one which will continue for a long period of time, then the written standard procedure would involve much greater detail than if the operation were a relatively short-run job.

The third class of information is the workplace, or flow, diagram for the work. These are usually the same as those made in step 5, detailing the new method, although it may be necessary to include more explicit instructions to the operator.

Figure 16-1 is the written standard procedure for a short-run operation. The number of units made at one time by the two men is only three or four hundred. Therefore, the description is in rather gross detail. The grossness is apparent because the cycle took over five minutes, yet the complete WSP is recorded on one and one-half 8½ by 11 sheets. Only gross activity of each man is recorded, with no definite hand pattern. The workplace diagram is shown in Fig. 16-2. (A flow diagram was not made, even though the operator moved from place to place, because the WSP detail level did not require it.)

Fig. 16-1. Written standard procedure for operation of bus duct assembly (short-run, low-volume operation for two-man crew).

Bus Duct Assembly (¼″ × 3″) *

(With or without end protectors, two-man method)

1st Man	2d Man
1. Go to covers, grasp cover at one end, and pick up with help of 2d man. Help carry cover to squeezer jig and place in position.	Go to covers, grasp cover at one end, and pick up with help of 1st man. Help carry cover to squeezer jig and place in position.
2. Pick up rabbet and two screws. Place and align rabbet and start 1st & 2d screws.	Pick up four insulators and place one in each of the four insulator brackets.
3. Go to copper bars. Grasp one bar at end and slide it toward near end of truck. Regrasp bar at center and pick up. Carry bar to cover and push through all four insulators.	Go to guide, pick it up, and place in position over insulators.
	Go to truckload of housings, grasp one at its center, and lift it over onto horses.
4. Same as step #3.	Pick up one coupling and four screws. Place and align coupling at end of housing and start each screw in its position.
5. Same as step #4.	
6. Go to center of cover, pick up guide and set it aside.	Go to labels, pick up, and place in water can to soak. Remove labels from water, bring them to housing, and put in place.†
7. Pick up four supports. Go to 1st and 2d positions and place 1st and 2d supports. Close the nearest two squeezers.	Go to end of cover and pick up rabbet and two screws. Place and align rabbet and start 1st and 2d screws.‡
8. Go to 3d & 4th positions and place 3d & 4th supports. Close the remaining two squeezers.‡	
9. Go to end of cover and pick up length of rope. Double the rope and thread it through holes in ends of bar. Tie the two ends of the rope together.†	Same as the 1st man.
10. Go to horses and grasp one end of housing. Pick up the housing with help of 2d man. Help carry housing to cover and place it on the cover so that the holes are aligned.	Same as the 1st man.
11. Pick up four screws and get power screwdriver from overhead hook. Run down the screws at the end of the duct. Place and run up one screw at each of the four screw positions. Replace screwdriver on hook.	Same as the 1st man.
12. Open all four squeezers.	
13. Go to one end of the assembled duct. Grasp and pick up with help of 2d man. Help carry duct to truck and place on truck.	Same as 1st man.

* This procedure may be used for assembly of ¼″ × 2″ duct by ignoring the second note below (‡).
† If wooden end protectors are used, place them on at this point in the cycle in the following manner:
     1st man: Pick up end protector and four screws. Hold the end protector in position and start the screws.
     2d man: Pick up end protector and four screws. Hold end protector in position and insert one screw, lock washer, and nut in each position. Tighten nut by hand until it is caught by the washer.
‡ If four copper bars are used, the 2d man puts on two supports and tightens two squeezers at this point.

Fig. 16-2. Workplace diagram for bus duct assembly.

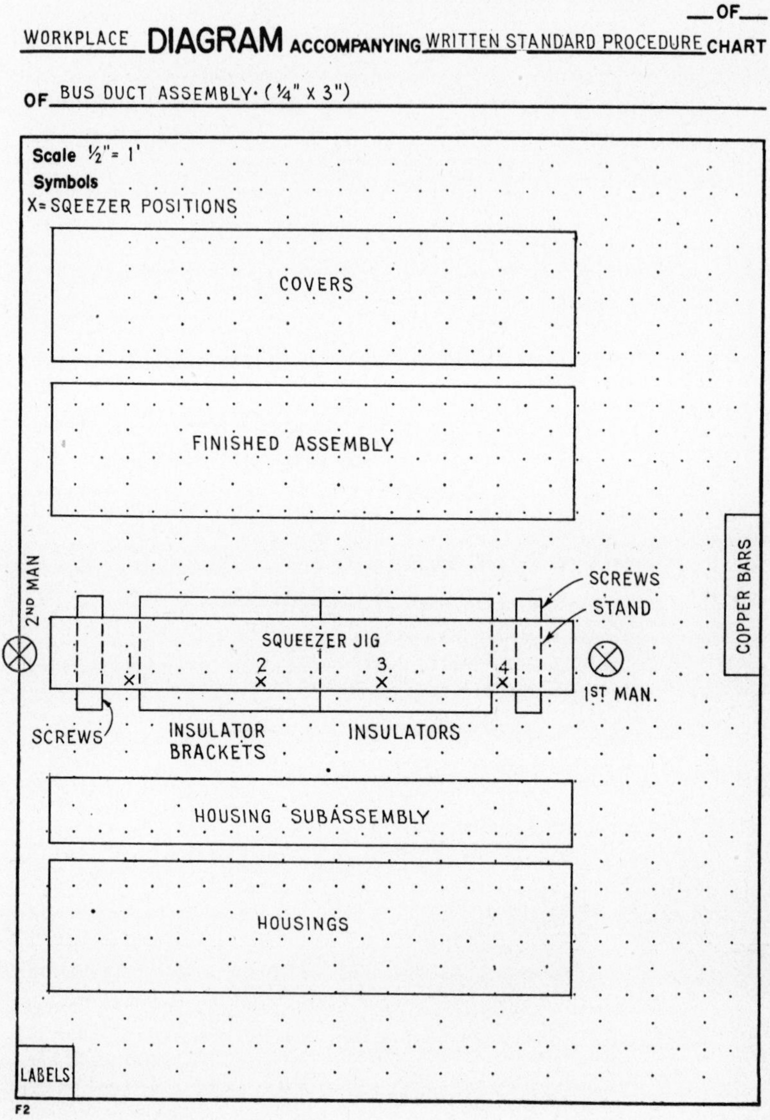

WORKPLACE **DIAGRAM** ACCOMPANYING <u>WRITTEN STANDARD PROCEDURE</u> CHART —OF—

OF <u>BUS DUCT ASSEMBLY· (¼" x 3")</u>

Scale ½"= 1'
Symbols
X= SQEEZER POSITIONS

COVERS

FINISHED ASSEMBLY

2ND MAN

SCREWS
STAND

SQUEEZER JIG

1.   2.   3.   4.
 X   X   X   X

1ST MAN.

SCREWS   INSULATOR   INSULATORS
          BRACKETS

COPPER BARS

HOUSING SUBASSEMBLY

HOUSINGS

LABELS

F2

Figure 16-3 is a WSP for a long-run, high-volume operation. Detail is so fine on this WSP that not only is the activity of each working finger noted but each working finger has the point at which it is to do its work distinctly noted. The workplace diagram is shown in Fig. 16-4.

In some cases, the WSP is enclosed in a transparent plastic cover and placed in a conspicuous location by the workplace. This permits the operator to check the method easily at any time. Such a reference is important when a new method is first installed.

3. Follow-up

Even after training, there is still a possibility that the new method will not be properly used. This could mean a poor installation, with the attendant waste of time and effort. Even though an excellent work simplification job may have been done up through training of an operator, it is still important to review periodically the method used by the employee to make certain that correct procedures are being followed. In some companies this responsibility falls on the foreman, and in other situations it falls on the work simplification analyst. In almost all situations, the supervisor will be responsible in some measure for the method being used by his operators. This is why the supervisor is a key person in work simplification. Regardless of whose responsibility it is to review methods and their performance, certainly the analyst should have enough interest and effort invested in the method to check the utilization of the new method. Many cases illustrate that if this is not done, it is possible to lose all the benefits of the work simplification procedure to this point.

In most cases the blame for not following methods falls on human beings. However, there are other reasons why a follow-up should be made. It permits a review and investigation of the whole picture. For example, a materials handling system might be good for the work originally studied. But after installation, the equipment may be utilized only 20

Fig. 16-3. Written standard procedure for operation of sewing lining, backing, and front (long-run, high-volume, short-cycle).

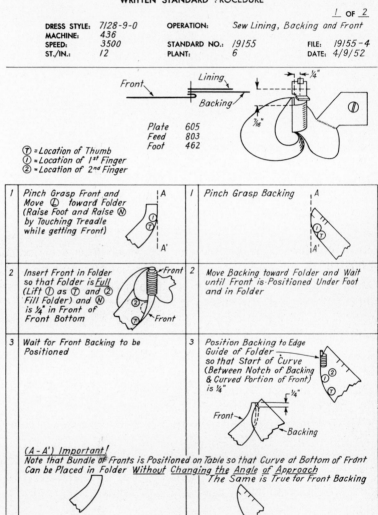

WRITTEN STANDARD PROCEDURE

_1_ OF _2_

DRESS STYLE:	7/28-9-0	OPERATION:	Sew Lining, Backing and Front		
MACHINE:	436				
SPEED:	3500	STANDARD NO.:	19155	FILE:	19155-4
ST./IN.:	12	PLANT:	6	DATE:	4/9/52

Front   Lining   ¼"
Backing

Plate   605
Feed   803
Foot   462

(T) = Location of Thumb
(1) = Location of 1st Finger
(2) = Location of 2nd Finger

1	Pinch Grasp Front and Move (L) toward Folder (Raise Foot and Raise (N) by Touching Treadle while getting Front)	1	Pinch Grasp Backing
2	Insert Front in Folder so that Folder is _Full_ (Lift (1) as (T) and (2) Fill Folder) and (N) is ¼" in Front of Front Bottom	2	Move Backing toward Folder and Wait until Front is Positioned Under Foot and in Folder
3	Wait for Front Backing to be Positioned	3	Position Backing to Edge Guide of Folder so that Start of Curve (Between Notch of Backing & Curved Portion of Front) is ¼"

(A-A') Important!
Note that Bundle of Fronts is Positioned on Table so that Curve at Bottom of Front
Can be Placed in Folder _Without Changing the Angle of Approach_
                                    The Same is True for Front Backing

FIG. 16-4. Workplace diagram for sewing lining, backing, and front.

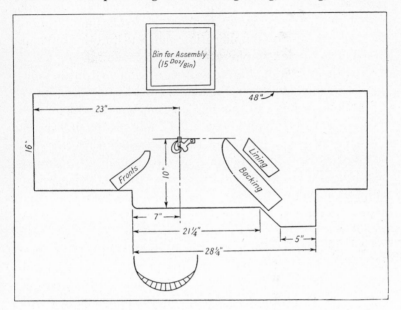

or 25 per cent of the time. So much idle time might make the whole concept more inefficient than the original work. Follow-up permits the work simplification analyst to develop complete utilization of his efforts. For example, a hospital introduced the method of keeping floor stocks of intravenous solutions. The method worked fine, but the analyst had to check on the utilization of the "saved" time because of this change. If this is not done, the free time may not become a realized benefit.

Follow-up is probably most important for operations not continually performed, but performed as needed. In these cases the worker may forget much of what was learned the last time the operation was worked on. Supposedly the supervisor is the person who assumes the greatest responsibility for methods in situations like this. Occasional checking by the analyst is not unwarranted. It is like insurance on the investment of time and effort.

The follow-up part is important for another reason: New problems develop with people and their reaction to work. Although there are many benefits of work simplification, the very process of simplification can lead to other difficulties. For example, simple work tends to make people bored with their jobs. Monotony can be a greater evil in preventing increasing effectiveness than no work simplification at all. Follow-up helps in this by detecting such problems and trying to do something about it. The answers to such problems are not always easy, but there are some ways they can be taken care of. Job rotation is an effective answer. Moving people from one job to another, even though the jobs are simple, can help eliminate some of the boredom associated with working with one job. This can almost always be done and is good to build up replacement skills.

Probably the most important way of making certain boredom and monotony do not enter the picture is to follow one of the basic tenets of work simplification: "When people know more about their own work, and help design and simplify it, they will be more interested in that work." Notice that this has been stressed throughout the various chapters on techniques and has been discussed in relation to the human relations approach in Chapter 2.

CHAPTER 17

FUNDAMENTALS OF WORK
MEASUREMENT

Many people think that work simplification consists only of the eight steps presented up to this point. After a work method has been installed, it is thought that work simplification has done its job. In many ways, this is true. Some people say there is no reason to establish a standard time after the new method has been installed. But, in most cases, these people are referring to the procedures of formal standards setting. In almost every case where work simplification is applied there is a need for some form of standards setting, although it might be informal. In this sense, work simplification requires the ninth step, standards setting. (A formal system of standards setting or work measurement is itself a large topic. It will not be possible to describe all the problems here, but this chapter will attempt to give the basic concepts.)

Whoever uses work simplification will find that there are certain types of information desired after the work simplification project has been installed. This is true even if a housewife has applied work simplification. For example, the housewife wants to know if the method she installed actually meets the objective she set up in step 1. She also wants to know what she should expect from future performances of the new method. If her objective was to save time for the purpose of using the time for charitable work, then she is interested in knowing how much time saved from her housework she can put into charitable work.

In the same way, this type of information is important in a business or industrial situation. Basically, the standards setting step tries to determine two things:

1. How well has the new method met the original objective (step 1), and how well do the final results compare with the estimate obtained in step 4?

2. What performance or production should be expected in the future from the work activity?

There are various ways of arriving at these answers. These range all the way from the complete informality of guessing what the "standard" time should be to a complete formal installation of a standards setting program to establish incentives rates. For these reasons, it is important to review the uses of such information, so that one can understand the effect of the decision to establish some sort of standards.

WHAT ARE USES OF STANDARDS?

Standards have many uses. But even more important are the requirements of organizations in relation to work performances. This will show how standards setting is important.

1. Balance work

One person cannot do everything in an organization. Work is broken up into smaller units for assignment division among many people. What is the proper division of the work? How much work should go into a specific operation? These questions must be answered properly to balance the work satisfactorily among all the operations to produce the desired end result.

2. Equipment requirements

This is a logical next use of standards. After work is balanced, it is possible to predict equipment requirements. Notice that work simplification plays an important role here. If present output on equipment is used as the basis for deciding whether or not new equipment is needed, there might be some inefficiencies included. However, if work simplification is applied first to eliminate or simplify the work, then there is a better basis for making the decision on equipment requirements. The final time, determined by standards setting, is used to establish this requirement.

3. Manpower requirements

This is another natural use after balancing the work. After the volume is established, it is necessary to determine how many people will be required for the various operations to produce the volume.

4. Production planning

What is the sequence, or order, of modifications for the product? What equipment should be used for each operation? Here again, knowing or estimating the amount of time for operations is essential.

5. Cost planning

How much should the company bid for special work or special products? How much should the selling price of a new product be? Here, it is necessary to use standards to plan costs.

6. Production control

Now that production has been planned, scheduling, dispatching, and keeping proper inventories become essential to effective operation of an organization. Time values are essential for establishing information about scheduling and inventories, or for determining how much to expect from future performances.

7. Cost control

This is likewise related to the question "How much should we expect from future performances?" Controlling costs depends on a measure, or standard, against which to compare performances. Time values are needed for many sections of cost control.

8. *Wage incentives*

Management needs to provide incentives of some sort for work activities. Although incentives are not essential, they are widely used. The other seven needs are relatively essential. This one is desirable and, if used, requires having accurate standards beyond which a person earns incentive. This is one need for which informal standards setting is not good. Formal standards setting is needed for establishing base production requirements.

BEFORE OR AFTER IMPROVEMENTS?

Why is standards setting the last step of the work simplification procedure? Some believe that it is actually a technique for work simplification. This use was presented in Chapter 11. But the problem is frequently one of whether or not to set a standard on a job which has not been improved. Basically, the techniques of a formal standards setting system can be applied to work which has not been improved. However, the best application of standards setting is to work properly designed or improved. This permits the least difficulty in bookkeeping and human relations; it is easier to establish standards for a new or simplified job. Newly designed or improved work divides itself into more readily discernible activities for the purpose of standards settings. It *is* possible to use the technique of standards setting on work not yet improved, but great care should be exercised in such cases.

STANDARDS SETTING AND THE EMPLOYEES

Any job improvement is important to the worker. The operation will have a new quota or goal, and such a change creates a problem. Of course, it is by far the most important problem, because the worker feels that this is the direct result he compares to his take-home pay. It is important to have worked with the employees through all stages, so that standards are established with a fair degree of understanding of what has gone on. Difficulty with operators can occur when no standards setting procedure is used, for example, when some form of informal arrangement governs the amount of production or service produced. A formal standards setting approach will probably be much better, because the participants know more about what is to be considered fair for both sides, as well as having a great deal more knowledge about how the final standard was established. The basic maxim is: "The more the people know about what and why, the more likely they are to cooperate."

RELATIONSHIP BETWEEN WORK SIMPLIFICATION AND WORK MEASUREMENT

There is a simple way to show the relationship of these two activities. The first eight steps of the problem-solving approach deal with the "qualitative" aspects of work, that is, "What does the work consist of?" The last step, standards setting, refers to the "quantitative" component, or "How much of the work should be done?" The information of "What work consists of" is important in establishing a "base" for standards setting. It is something like analyzing a piece of metal. The various components of the metal can be determined. But this would not be sufficient information if the amount of each material in the piece of metal were not determined. Getting both does a relatively complete job.

WHAT IS STANDARDS SETTING?

Standards setting techniques determine the time an operation should take. Of course, there are other limiting circumstances within the definition. For example, there should be a given method, given job conditions, an operator with necessary skill, and necessary training, and specified pace require-ments. Under ordinary circumstances this amount of time is called the allowed, or standard, time.

Standards setting consists of two procedures:

1. Time study for determining standard times on indi-vidual operations by a complete study of that operation while it is being performed.

2. Standard data, for determining standard times on indi-vidual operations by reference to information from indi-vidual studies, collected and arranged properly, either be-fore or during the actual performance of the operation. Since time studies form an important source for standard data, and for standard times on individual operations, more people know about it, and it is used widely because it does not need a compilation of previous information. Therefore, we will discuss time study first.

PARTS OF TIME STUDY

In general, five steps are used in the time study process. Time study is a measurement procedure, and the various steps are designed to make certain that the measurements are accurate, that all measurements are made. Of course, dealing with human beings presents problems. It will not be the purpose of this presentation to dissect completely every part of time study to present its problems and its good points. Rather, it is desired to give some idea of what time study consists in actual application, and to provide other sources for more complete and detailed descriptions of the time study procedure.[1]

1. Methods description

This step requires that the method for which the time will be determined be recorded in detail in relation to the accuracy required. This is somewhat different from the

[1] See G. Nadler, *Motion and Time Study*, New York: McGraw-Hill Book Company, Inc., 1955, chaps. 20–25.

methods description obtained in step 5, detailing the new method. In step 5 the problem was to determine the method to be used in terms of workability.

In methods description, there are several problems. People perform the "same" method in slightly different ways. The first problem in this area is to determine what method should be recorded from among the slight variations present. Another problem concerns the amount of detail adequate for the description under the conditions of the operation. Is the operation long-run and high-volume? Then much accuracy and detail will be required. The third problem represents a serious one in relation to maintenance of time standards. What means can be used to detect methods differences between operators and within one operator from one cycle to another?

In many ways if the third question is answered by saying that we need a lot of detail, then the second problem and, in many cases, the first problem are taken care of as well.

The purpose for asking these questions becomes apparent when you realize that a time value (quantitative) must always be associated with a method (qualitative) of work. If the work changes, then the time value is no good. The times obtained must be related to a specific method. Detailed methods descriptions are desirable. Then a change in the method will be more easily detected, and subsequent changes in time values can be made too.

Methods Description Objectives. To accomplish the task, three objectives should be met:

1. All conditions surrounding the job must be recorded. This includes everything, like machine numbers, materials handling requirements, general working conditions, tooling, and even parts drawings.

2. Everything the operator does on and for the operation should be recorded. This includes maintenance requirements, tool maintenance and requisition requirements, materials handling activities, inspection requirements.

3. All the above information should be recorded with

enough detail so that the operation could be performed again at a later time or another place as recorded. This reiterates the problem of making certain that a given method is associated with a given standard time.

Recording the method does not involve too many special techniques. An important one is methods consciousness and the ability to "look" into a method. Generally, this requires that the work be divided into elements to make the measurements more realistic and simple. It then becomes possible to use these elements in standard data, described later.

An element is a series of therbligs which tend to be grouped together to make a realistic work unit. This work unit is more readily observable, and even at this stage of the work simplification procedure, it might even be possible to find some slight improvements. The elements permit such improvements to be made, because making elements forces the analyst to look into all parts of the method even though he may have been the one to improve or design it. *All* the work the operator must do should be described in elements.

Figure 17-1 shows a typical time study sheet with a typical methods description on it. The underlined words in the elemental descriptions refer to the end point of the element at which point the time value is obtained.

2. *Timing*

The timing step obtains information about the actual time an operator takes on the job. There are various ways of getting these time values, but all of them obtain information in terms of elements. The basic purpose of the timing step is to determine the average time the operator takes to perform each element.

Depending upon the accuracy required, there are many techniques for timing. Electronic devices determine very accurate information. Motion pictures are another way of obtaining highly accurate information. The paper-tape recording machine is activated by pushing buttons to give somewhat accurate results. The most usual way of obtaining

Fig. 17-1. Methods description for packing belts (finer detail without therbligs).

TIME STUDY SHEET

—OF—
Workplace
Diagram
Attached

FOR PACK BELT

DATE 6/22/50 PART BELT-CARD-BOX Operator E.V. Mach SEALER

By H.L. No. 570 - 4 - 28 No. 62 No. 14

Appr Drawing SPEC.570 Dept. PACKING Fixtures —

Appr Time started Time finished Tools —

Remarks

No.	Left hand description	Right hand description	Notes	Rating	Allow. time
1	Idle While Right Hand Grasps Belt Overarm, Left Hand Grasps and Straightens Belt, Release and Get Card, Hold While Right Hand Assembles Tab, Hold and Fold Belt Around Right Side, then Left Side, Hold Assembly.	Grasp Belt from Left Arm, Move to Table, Straighten with Left Hand Hold Until Left Hand Gets Card, Insert Tab in Slot, Fold Belt Around Right Side of Card, Then Left Side, Release Assembly.			
2	Hold Assembly for Right Hand Release Assembly	Move to Printed Tape, Pick Up and Move to Assembly, Fold Tape Around Assembly, Hold Assembly			
3	Move to Boxes, Pick Up and Place on Table, Grasp Assembly, Place in Box, Adjust Pin, Release Assembly in Box.	Hold Until Left Hand Gets Box, Move to Left Hand, Help Assemble in Box, Hold in Box			
4	Move to Cellophane Pick Up Piece, to Box, Place on Box, Help Turn Box Over, Fold Up Bottom of Cello, Hold for Seal.	Hold for Left Hand to Place Cello on Top, Turn Box Over, Fold Down Top of Cello, Place Under Sealer, Right Foot Press Pedal, Sealer Strikes Cello First Time.			
5	Fold Over Left Side of Cello, Seal, Hold for Right Side Fold and Seal, Slide to Chute, Release Box.	Hold for Leftside Seal, Fold Over Right Side, Hold for Seal, Slide to Chute, Release Box.			
a	Get Supply of Belts from Rack Behind Operator		$1/15$		
	TOTAL ALLOWED TIME per _____ pieces, in_____				

F4F

the time values is through stop watches. This is not the most accurate means of obtaining time, as indicated by its placement in this list of timing devices from most accurate to least accurate. But stop watches represent a good way of obtaining time values. Sweep-second wrist watches are another way, of slightly less accuracy. The occurrence study, or work sampling, can be used to obtain some time values of a relatively inaccurate nature for some gross work. It is even possible to use the wall clock for inaccurate timing. And last, and probably most inaccurate, is the procedure where the operator records his work times. Here, the elements become long, and the inaccuracies are quite apparent. However, all the techniques are usable, and they should be selected when the requirements indicate their amount of accuracy.

A frequent problem in timing concerns the number of readings that should be taken to obtain an average time. There are many statistical techniques which can be used to check accuracy of the number of readings, if anyone gets into this problem.

Figure 17-2 shows the back of the time study sheet shown in Fig. 17-1. On this side the time values are recorded.

FIG. 17-2. An example of one type of time value recording, continuous readings of decimal-minute stop watch.

Cycles		1		2		3		4		5		6		7		8		9		10		11		12		13		14		15		Notes and Irregular
No	Element end point	R	T	R	T	R	T	R	T	R	T	R	T	R	T	R	T	R	T	R	T	R	T	R	T	R	T	R	T	R	T	Element Descriptions
1	RH−RL Assem	11	11	50	15	88	15	28	14	68	16	10	14	53	15	93	15	19	19	60	16	18	18	55	16	17	17	57	15	98	16	
2	LH−RL Assem	17	6	56	6	96	8	32	4	76	8	16	6	61	8	99	6	25	6	65	5	22	4	60	5	21	4	62	5	03	5	
3	LH−RL In Box	22	5	61	5	02	6	38	6	82	6	22	6	67	6	05	6	31	6	73	8	28	6	65	5	29	8	68	6	10	7	
4	RH−Sealer 1st Time	28	6	67	6	07	5	45	7	88	6	29	7	72	5	09	4	38	7	79	6	32	4	92f		35	6	75	7	15	5	
5	RH−RL Box	35	7	73	6	14	7	52	7	96	8	38	9	78	6	15	6	44	6	85	6	39	7	00	8	42	7	82	7	21	6	
6	a − Get Belts															00	85			X				00						98	77	
7																																
8																																
9	1	16	18	73f		17	17																									
10	2	21	5	80	7	23	6																									
11	3	27	6	88	8	29	6																									
12	4	32	5	94	6	35	6																									f = Fumble
13	5	40	8	00	6	41	6																									X = Personal
	ELEMENT	1		2		3		4		5		6		7		8		9		10		11		12		13		14		15		Symbols
	BODY MEMBER																															
Elemental	FOOT PEDAL																															
	TWO HANDS																															
Difficulty	WEIGHT																															
	POS. E−H																															
Comparison	DIR. E−H																															
	PRES. CONT.																															
	CONT.																															

Notice that the elemental end points are listed down the left side of the sheet.

3. Measuring operator performance

Everyone knows that two people performing on the same job will not likely produce the same amount. It is possible that two people could do this, but most of the time this would not happen. When timing is done on one operator, it must be recognized that this operator might be faster than another, or slower, or take just about the average amount of time that we *should* allow for the work. This means that when there is only one operator on the job, it is important to measure his performance to see how it compares with the rest of the people in the plant or organization. The measurement of an operator's performance is used to modify the average time. For example, if the performance of the operator is better than what might be expected of the "average," or "standard," operator, the time values obtained from his performance would have to be adjusted to include more time. If the person on whom the time study was taken was performing at a level below the expected, then his time values would have to be reduced. This process is called rating.

Rating represents one of the biggest problems in time study. It requires the time study man to make some sort of judgment of what the operator is doing. Much research work is going on to eliminate the judgment, but at the present time this judgment still remains. There have been many systems proposed for the rating process, but all of them presently still require judgment. Some of the "systems" are the over-all evaluation procedure, which gives a general performance per cent to over-all production; a good-performance measurement, which uses much mental judgment; mathematical or statistical procedures (none of which are anywhere near effective, because they still leave the problem of adjustment); the Westinghouse system, sometimes called the leveling system, which tries to measure the skill and effort of individuals; and the most common system today—that of measuring speed—where the time study man compares the speed of the operator to a standard speed. In most cases speed seems to be the correct measurement, but the means of making the measurement are still in question and can present some problems.

The important consideration about rating is that, even with its problems, it attempts to make a much better prediction of how long an operation should take than if we use the plain time values obtained from the timing step. At least, rating tends to bring the time values closer to the amount of time the operation "should take."

As mentioned above, the most common procedure for rating is to compare the speed of motions of the operator being studied to a standard speed of motions. This permits a measurement of whether an operator is faster or slower than the standard, and then the average time values can be adjusted. All supervisors and operators should know about how time studies are made, because this information in their hands can help immeasurably to make this measurement more realistic.

Figure 17-3 shows the bottom of an ordinary time study sheet filled in with the average time for each element and the measurement of pace (called rating, or pace comparison) included. The time values have now been adjusted to the point which is representative of a standard speed.

4. Difficulty measurements

The measurement of speed has been made in comparison with a standard speed, but this standard does not include any difficulty. It is important to determine how much difficulty is present in the job being studied to determine how much it affected the pace of the operator. The difficulty measurement, in effect, adds time to the operation, because the difficulty factors reduce the pace, or speed, at which an

Fig. 17-3. Bottom of back of time study sheet of first man on bus duct assembly, showing how pace comparisons and time at standard pace for each element are entered on the sheet.

1st Man — Elements

No.	Element end point
1	RL Cover in Jig
2	RL 2nd Screw
3	RL 1st Copper Bar
4	RL 2nd "
5	RL 3rd "
6	RL Guide
7	RL 2nd Squeezer
8	RL 4th Squeezer
9	RL Tied Rope
10	Finish Aligning
11	RL Screwdriver
12	Open 4th Squeezer
13	RL Duct

Notes and Irregular Element Descriptions

a - Retap Hole
b - Adjust Protector
c - Copper Bar Jam
d - Get Truck
e - Move Skids
f - Relocate Guides
g - Hammer Points
h - Difficult Start on Rabbets
j - Bad Fit on Housing
k - Adjust Duct on Truck

Symbols

M - Wait for 2nd Man
⊗ - Personal Time
D - Unavoidable Delay
S - Drop Screw
* = Letter is the Sequence on the Step Film which was Closest to Operator Pace on Element

For Summary of Times of Irregular Occurrences, See Sheet Attached

Summary rows (Elements 1–13)

	1	2	3	4	5	6	7	8	9	10	11	12	13
Total time in Sec	49	201	196	90	148	158	133	377	328	106	239	168	82
No. of observations	11	9	11	7	11	11	9	11	10	8	6	12	10
Average time	4.5	22.3	17.8	12.9	13.5	14.4	14.8	34.3	32.8	13.2	39.8	14.0	8.2
Pace comparison *	E93	C80	C80	C80	C80	C80	C80	B73	C80	C80	C80	D87	E93
Time at std. pace	4.2	17.8	14.2	10.3	10.8	11.5	11.8	25.0	26.2	10.6	31.8	12.2	7.6

Left-side row labels (below element data):

ELEMENT

Elemental — BODY MEMBER, FOOT PEDAL, TWO HANDS
Difficulty — WEIGHT, POS. E–H, DIR. E–H
Comparison — PRES. CONT., TILT CONT.
Details
TOTAL

Cycle Allowance — PERSONAL, IRREGULAR, DELAY
Details — MACH. CONT.
TOTAL

Total time in Sec
No. of observations
Average time
Pace comparison *
Time at std. pace
I — Difficulty comp.
Base time
I + Allowances
ALLOWED TIME

↑ Frame = 1 Sec

259

operator can work. This step is sometimes performed at the same time as the measurement of speed. It all depends on the system that is being used. If the latest system of using motion pictures as step, or standard speed, film is used, then the measurement of difficulty is separated as indicated here.

Measuring difficulty is simplified somewhat because much industrial installation and research have been able to find adjustment values for the various difficulty factors. The factors now being used in measuring difficulty are amount of body used, foot pedals, simultaneous symmetrical or alternate hand pattern, weight or resistance, positional eye-hand coordination, directional eye-hand coordination, muscular pressure control, and muscular tilt control. Even a rough study would show how these factors tend to reduce the pace of the operator. The procedure uses a table [2] of values for each difficulty factor found to affect the speed, or pace, of the work being studied. The amount of pace reduction for each factor is listed, and this value would be entered on the time study sheet, as illustrated in Fig. 17-4, to permit complete adjustment. The time values at the bottom of Fig. 17-4 give the amount of time that the *element* should take.

FIG. 17-4. Bottom of back of time study sheet of first man on bus duct assembly, showing how difficulty comparison and base time for each element are entered on the sheet.

	ELEMENT	1	2	3	4	5	6	7	8	9	10	11	12	13	14	15	Symbols
Elemental Difficulty Comparison Details	BODY MEMBER	5	2	5	5	5	5	2	5	1	5	3	2	5			
	FOOT PEDAL	0	0	0	0	0	0	0	0	0	0	0	0	0			
	TWO HANDS	0	0	0	0	0	0	0	0	0	0	0	0	0			
	WEIGHT	$^E15$	$_B4$	$^{30m}26$	$_B26$	$_B26$	$_B2$	$_B5$	$_B3$	$_B0$	$^{B}13$	$^{20m}18$	$_B3$	$^{75m}40$			
	POS. E-H	B1	A2	A3	A3	A3	B4	A1	A2	A1	A1	A4	0	B1			Occurrences,
	DIR. E-H	0	0	1	1	1	0	0	0	1	1	0	1	0			
	PRES. CONT.	0	0	0	0	0	0	0	0	0	0	2	0	0			
	TILT CONT.	0	0	2	2	2	2	0	0	0	0	0	0	2			
	TOTAL	21	8	37	37	37	13	8	10	3	20	27	6	48			Irregular
Cycle Allowance Details	PERSONAL																of Times of
	IRREGULAR																2 Attached
	DELAY																Sheet
	MACH. CONT.																See
	TOTAL																
Total time in Sec.		49	201	196	90	148	158	133	377	328	106	239	168	82			
No. of observations		11	9	11	7	11	11	9	11	10	8	6	12	10			Times of
Average time		4.5	22.3	17.8	12.9	13.5	14.4	14.8	34.3	32.8	13.2	39.8	14.0	8.2			
Pace comparison		E93	C80	C80	C80	C80	C80	C80	B73	C80	C80	C80	D87	E93			Summary of
Time at std. pace		4.2	17.8	14.2	10.3	10.8	11.5	11.8	25.0	26.2	10.6	31.8	12.2	7.6			
1 — Difficulty comp.		.79	.92	.63	.63	.63	.87	.92	.90	.97	.80	.73	.94	.52			For
Base time		5.32	19.3	22.3	16.3	17.1	13.2	12.8	27.8	27.0	13.4	43.5	13.0	14.6			
1 + Allowances																	
ALLOWED TIME																	

[2] *Ibid.*, chap. 24.

5. *Allowances*

The elements of an ordinary job are not always performed without some other factors affecting the continual performance of the elements. For example, each individual must have some personal time. Likewise, there are requirements for getting material, getting trucks, moving material, tool replacement, etc. In addition, there are delays, like a machine breakdown, maintenance men coming into the area and stopping work, or no parts to work on. All these factors tend to stop a person from working at the regular job. Therefore, allowances for these personal times, irregular occurrences, and delays must be made to permit complete and fair standard times to be developed. Most of the time, this information is determined within the plant, and from the operation involved. There are various techniques used to do this. Even the occurrence study is an important technique in developing information on irregular occurrences and delays. By finding this information, it is possible to convert all the time values and measurements into the final desired standard time. A complete time study sheet is shown in Fig. 17-5, and all the time values are added to give the total shown in the lower right-hand corner. This is the time value for a unit of production, the end results of the time study procedure.

STANDARD DATA

There are many advantages to using standard data. Less time is required; simplification and balance of work can be done before production actually starts; costs and schedules can be predicted before work is started; somewhat greater accuracy and consistency can be obtained from standard data; and standard data are more economical to apply for arriving at standards. To accomplish these objectives and advantages, there are two types of standard data: One is

No.	Element end point	1 R	1 T	2 R	2 T	3 R	3 T	4 R	4 T	5 R	5 T	6 R	6 T	7 R	7 T	8 R	8 T	9 R	9 T	10 R	10 T	11 R	11 T	12 R	12 T	13 R	13 T	14 R	14 T	15 R	15 T	Notes and Irregular Element Descriptions
	1st Man Cycles																															
1	RL Cover in Jig	20	X	4	5	35	4	05	5	82	5	03	4	44	4	95	4	51	5	60	4	07	4	89	5							a- Retap Hole
2	RL 2nd Screw	40	20	27	23	57	22	32	27	08	26	21	18	65	21	14	19	87^b		94^s		52^s	45	14	25							b- Adjust Protector
3	RL 1st Copper Bar	63	23	43	16	78	21	53	21	46^c	38	39	18	82	17	29	15	02	15	11	17	69	17	30	16							c- Copper Bar Jam
4	RL 2nd " "	91^k		57	14	07^x		89^c	36	61	15	50	11	04^h	22	43	14	14	12	23	12	81	12	54^c	24							d- Get Truck
5	RL 3rd " "	10^α		69	12	19	12	03	14	75	14	65	15	16	12	60	17	26	12	36	13	95	14	67	13							e- Move Skids
6	RL Guide	23	13	88^x		35	16	19	16	89	14	79	14	33	17	75	15	39	13	48	12	09	14	81	14							f- Relocate Guides
7	RL 2nd Squeezer	36	13	01	13	51	16	34	15	16^g	27	03^x		49	16	90	15	55	16	63	15	23	14	03^x								
8	RL 4th Squeezer	73	37	34	33	91	40	68	34	51	35	32	29	80	31	31	41	37^x		98	35	53	30	35	32							g- Hammer Points
9	RL Tied Rope	04	31	68	34	32^x		05^f	37	84	33	62	30	14	34	65	34	75	38	33	35	82	29	65	30							h- Difficult Start on Rabbets
10	Finish Aligning	20	16	82	14	48	16	22	17	10^j	26	75	13	36^x		74	9	85	10	44	11	19^g		86^j	21							
11	RL Screwdriver	61	41	96^g	14	14	33	81	33	51^e	29	76^g	76	15	40	71	35	26^h	52	31	46	83	39	65^g	70	24	38					j- Bad Fit on Housing
12	Open 4th Squeezer	75	14	12	16	93	12	66	15	91	15	30	15	84	13	38	12	48	17	96	13	77	12	38	14							k- Adjust Duct on Truck
13	RL Duct	99^k	24	22^m		00	7	77	11	99	8	40	10	91	7	46	8	56	8	03	7	84	7									

	ELEMENT	1	2	3	4	5	6	7	8	9	10	11	12	13	14	15	Symbols
		1	31 2 9	3	4	5	6	7	8	9	10	841 200	12	13	14	15	
Elemental Difficulty	BODY MEMBER	5	2	5	5	5	5	2	5	1	5	3	2	5			M- Wait for 2nd Man
	FOOT PEDAL	0	0	0	0	0	0	0	0	0	0	0	0	0			Ⓧ- Personal Time
	TWO HANDS	0	0	0	0	0	0	0	0	0	0	0	0	0			D- Unavoidable Delay
	WEIGHT	10^{H}B15	B4	30^{H}B26	B26	B26	B2	B5	B3	B0	8^{H}B13	20^{H}B18	B3	75^{H}B40			S- Drop Screw
Comparison Details	POS. E-H	B1	A2	A3	A3	A3	B4	A1	A2	A1	A1	A4	0	B1			
	DIR. E-H	0	0	1	1	1	0	0	0	1	0	1	0				
	PRES. CONT.	0	0	0	0	0	0	0	0	0	0	2	0	0			
	TILT CONT.	0	0	2	2	2	1	0	0	0	0	0	0	2			
	TOTAL	21	8	37	37	37	13	8	10	3	20	27	6	48			
Cycle Allowance Details	PERSONAL	30															
	IRREGULAR	84	From Ratio Delay					121 x 100		12100		=34%					
	DELAY	7			121			480-121		359							
	MACH. CONT.										0						
	TOTAL										34%						
	Total time in Sec.	49	201	196	90	148	158	133	377	328	106	239	168	82			
	No. of observations	11	9	11	7	11	11	9	11	10	8	6	12	10			
	Average time	4.5	22.3	17.8	12.9	13.5	14.4	14.8	34.3	32.8	13.2	39.8	14.0	8.2			
	Pace comparison	E 93	C 80	C 80	C 80	C 80	C 80	C 80	B 73	C 80	B 80	C 80	D 87	E 93			
	Time at std. pace	4.2	17.8	14.2	10.3	10.8	11.5	11.8	25.0	26.2	10.6	31.8	12.2	7.6			
	I — Difficulty comp.	.79	.92	.63	.63	.63	.87	.92	.90	.97	.80	.73	.94	.52			
	Base time	5.32	19.3	22.3	16.3	17.1	13.2	12.8	27.8	27.0	13.4	43.5	13.0	14.6		245.6	Total of Reg. Elem.
	I + Allowances															1.34	
	ALLOWED TIME															329.5	For Regular Elements

I Frame = I Sec

For Summary of Times of Irregular Occurrences, See Sheet 2 Attached

FIG. 17-5. Back of time study sheet, showing the complete information recorded for the first operator of the bus duct assembly.

called basic motion standard data, and the second is called elemental standard data.

1. Basic motion standard data

This type is similar to the approximate therblig times presented in Chapter 8. As presented there, such a system is not highly accurate because of the nature of motions, combinations of motions, and the inability to get time values at the proper pace level for each motion. Although the time values for these therblig times are "average," there is nothing to indicate that the organizations to which they are being applied have "average" activities or motions. The therblig times can be used for approximation of the standards for operations. This might be somewhat similar to using an informal, or closer to the informal, type of standards setting system.

In addition to the approximate therblig times presented in Chapter 8, there are many commercial systems of predetermined time values available for establishing estimates of time standards. They have various names, such as Motion-Time-Analysis, Methods-Time-Measurement, Work-Factor, Dimensional-Motion-Times, and Basic Motion-Timestudy. These systems and the approximate therblig time should be used with care when attempting to establish quotas or goals, and especially incentive standards, for operations.

2. Elemental standard data

This type is the direct result of time studies. Elemental standard data, because they come from time studies within the organization, are usually more accurate and consistent than basic motion standard data. At least, elemental standard data will more likely fit the organization for which it was developed.

The basic concept behind elemental standard data is that similar elements appearing in various jobs in the plants should be combined and organized for use later. Some elements might require the same amount of time. These are called constant elements. There are elements which might vary with certain physical characteristics, like weight, size, or number of slots. These are called variable elements, and the various time studies are used to determine how the variations affect time. These relationships are expressed in terms of curves, tables, graphs, or formulas.

The analyst determines what elements are present in a job and then looks in the tables or graphs to determine how much time should be allowed for each element. These element times are added to arrive at the standard time for the job.

Some types of elemental standard data can be developed from past performances, rather than from a formal standards setting system. Such data involve large errors. They require someone familiar with formal time study and elemental standard data, so that the values are meaningful for their purposes. Where applicable, past performance data are useful in work simplification and work measurement.

FUTURE OF WORK SIMPLIFICATION

The challenge for work simplification is ever increasing. Automation needs are going to increase the requirements for work simplification even further. Simplifying work before it is automated is important. Simplifying and arranging the work of the engineers and technicians needed for automated factories is even still more important, so that we can better utilize this class of skilled personnel.

The advent of more nonrepetitive work in all organizations and activities, and higher labor costs, are other reasons why more work simplification will be needed.

Work simplification will grow in usage, because it is being accepted more. Labor is starting to learn more about what work simplification is and why it is needed. It is willing to adopt methods of work simplification. Management understands employees better. This means more understanding about who should get the results and benefits.

Research is going on in many areas (like industrial engineering, electronics, psychology, and physiology) to develop new techniques to help supervisors and engineers in performing work simplification. These activities promise a good future for work simplification too.

Work simplification has helped increase our standard of living by increasing productivity and reducing waste effort. It is important for everyone to be concerned with simplifying their own work and the work of those they supervise. Work simplification provides techniques which give any individual a clear insight into what work is and what it is composed of. This book has presented some of the simple techniques which can be used to gather the facts and to pursue the objective of making the most of our time.

A BRIEF BIBLIOGRAPHY

BOOKS

Alford, L. P., and J. R. Bangs (eds.): *Production Handbook,* New York: The Ronald Press Company, 1944.

Apple, J. M.: *Plant Layout and Materials Handling,* New York: The Ronald Press Company, 1950.

Bailey, N. R.: *Motion Study for the Supervisor,* New York: McGraw-Hill Book Company, Inc., 1942.

Barish, N. N.: *Systems Analysis for Effective Administration,* New York: Funk & Wagnalls Company, 1951.

Barnes, R. M.: *Motion and Time Study,* 3d ed., New York: John Wiley & Sons, Inc., 1948.

Barnes, R. M.: *Work Methods Manual,* New York: John Wiley & Sons, Inc., 1944.

Barnes, R. M.: *Work Methods Training Manual,* 3d ed., Dubuque, Iowa: William C. Brown Company, 1950.

Beckman, R. O.: *How to Train Supervisors,* 4th ed., New York: Harper & Brothers, 1952.

Chane, G. W.: *Motion and Time Study,* New York: Harper & Brothers, 1942.

Chapanis, A., W. R. Garner, and C. T. Morgan: *Applied Experimental Psychology,* New York: John Wiley & Sons, Inc., 1949.

Copley, F. B.: *Frederick W. Taylor, Father of Scientific Management,* vols. 1 and 2, New York: Harper & Brothers, 1923.

Emerson, H.: *The Twelve Principles of Efficiency,* 5th ed., Engineering Management Co., New York, 1917.

Gilbreth, F. B.: *Motion Study,* Princeton, N.J.: D. Van Nostrand Company, Inc., 1911.

Gilbreth, F. B., and L. M. Gilbreth: *Applied Motion Study,* New York: Sturgis & Walton Co., 1917.

Gilbreth, F. B., and L. M. Gilbreth: *Motion Study for the Handicapped*, London: Routledge and Kegan Paul, Ltd., 1920.

Grant, E. L.: *Principles of Engineering Economy*, New York: The Ronald Press Company, 1938.

Hendry, J. W.: *A Manual of Time and Motion Study*, New York: Pitman Publishing Corporation, 1946.

Holmes, W. G.: *Applied Time and Motion Study*, New York: The Ronald Press Company, 1938.

Hoslett, S. D.: *Human Factors in Management*, New York: Harper & Brothers, 1946.

Kosma, A. R.: *The A.B.C.'s of Motion Economy*, Institute of Motion Analysis and Human Relations, Newark, N.J., 1943.

Lesperance, J. P.: *Economics and Techniques of Motion and Time Study*, Dubuque, Iowa: William C. Brown Company, 1953.

Mathewson, S. B.: *Restriction of Output among Unorganized Workers*, New York: The Viking Press, Inc., 1931.

Maynard, H. B., and G. J. Stegemerten: *Operation Analysis*, New York: McGraw-Hill Book Company, Inc., 1939.

Maynard, H. B., G. J. Stegemerten, and J. L. Schwab: *Methods–Time Measurement*, New York: McGraw-Hill Book Company, Inc., 1948.

Mayo, E.: *The Human Problems of an Industrial Civilization*, New York: The Macmillan Company, 1933.

Mogensen, A. H.: *Common Sense Applied to Motion and Time Study*, New York: McGraw-Hill Book Company, Inc., 1932.

Morrow, R. L.: *Time Study and Motion Economy*, New York: The Ronald Press Company, 1946.

Mundel, M. E.: *Motion and Time Study Principles and Practice*, 2d ed., Englewood Cliffs, N.J.: Prentice-Hall, Inc., 1955.

Nadler, G.: *Motion and Time Study*, New York: McGraw-Hill Book Company, Inc., 1955.

Parton, J. A., Jr.: *Motion and Time Study Manual*, New York: Conover–Mast Corporation, 1952.

Pear, T. H.: *Skill in Work and Play*, New York: E. P. Dutton & Co., Inc., 1924.

Ryan, T. A.: *Work and Effort*, New York: The Ronald Press Company, 1947.

Sampter, H. C.: *Motion Study*, New York: Pitman Publishing Corporation, 1941.

Scott, M. G.: *Analysis of Human Motion*, New York: A. S. Barnes and Company, 1942.

Shaw, A. G.: *The Purpose and Practice of Motion Study*, Manchester: Harlequin Press Co., Ltd., 1952.

Shevlin, J. D.: *Time Study and Motion Economy for Supervisors*, National Foremen's Institute, Deep River, Conn., 1945.

Thuesen, H. B.: *Engineering Economy*, Englewood Cliffs, N.J.: Prentice-Hall, Inc., 1951.

Tiffin, J.: *Industrial Psychology*, 2d ed., Englewood Cliffs, N.J.: Prentice-Hall, Inc., 1947.

Vaughan, L. M., and L. S. Hardin: *Farm Work Simplification*, New York: John Wiley & Sons, Inc., 1949.

Viteles, M. S.: *The Science of Work*, New York: W. W. Norton & Company, Inc., 1934.

BULLETINS, PERIODICALS, AND SPECIAL REPORTS

Advanced Management, monthly, Society for Advancement of Management, Inc., New York.

Bibliography of Time and Motion Study, 1933–1939, The John Crerar Library, Chicago.

Bibliography of Time Study Engineering, Society of Industrial Engineers, New York: The H. W. Wilson Company, 1933.

Factory Management and Maintenance, monthly, McGraw-Hill Publishing Company, Inc., New York.

Glossary of Terms Used in Methods Time Study and Wage Incentives, Society for Advancement of Management, Inc., New York, 1952.

Handbook of Human Engineering Data, 2d ed., Technical Report SDC 199-1-2, Tufts College Institute of Applied Experimental Psychology, Office of Naval Research, Special Devices Center, Medford, Mass., 1951.

Heinle, G. F.: *A Method of Measuring Delays in Production*, Bemis Bag Co., Engineering Dept., St. Louis, Mo., 1952.

Industrial Engineering Institute Proceedings, annual from 1949, University of California, Berkeley, Calif.

Industrial Fatigue (Health) Research Board, H.M. Stationery Office, London.

Iron Age, weekly, Chilton Co., Philadelphia.

Journal of Industrial Engineering, bimonthly, American Institute of Industrial Engineers, Columbus, Ohio.

Management Engineering Conference Proceedings, annual from 1949, A. & M. College of Texas, College Station, Texas.

Management Review, monthly, American Management Association, New York.

Manufacturing Series Reports, American Management Association, New York.

Mill and Factory, monthly, Conover–Mast Corporation, New York.

Motion and Time Study Work Sessions, 5 reports, Purdue University, Lafayette, Ind.

Fatigue of Workers, Its Relation to Industrial Production, National Research Council, New York: Reinhold Publishing Corporation, 1941.

Personnel, monthly, American Management Association, New York.

Proceedings, Annual Conference and Convention, American Institute of Industrial Engineers, Columbus, Ohio.

Research Reports, MTM Association for Standards and Research, Ann Arbor, Mich.

Simplifying Procedures through Forms Control, Management Bulletin, Government Printing Office, 1948.

Smalley, H. E.: *Predetermined Standards for Typing,* preliminary study, University of Connecticut, Storrs, Conn., 1954.

Studies in Engineering, Bulletins 6, 12, 16, 17, 21, and 22, University of Iowa, Iowa City, Iowa.

Supervisor's Guide to the Process Chart, Work Simplification Program, Government Printing Office, 1948.

Supervisor's Guide to the Work Distribution Chart, Work Simplification Program, Government Printing Office, 1948.

T. Mangan: *The Knack of Selling Yourself,* The Dartwell Corp., Chicago, 1951.

Time and Motion Study Clinic Proceedings, annual from 1937, Industrial Management Society, Chicago.

Time Study and Methods Conference Proceedings, annual from 1946, Society for Advancement of Management, Inc., New York.

Turret Lathe and Hand Screw Machine Standard Data, E. A. Cyrol & Company, Chicago, 1952.

A Work Measurement System–Development and Use (*A Case Study*), Management Bulletin, Government Printing Office, 1950.

Work Simplification, Maytag Co., Newton, Iowa.

Work Simplification Manual, Servel, Inc., Evansville, Ind., 1951.

MOTION-PICTURE BIBLIOGRAPHY

Motion pictures have become an indispensable aid to the teaching of work simplification classes in the university, plant, hospital, etc. Many motion pictures have been produced to demonstrate various aspects of the subject matter. Problems for solution by the group are also recorded on film as a further assistance in explaining concept. The following list of films is arranged to correspond with the chapters of this book. The potential users of any film, however, should review it before using in order to determine its suitability for a particular group. The title of a film is generally followed by the name of a source for the film. In many cases the film is available only from the source named. However, it probably will be more convenient for film users to contact the nearest film library before trying any other source. The addresses of the sources mentioned below follow the bibliography. Unless otherwise indicated, the motion pictures are 16mm sound black-and-white film.

Because work simplification has been applied in so many work situations, the films included under Chapter 1 have been divided into general illustrations of work simplification concepts and application, and specific applications of work simplification principles (under which *some* of the available films have been listed; it would be virtually impossible to list all the available specific-application films).

This bibliography has been assembled from many sources, and only those films which have a direct bearing on the subject have been included. Additional film titles can be obtained from the bibliographies listed below:

Film Guide on Production and Management Methods, Film Research Associates, 135 W. 52d St., New York 19, N.Y.

Educational Film Guide, The H. W. Wilson Company, New York. Available in most libraries.

"The Index of Training Films," *Business Screen Magazine,* 150 E. Superior, Chicago 11, Ill.

The Material Handling Institute, Inc., 1108 Clark Bldg., Pittsburgh 22, Pa.

Industrial Film Bibliography, National Metal Trades Association, 122 S. Michigan, Chicago 3, Ill.

A Guide to Audio-Visual Materials in Industrial and Labor Relations, New York State School of Industrial and Labor Relations, Cornell University, Ithaca, N.Y.

Film Guide on Industrial Relations, Film Research Associates, 135 W. 52d St., New York 19, N.Y.

U.S. Government Films for School and Industry, United World Films, Inc., 1445 Park Ave., New York 29, N.Y.

Pocket Guide to Titles and Descriptions of Free 16mm. Sound Films, Modern Talking Picture Service, Inc., 45 Rockefeller Plaza, New York 20, N.Y.

CHAPTER 1

General illustrations of concepts and application

The Assembly of Small Parts (Iowa 9min si). The application of motion economy principles to four different assembly operations with actual increases in production.

The Easier Way (GM 12min). How various operations have been made simpler, more productive, and easier to handle. Pegboard illustration is used as a basic demonstration.

Effective Working Methods (MEC 9min si). One inspection and two small assembly operations with original and improved methods.

A Hidden World (AC 26min col). The role of industrial and other engineers in our daily lives.

Improved Methods (MEC 16min si). How costs are reduced by the operators and/or supervisor, as well as the motion and time study analyst.

Improved Methods at Work—Part I (MEC 16min si). Original and improved methods for three operations.

Improved Methods at Work—Part II (MEC 16min si). A continuation of Part I for four additional operations.

Make Every Movement Count (Purdue 24min si col). Eight

operations with original and improved methods. Another operation is presented for class discussion, and then the improved method is shown.

Method Improvement Applications (MEC 16min si). Six original and improved methods.

Mighty Labors (IEC 34min). The importance of industrial engineering to the industrial world.

Modern Methods (MEC 16min si). Original and improved methods for heavy processing and light manual operations.

More Production through Motion Study (Purdue 24min si col). Original and improved methods for 11 operations of a wide variety.

Motion Study in Action (Iowa 21min). Original and improved methods for 12 operations.

Motion and Time Study (USC 9min). The concept of motion and time study and specific exercises for class instruction.

Original Gilbreth Film (Iowa 48min si). How principles developed by the Gilbreths are applied in present-day activities. Some of the original film is included.

Productivity: Key to Plenty (EB 20min). The increases of the American standard of living through technological progress.

Illustrations of specific applications

Carding and Packing Steel Pins (Iowa 14min si).

Coil Winding and Miscellaneous Operations (Iowa 9min si).

Cresting Letters on Glasses (Iowa 11min si).

Disassemble Bicycle Coaster Brake (Huffman 10min).

Dusting (ATT 20min col).

Extractor Operations in a Commercial Laundry (Iowa 11min si).

Farm Work Simplification (Sinclair 14min).

Folding and Packing Operations (Iowa 4min si).

Folding Napkins on Napkin Ironer (Iowa 6min si).

Forging and Machine Shop Operations (Iowa 15min si).

Forming Links for Portable Typewriters (Iowa 3min si).

Handling a Flour Sack (General Mills 28min). Describes the technique of process analysis using the flow process chart. Presents appropriate symbols and nomenclature.

Harvesting Vegetables and Preparing Them for Market (Iowa 15min si).

Ideas Unlimited: Work simplification (U.S. Army), six parts: I (20min), II, III, IV, V, and VI (18min each).

Identification and Assembly of Laundry Bundles (Iowa 24min si col).

Industrial Motion Analysis (in garment factories) (IFC 15min si).

Inserting Liner and Partition in Paper Boxes (Iowa 7min si).

Inspection and Small Assembly Operations (Iowa 12min si).

Job Design as Applied to Petroleum Production (Iowa 12min si).

Knitting Mill Operations (Iowa 19min si).

Laundry Work (Iowa 8min si).

Maiden Form Brassiere (needle trades illustration) (AHM 8min si).

Making Minutes Count (on farms) (Iowa 32min si).

Material Handling in Receiving, Warehousing and Shipping (GE 24min col).

Miscellaneous Operations in a Metal Furniture and Cabinet Plant (Iowa 11min si).

Motion Economy and Tool Design (Iowa 48min si).

Motion Study Applied to Clinical Dentistry (Iowa 32min si).

Motion Study Applied to Factory Cleanup (Iowa 6min si).

Motion Study Applied to Letter Indexing (TVA 11min).

Motion Study Helps Plumbing Assembly (Purdue 16min si).

Motion Study of the Simplified Typewriter Keyboard (Iowa 26min si).

Packing Cheddar Cheese in Cups (Iowa 6min si).

Painting Refrigerator Units with Spray Gun (Iowa 4min si).

Paper Can Assembly (HPH). Illustrates micromotion analysis.

Reclaiming Surgical Sponges (Iowa 8min si).

Shipping Room Operations (Iowa 7min si).

A Shirt Finishing Method (garment plant) (Iowa 8min si).

Simplifying Work in the Office (Iowa 64min si).

Snap Flask Molding Methods (MEC 16min si). Also shows how operators help develop better methods.

Soldering and Small Assembly Operations (Iowa 14min si).

Sorting Operations (Iowa 4min si).

Sorting Personal Laundry (Iowa 8min si).

Work Simplification Applied to Clerical Operations (Standard Register 14min).

CHAPTER 2

Compliment Club (IU 30min). "Before and after" or how compliments cause other people to do their best.

Dollars and Cents (Marshall Field & Co. 11min col). Techniques of stimulating cost reductions through methods analysis.

Experiment (GM 12min). Understanding of fundamentals in getting along with people.

Job Analysis (MEC 16min si). Nine steps (different from those presented in Chapter 2) of job analysis and the questioning attitude are applied to six operations. The film is mainly before and after demonstrations.

By Jupiter (30min). Value of courtesy, kindness, and thoughtfulness.

Machines, Master or Slave? (NYU 14min). Problems raised by technological advances.

The Open Door (GM 60min sd). The role a foreman plays in the present industrial organization.

The Questioning Attitude (MEC 16min si). A questioning attitude on the part of supervisors can introduce many methods improvements.

Snap Flask Molding Methods (MEC 16min si). Also shows how operators help develop better methods.

Work Simplification in Action (Wolverine 10min). The foreman group approach to problems in work simplification.

CHAPTER 3

Film Tactics (USN 22min). The proper and wrong ways of using a training film.

Instructional Films—The New Way to Greater Education (25min). Advantages of film over other methods of teaching.

How to Peel Tomatoes in Canning Factories (Purdue 6min si). Demonstrates how a film may help teach the correct way to do a job.

Record of a Job Procedure (Purdue 3min si). Slow-motion pictures to assist in demonstrating and teaching the correct way to do a job.

Time Magnification (EK 17min si). The use of high-speed motion pictures to study rapid motion.

CHAPTER 4

The Flow Process Chart and How to Use It (USOSRD 15min col). The preparation of a flow process chart (with symbols only slightly different from those found in Chapter 5) is illustrated with shaving. Proposed chart is also shown.

Handling a Flour Sack (General Mills 28min). Describes the technique of process analysis using the flow process chart. Presents appropriate symbols and nomenclature.

Stockroom Sam (Marshall Field & Co. 10min col). An employee can improve his work with assistance of a flow process chart.

CHAPTER 6

Process Charts—How They Are Made and Used (Iowa 16min). Explains the purposes, preparation, and values of process charts and flow diagrams as used in business and industry. Illustrates through analysis of a specific familiar work operation how a process chart is made, and the correlation of a flow diagram to this chart. Applications of process charting and flow diagramming in a variety of work situations are suggested.

CHAPTER 7

Operation Analysis (MEC 16min si). Operation charts (with slightly different symbols) applied to eight operations with resulting improvements.

Three Operations for Operation Analysis—Original Method (Purdue 4min si).

CHAPTER 8

Definition of Therbligs (Purdue 6min si). Examples of each basic therblig without reference to fine-detail therbligs.

Film for Film Analysis—Plastic Knob (Purdue 13min si). Sixteen different methods (sixteen reels) of assembling a plastic-drawer pull knob for making film analyses.

Film for Film Analysis—Radio Tube (Purdue 4min si). The original methods for three operations for film-analysis purposes.

Miscellaneous Research Studies (Iowa 7min si). The effect of practice on motions used to perform operations, and other studies.

Paper Can Assembly (HPH). Illustrates micromotion analysis.

CHAPTER 9

Building Motion Economy into Tools and Equipment (GM-Saginaw 67min si col). Rebuilding standard machines or designing special machines results in many savings. Actual operations are shown, with detail on how changes were made.

Machine Tools and Motions (Iowa 22min). Motion study applied to the location and design of machine tool controls.

Man-Machine Charts—How They Are Made and Used (Iowa 22min). An effective demonstration with slightly different symbols. How to improve this type of activity.

Motion Economy and Tool Design (Iowa 48min si).

CHAPTER 10

Training Film on Work Sampling (Wolverine 15min si). Practice for a group with work sampling.

The Work Sampling Technique (MEC 16min col). An explanation of this technique to operators, foremen, and supervisors. Illustrated by determining delay allowances for time study.

CHAPTER 11

Materials Handling Methods (MEC 27min col). Shows a wide variety of materials handling problems, equipment, and methods. The objective of any materials handling operation is to move materials in the *shortest* possible time and with the *least* expenditure of money and energy.

Methods Improvements Applied to Large Machine Work (MEC 12min si). The application of methods analysis to basically nonrepetitive work.

CHAPTER 12

Conveyor Design and Application (Bosworth 10min). Basic concepts of conveyors.

Correct Working Methods (MEC 33min si). Illustrations of the principles of motion economy and work simplification applied to some light manual operations.

Demonstrations in Reaction Time (Iowa 16min si).

Ford Rouge Plant (Ford 30min). Mass-production techniques of the automobile industry.

Illustration of a Therblig Check List (Purdue 6min si). Applying principles of methods design to individual therbligs occurring in operations.

The Investigation of Some Hand Motions (Iowa 8min si).

It's Your Money (Yale 38min). Complete range of electrical industrial trucks.

Job Simplification through Motion Study (MEC 16min si). Improvement of operations by elimination of violations of laws of motion economy.

Jobs for Application of Motion Economy (Purdue 3min si). Two operations to which the principles of methods design and motion economy are to be applied. Suggestion lists may be made. The improved methods are shown.

Man-Machine Charts—How They Are Made and Used (Iowa 22min). An effective demonstration with slightly different symbols. How to improve this type of activity.

Materials Handling (GE 24min col). Some fundamental materials handling concepts.

Materials Handling Methods (MEC 27min col). Shows a wide variety of materials handling problems, equipment, and methods. The objective of any materials handling operation is to move materials in the *shortest* possible time and with the *least* expenditure of money and energy.

Motion Study Applications (CCNY 21min). Some basic principles of motion economy applied to four manual operations.

Motion Study Is Everybody's Job (Purdue 26min col). Illustrations of the five basic principles of methods design for eleven operations.

Motion Study Principles (CCNY 22 min). Some of the basic principles of motion economy with applications.

Pay Loads Pay Off (ATC 35min). Study of the "science" of materials handling.

Permanent Belt Conveyors (Barber-Greene 36min si col).

Pictorial Study of Methods Improvement Principles (GM-Saginaw 45min col). The application of seven different methods improvement principles in production operations.

Pin Board Study (Iowa 3min si). Demonstrates the application of motion economy principles to the assembly of pins in a board giving a substantial increase in efficiency.

Portable Conveyors (Barber-Greene 12min si col).

Project Tinkertoy (USN 28min). Describes new automatic production methods using the "building-block" principle by which resistors, capacitors, tube sockets, and other parts of common design are machine assembled into electronic products.

Steps to Effective Production (MEC 16min si). Decrease unnecessary walking to increase efficiency.

Study of Eye and Hand Movements in Inspection Work (Iowa 9min si). Analyzes fundamental eye and hand movements with a view to increasing the over-all efficiency of the inspection operation.

Study of Pedal Design (Iowa 4min si).

Study of Simultaneous Symmetrical and Asymmetrical Hand Motions in Three Planes (Iowa 8min si).

Study of Symmetrical Simultaneous Hand Motions (Iowa 8min si).

Study of Two Handed Work with Variations in Weights and Transport Distances (Iowa 13min si).

Technique for Tomorrow (Ford 24min). The automation built into Ford's foundry and engine plant.

Time and Motion Study Principles (CCNY 20min). Important principles of motion economy and their application to specific operations.

Transporter Newsreel (ATC 18min). Progress from hand trucks to motorized units moving heavy loads.

CHAPTER 13

Better Methods (MEC 10min si). Illustrates short- and long-range improvements by showing the development over a period of time of the "best" method for an operation.

Miscellaneous Research Studies (Iowa 7min si). The effect of practice on motions used to perform certain operations, and other studies.

A Theoretical Problem in Time and Motion Study (IIT 15min si). Comparing and evaluating four different methods of solution for an operation.

CHAPTER 14

The Flow Process Chart and How to Use It (USOSRD 15min col). The preparation of a flow process chart (with symbols only slightly different from those in Chapter 5) is illustrated with shaving. Proposed chart is shown.

Planning and Laying Out Work (FRA 10min). The importance of careful planning before starting the job. Bad results of poor planning are shown.

Planning Tomorrow's Methods Today (MEC 17min col). An industrial engineer and a shop foreman plan the operations of a difficult assembly job and work out the details in a methods laboratory.

CHAPTER 15

Assembly of Parts for Rubber Boots and Shoes (Iowa 15min si).

How to Peel Tomatoes in Canning Factories (Purdue 6min si). Demonstrates how a film may help teach the correct way of doing a job.

Planning Tomorrow's Methods Today (MEC 17min col). An industrial engineer and a shop foreman plan the operations of a difficult assembly job and work out the details in a methods laboratory.

CHAPTER 16

Effect of Practice (Iowa 9min si).

How to Peel Tomatoes in Canning Factories (Purdue 6min si). Shows how film may help teach correct way of doing a job.

Instructing the Worker on the Job (USOE 14min). Demonstrates difference between telling, showing, instructing.

Miscellaneous Research Studies (Iowa 7min si). The effect of practice on motions used to perform operations, and other studies.

Record of a Job Procedure (Purdue 3min si). Slow-motion pictures help demonstrate and teach the correct way to do a job.

The Western Electric–Iowa Skill Study (Iowa 20min si col). A study of development in skill in a manufacturing operation.

CHAPTER 17

An American Miracle (GM 18min). How a manufacturing sequence is set up and operated by "balanced" mass-production.

And in Return (AC 40min). Explains the concept of a fair day's work (pace) in terms of most present-day practices.

The Engineered Performance Standards Program (USN 16min). The Navy's approach to job performance in ordnance and repair. The official Navy policy on performance standards and a plan for improving manpower utilization and manpower control through scientific engineering techniques.

A Fair Day's Work (P&G 24min col). The concepts of work measurement as applied in one company.

Idler Gear Rating Film (IEC 14min si col). An explanation of rating and several speed sequences of several operations.

Rating–Explanation (PC 15min si). Introduces the subject of performance rating.

Time Study Methods (MEC 19min col). Shows the analysis of a representative industrial job—breaking the job into elements, timing those elements with a stop watch, recording the elemental times and other important aspects of the job, making the necessary computations and allowances.

SOURCES

Allis-Chalmers Mfg. Co.
Advertising and Industrial
  Press Dept.
P.O. Box 512
Milwaukee, Wis.

American Association of
  Consultants, Inc.
Pittsburgh, Pa.

American Telephone and
  Telegraph
New York, N.Y.

Automatic Transportation Co.
101 W. 87th St.
Chicago 20, Ill.

Barber-Greene Company
Aurora, Ill.

Bosworth Engineering Co.
P.O. Box 2676
Lakewood 7, Ohio

Phil Carroll, Jr.
6 Crestwood Dr.
Maplewood, N.J.

City College of New York
Audio-Visual Extension Service
17 Lexington Ave.
New York 10, N.Y.

Clark Equipment Company
Clark Tructractor Division
Battle Creek, Mich.

Conveyor Equipment Mfgrs.
  Assn.
1129 Vermont Ave.
Washington 5, D.C.

Eastman Kodak Company
343 State St.
Rochester 4, N.Y.

Encyclopaedia Britannica
  Films, Inc.
1150 Wilmette Ave.
Wilmette, Ill.

Film Research Associates
135 W. 52d St.
New York 19, N.Y.

Ford Motor Company
Ford Film Library
3000 Schaefer Rd.
Dearborn, Mich.

General Electric Co.
Schenectady, N.Y.

General Mills
400 Second Ave. So.
Minneapolis 1, Minn.

General Motors Corp.
Dept. of Public Relations
Film Distribution Section
3044 W. Grand Blvd.
Detroit 2, Mich.

H. P. Hood & Sons
Providence, R.I.

Huffman Mfg. Co.
Dayton, Ohio

Indiana University
Bloomington, Ind.

Illinois Institute of Technology
3300 Federal St.
Chicago 16, Ill.

Industrial Engineering College
3309 W. Washington Blvd.
Chicago 24, Ill.

International Film Center
6 N. Michigan Ave.
Chicago 2, Ill.

Marshall Field & Co.
111 N. State St.
Chicago, Ill.

Methods Engineering Council
822 Wood St.
Pittsburgh 21, Pa.

Allan H. Mogensen
330 W. 42d St.
New York 18, N.Y.

New York University Film
   Library
27 Washington Pl. So.
New York 3, N.Y.

Procter and Gamble Co.
Ivorydale, Ohio

Purdue University
Film Rental Service
Lafayette, Ind.

Saginaw Steering Division
General Motors Corporation
Saginaw, Mich.

Sinclair Refining Company
Chicago, Ill.

Society for Advancement of
   Management, Inc.
411 Fifth Ave.
New York 16, N.Y.

Socony-Vacuum Co.
26 Broadway
New York 4, N.Y.

Standard Register Company
Campbell and Albany Sts.
Dayton 1, Ohio

Tennessee Valley Authority
Knoxville, Tenn.

U.S. Army—any Army base
   with a library, such as Fifth
   Army Sub-library
Fort Leonard Wood, Mo.

U.S. Navy Department
Office of Public Information
Washington 25, D.C.

U.S. Office of Education
Washington 25, D.C.

U.S. Office of Scientific
Research and Development
Washington 25, D.C.

United World Films Inc.
1445 Park Ave.
New York 29, N.Y.

University of Iowa
Visual Education Bureau
Iowa City, Iowa

University of Southern
   California
Los Angeles, Calif.

Wolverine Tube Division
Calumet & Hecla
Detroit 9, Mich.

Yale & Towne Mfg. Co.
4530 Tacony St.
Philadelphia 24, Pa.

INDEX